THREE CARDINALS

THREE CARDINALS

NEWMAN — WISEMAN — MANNING

by

E. E. REYNOLDS

P. J. KENEDY & SONS

NEW YORK

NIHIL OBSTAT: ANDREAS MOORE, L.C.L.

CENSOR DEPVTATVS

IMPRIMATVR: E. MORROGH BERNARD

VICARIVS GENERALIS

WESTMONASTERII: DIE XVIII MARTII MCMLVIII

Library of Congress Catalog Card No. : 58–10991

Printed in Great Britain

CONTENTS

ILLUSTRATIONS

(between pp. 134 and 135)

PREFACE

THIS book is a biographical study of the three Cardinals who played the leading parts in the development of the Roman Catholic Church in England during the second half of the nineteenth century.

It seemed to me of interest to compare their personalities, development and achievements and, at the same time, to note their relations one with another. To give accounts of the lives of three men *pari passu* has inevitably meant occasional overlapping and some repetition, but there appeared no other way of recording the development of each as seen side by side with the other two. Careful selection of material had to be made otherwise the book would have become unwieldy and so overladen with detail that the picture would have been lost. I have preferred those matters that would best reveal intellectual and religious development, or would help to bring out personal characteristics, or emphasize their relations one with another.

As this book is not based on unpublished material, I have not thought it necessary to give a multitude of references; the sources of information and of most quotations will usually be obvious. The notes at the end indicate the books I have found most useful, but it is far from being a complete list of those read over the years from which I have gained ideas and impressions, many of which I should now find it hard to trace to their sources.

E. E. R.

CHAPTER I

AT THE OPENING OF THE
NINETEENTH CENTURY

BETWEEN the birth of Cardinal Newman in 1801 and the death of Cardinal Manning in 1892, the religious life of England was transformed. The Anglican Church gained a new impetus; the Nonconformists increased their influence, and the Catholic Church came out of the shadows into the stronger light.

An engraving of a drawing by Frederick Nash of the interior of St Bartholomew-the-Great, Smithfield, in 1805 may serve as an introduction to the Anglican Church at the opening of the century. The floor, except for the aisle, is filled with private pews enclosed by high panelling. The great window is obscured by an organ and a gallery. The rector, in wig, bands and black gown, is in the pulpit with his clerk below him. A dozen people in the gallery may have been a choir. Two bewigged heads show above the pews, and on a bench along the aisle sit three adults and a child. Such accommodation was provided for those who could not afford a pew. The atmosphere must have been humid and pervaded by the charnel smell of the many dead parishioners buried beneath the stone flags.

The rector since 1768 had been Owen Edwardes, and he remained at St Bartholomew's until his death in 1814. The few records of his ministry show that he carried out his duties conscientiously and won the respect of his parishioners.

This placid scene displays one aspect of the Anglican Church of that period—decorous, uninspired and uninspiring. There was little fervour, nor would the congregation have welcomed a more zealous apostleship.

The counterpart of this London church was to be found in other towns and in the country parishes. The Rev. Robert Hurrell Froude became rector of Dartington in Devonshire in 1799, and was there for sixty years. He was rector, squire, and magistrate. His historian son, J. A. Froude, recalled that "our spiritual lessons did not go beyond the catechism. . . . About doctrine, evangelical or catholic, I do not think that in my early boyhood I ever heard a single word, in church or out of it."

We can turn to the novels of Jane Austen to learn something of the country livings held by the junior relatives of the landed gentry. Again it is a picture of complacency with established order rather than of spiritual or intellectual ardour.

A wider view would take note of many benefices held in plurality which were served by curates struggling to live on less than a pound a week; many a country church had only one service on Sundays as the same parson or curate had to include two or three in his circuit; there would be Holy Communion on a few occasions in the year, and Confirmations were so rare that crowds of candidates had to be assembled at any one time. We should also have to note the wealth accumulated by some of the bishops whose qualifications were more often political or territorial than religious; the needs of the House of Lords were more pressing than those of the House of God.

The clergy were untrained; if a parson knew any theology, it was the outcome of his own inclinations and not of necessity. A brief interview with the bishop was often sufficient to secure ordination which was often done in a perfunctory manner.

If this gave the full picture, the survival of the Anglican Church would have been against expectation. There is much evidence of its unpopularity in the country; its Tory and territorial affiliations and its opposition to needed reforms, both of itself and of social conditions, made men feel that the Church was an obstacle to development and an opponent of improvements in the lives of the majority of people. Even in the thirties of the century, Thomas Arnold could write, "The Church as it now stands, no human power can save."

So we must not forget the quiet influence of those of the clergy who were devout pastors, earnest in their ministrations and full of charity towards their neighbours. They were the salt of the Church.

There were many country parsonages like Burnham Thorpe,

the home of Horatio Nelson, which were then and later during the century to produce many notable sons. The accounts we can read of such households tell of a healthy family life, of simple fare, of friendly relations with the local gentry, and of a genuine care for the people of the parish. Those who held such livings, above the clerical poverty line, were usually University men, themselves the younger sons of the squirarchy, and not infrequently of cultured interests. It was part of a social pattern to which the country owes much, but it was not fervently religious nor intellectually venturesome.

However complacent some sections of the Anglican Church may have been, there were stirrings within its ranks that promised a more vigorous life. The preaching of the Wesleys and of Whitfield during the second half of the eighteenth century had influenced a Church that was unable to retain these followers of unorthodox ways. The Methodist Movement had reached the many thousands of workmen and labourers who had been displaced by the Industrial Revolution or for whom the Anglican Church had been slow to make provision. It is true that in the early nineteenth century the Methodists had been split by controversy into contending groups, but they, and the revived dissenting sects, formed a separate community that was to become the powerful Nonconformist body of the latter part of the century.

The disturbing and even disruptive ideas of the French Revolution had also affected men's minds and had sharpened their opposition to an Established Church that seemed the ally of the landed gentry and the supporter of outworn privilege.

Within the Church, these influences were reflected in the rise of the Evangelicals. They might be described as the extreme Protestant party within the Church; they believed in the plenary inspiration of the Bible and regarded it as the sole authority for belief and doctrine; they accepted the Calvinist teaching of justification by faith alone, and they held that each must experience a conversion from the ways of the world. Their view of life was stern and often gloomy, and it is from them that our popular conception of the joyless Victorian Sunday is mainly derived. An influential body of laymen who held these tenets promoted missionary and educational work as well as being the leaders in such humanitarian causes as the abolition of slavery. By the middle of the century, much of the fire of evangelicalism had died down and a suppressive formalism had replaced the early zeal.

There were other parties in the Anglican Church, though "party" is not perhaps the best term to use as it now implies a degree of organization that did not then exist. The old High Churchman was an Erastian who accepted the subordination of the Established Church to the State. Other High Churchmen were the heirs of the Laudian tradition and were the forerunners of those who were to stress the Catholic nature of the Church. A Low Churchman was inclined to lay little emphasis on the importance of the Episcopate, nor did he have an exalted view of the position of the clergy. Latitudinarian and Broad Churchman were other terms in use for those who did not give much importance to ecclesiastical discipline; they were ready to come to terms with the thought of the day. Such labels varied in their significance as the years passed and their application must not be made rigidly; they may be taken as representing trends of thought or attitudes of mind rather than clearly defined positions.

During the first quarter of the century there was growing uneasiness within the Church itself; no body of men enjoys being unpopular or of feeling that its influence is declining. The spirit of inquiry was at work and many were ready to question long-established beliefs and practices. This spirit was not peculiar to this country; in France and Germany and elsewhere men were turning their minds to similar problems; in each country these took local forms, but fundamentally all were concerned with questions of teaching and authority. The nineteenth century was to experience religious and intellectual controversies that were to affect the most placid country parsonages.

At the opening of the century the Catholic Church in England was beginning to revive after the long years of suppression under the penal laws. The Relief Acts of 1778 and 1791 permitted Catholics freedom of worship. They had still to suffer some civil disabilities until the Emancipation Act of 1829, but they had gained the primary liberty of not being penalized for attending

Mass; nor were their priests any longer compelled to live in fear of the informer; their schools were allowed to provide for the education of Catholic children.

The generations of proscription had produced a state of mind that could not immediately be changed. Catholics had been forced to live quietly to avoid drawing attention to themselves; they had become, as it were, a secret people without any share in the civil or military or official life of the country. They even had their own language; they did not speak of "Mass", but of "Prayers", and "Confession" was "Duty". Even after the Emancipation Act, the older generation found it impossible to throw off established habits of secrecy, and they looked askance at those who dared to come out into the open and freely proclaim their faith. All this must be kept in mind when considering the history of the Catholic Church in this country during the nineteenth century; it provides the explanation of much that may now seem perverse and even obstructive.

Catholics formed about one per cent. of the population. These numbers were increased by a steady flow of immigrants from Ireland; in later years this became a flood. The French Revolution had an important effect on the Catholic Church; many of the emigrés were Catholics and their plight excited the sympathy of those who knew them. The priests amongst them gave valued service until they were able to return to France. The same cause compelled the English schools and colleges and convents on the Continent to return to their home country. So it happened that soon after the Relief Acts were passed, it became necessary for such institutions to re-establish themselves in England. Some schools had been carried on discreetly even in penal days, but a new era opened when young men could again be trained for the priesthood in their native land.

Rome regarded England as a missionary country.[1] Four vicars-apostolic were appointed to direct Catholic affairs; although

[1] Catholic affairs were under the direction of the Congregation of Propaganda in Rome. Even after the restoration of the Hierarchy, some measure of control was retained by Propaganda; it was not until 1908 that the Hierarchy was allowed full direction of the Church in England.

they were titular bishops, they did not have the full authority of ordinary bishops, and this was one cause of the difficulties that arose between the vicars-apostolic and the leading Catholic laymen of the old families during the early decades of the century.

To the vast majority of the people in the country, Catholics were an unknown people. Old fears and prejudices persisted as had been shown in the Gordon Riots of 1780; nor was this the last demonstration of blind mistrust; indeed, even today, fear of Rome lingers in some minds. At the beginning of the nineteenth century, few could say that they had spoken to a Catholic priest, and few had any knowledge of the Catholic Church.

CHAPTER II

JOHN HENRY NEWMAN
1801–1832

JOHN HENRY NEWMAN was born on 21 February 1801 at 80 Old Broad Street in the City of London. His father, John Newman (1767–1824), was at that date a partner in a banking firm. His side of the family came from Swaffham Bulbeck in Cambridgeshire where his great-grandfather had been a tailor who died in possession of a few acres of land. His eldest son, Francis, added to his patrimony, but even this did little more than raise the family out of the landless class. The eldest son of Francis came to London and made a moderate livelihood as a grocer. It was his son John who became the father of John Henry Newman.

We know nothing of John Newman's schooling, but, judged by his career, he must have been reasonably well educated. Our next information is that in 1794 he was a partner in a banking firm. This seems a remarkable leap for the son of a small grocer, though we should not attach to his position the importance we should now give to a Bank Director. Perhaps he entered the firm as a clerk and proved so competent that he was made a partner.

Three months after the death of his father in 1799, John Newman married Jemima Fourdrinier the daughter of a wealthy family of paper manufacturers. She brought a dowry of £5,000 which, fortunately, as events proved, remained under her control. The Fourdriniers were of Huguenot stock; they had fled from Caen in Normandy to Gronigen in Holland and came to England early in the eighteenth century. Jemima's grandfather had married into another refugee family from Caen; there was therefore a strong French strain in the Newman children.

John Henry was the eldest son; he was to have two brothers and three sisters: Charles (1802–84), Harriett (1803–52), Francis (1805–97), Jemima (1808–79), and Mary (1809–28).

In 1802 the family moved from Old Broad Street to the more fashionable Southampton Place, off Bloomsbury Square, and, in the following year, John Newman took Grey Court House at Ham near Richmond as his country house. A few years later, the family left Ham for a small farm at Norwood. John Henry to the end of his life treasured memories of those early years, especially of the summer days at Richmond. It was a happy childhood warmed by a strong family affection.

The personality of John Newman remains shadowy; he must have been a man of ability, and the uprightness of his character was shown in the troubles that came upon him. His love of music, both as a listener and as a performer, was shared by his wife, and was passed on to his eldest son. In religious belief he seems to have had no determined convictions. Jemima Newman was a devout woman who accepted the teaching of the Church as it came to her from the clergymen of the parishes in which she lived. The place given to the Bible in the teaching of her children suggests Evangelical leanings, but she was not a strict adherent of either the Evangelical or the Calvinist doctrines. Her eldest son wrote, "I was brought up from a child to take a great delight in reading the Bible; but I had no formed religious convictions till I was fifteen. Of course I had a perfect knowledge of my Catechism."

He had just had his fifteenth birthday when the family fortunes were reversed by the failure of the bank of which John Newman was a partner; it was but one of the thirty-seven banks that closed their doors after the defeat of Napoleon. John Newman and his partners were able to avoid bankruptcy but the business was ended. He found a position as manager of a brewery at Alton, and there the family went to live. Happily Jemima's own £5,000 remained secure.

John Newman was not a success at Alton, nor in his later ventures of a more humble character. We need not follow his declining fortunes in detail; he died at the end of September 1824. By that date his eldest son was a Fellow of Oriel College, Oxford.

In the spring of 1808, John Henry Newman was sent as a boarder to the flourishing Great Ealing School; his younger brothers joined him later. His progress in learning was rapid; his one regret in later life was that instruction in the classics had not been of the highest quality; mathematics was his best subject. The school was conducted on sensible lines; there seems to have been none of the coarse bullying to be found in the Public Schools of the day; fortunately there were no compulsory games, nor did Newman show any interest in such activities; his shortsightedness may have accounted partly for this indifference, but his natural inclinations were in other directions in his out-of-school time. He read omnivorously; in his last years at the school he had the excitement of reading the early Waverley novels as they came out, and this gave him a lifelong love of Scott. He wrote verses, made speeches in debates, took part in Latin plays, formed a Club and edited a magazine; it is the pattern of the scholarly boy with literary tastes. No doubt the other boys thought him a bit odd, but he was allowed to go his own way, and, in his own circle, was accepted as a leader.

In the *Apologia* he wrote:

When I was fifteen, (in the autumn of 1816) a great change of thought took place in me. I fell under the influence of a definite Creed, and received into my intellect impressions of dogma, which, through God's mercy, have never been effaced or obscured. Above and beyond the conversations and sermons of the excellent man, the Rev. Walter Mayers, of Pembroke College, Oxford, who was the human means of this beginning of divine faith in me, was the effect of the books which he put into my hands, all of the school of Calvin. One of the first books I read was a work of Romaine's;[1] I neither recollect the title nor the contents, except one doctrine, which of course I include among those which I believe to have come from a divine source, viz. the doctrine of final perseverance. I received it at once, and believed that the inward conversion of which I was conscious, (and of which I still am more certain than that I have hands and feet,) would last into the next life, and that I

[1] William Romaine (1714–95), of Huguenot descent; Oxford, 1731–7; adopted most rigorous tenets of Calvinism; became a popular preacher and had to suffer some persecution. Probably Newman read one of Romaine's chief books, *The Life of Faith*, *The Walk of Faith*, and *The Triumph of Faith*.

was elected to eternal glory. I have no consciousness that this belief had any tendency whatever to lead me to be careless about pleasing God. I retained it till the age of twenty-one, when it gradually faded away; but I believe that it had some influence on my opinions, in the direction of those childish imaginations which I have already mentioned, viz. in isolating me from the objects which surrounded me, in confirming me in my mistrust of the reality of material phenomena, and making me rest in the thought of two and two only absolute and luminously self-evident beings, myself and my Creator;— for while I considered myself predestined to salvation, my mind did not dwell upon others, as fancying them simply passed over, not predestined to eternal death. I only thought of the mercy to myself.

The detestable doctrine last mentioned is simply denied and abjured, unless my memory strangely deceives me, by the writer who made a deeper impression on my mind than any other, and to whom (humanly speaking) I almost owe my soul,—Thomas Scott[1] of Aston Sandford. . . .

What, I suppose, will strike any reader of Scott's history and writings, is his bold unworldliness and vigorous independence of mind. He followed truth wherever it led him, beginning with Unitarianism, and ending in a zealous faith in the Holy Trinity. It was he who first planted deep in my mind that fundamental truth of religion. . . .

Besides his unworldliness, what I also admired in Scott was his resolute opposition to Antinomianism, and the minutely practical character of his writings. They show him to be a true Englishman, and I deeply felt his influence; and for years I used almost as proverbs what I considered to be the scope and issue of his doctrine, *Holiness rather than peace*, and *Growth the only evidence of life*.

He goes on to note other influences that came from books:

[1] Thomas Scott (1747–1821), self-educated; ordained, Church of England, 1773; began commentary on Bible in 1788; appointed to Aston Sandford, Bucks, in 1801.

Law's[1] *Serious Call,* Joseph Milner's[2] *Church History,* which introduced him to the Fathers, and Thomas Newton's[3] *Dissertation on
the Prophecies,* from which he received the notion that the Pope is
Antichrist.

These early impressions and opinions were to be developed or
discarded through the years, but one factor was constant.

> I have changed in many things; in this I have not. From the
> age of 15 dogma has been the fundamental principle of my
> religion. I cannot enter into the idea of any other sort of re-
> ligion; religion, as a mere sentiment, is to me a dream and a
> mockery. As well can there be filial love without the fact of a
> father, as devotion without the fact of a Supreme Being. What
> I held in 1816, I held in 1833, and I hold in 1864. Please God I
> shall hold it to the end.

The boy who went up to Trinity College, Oxford, at the age
of sixteen, was shy and sensitive. He had had as happy a childhood
as any child could have; his home had not provided much in the
way of intellectual or religious stimulus, but he had found both
in a school which he had come to like so much that he resisted a
suggestion that he should be transferred to Winchester. He described himself as "of a studious turn and of a quick apprehension
. . . though in no respect a precocious boy."

He arrived at Oxford at a period when the old complacency
was yielding to a revived interest in learning. His own tutor,
Thomas Short, was a sound if not enterprising scholar; he appreciated his new pupil's quickness of mind and was evidently glad
to guide his studies, but perhaps his greatest service was to bring
Newman and John William Bowden together. This was the beginning of one of those friendships that were to mean so much to
Newman; they were, indeed, a necessity of his nature and had a

---

[1] William Law (1686–1761), Anglican divine; his *Serious Call* was published
in 1729.

[2] Joseph Milner (1744–97), Evangelical. His history began publication in
1794.

[3] Thomas Newton (1704–82), Bishop of Bristol and Dean of St Paul's; the
first volume of his *Prophecies* was published in 1754.

formative part in his life. The two boys—for they were little more—
had the same serious outlook on life, and in their long talks they
exercised their minds and formed their opinions. When they were
not studying—and both were rigorous workers—they spent their
time together. "We used to live in each other's rooms as undergraduates," wrote Newman, "and men used to mistake our names,
and call us by each other's."

Newman set himself an exacting course of reading; nothing
was allowed to break into that; he was studying for nine or more
hours daily. He found relaxation in some mild boating, in walking
and in playing his fiddle. The wilder spirits of the college soon
gave up trying to bait him or to lure him to wine parties; they
came up against a strength of will that was part of his personality.
His over-concentration on his studies, and the worry of the increasing decline of the family fortunes, combined to ruin his
chances of a good degree in 1820. In the following year, his father
was declared bankrupt, and all the resources and possessions of the
family had to be sacrificed. Mrs Newman came to rely more and
more on the judgment of her eldest son; her own small fortune
was declining in value, and the outlook was dark. Newman had a
Trinity scholarship, and by taking pupils and accepting commissions for writing he was able to bring his brother Francis to
Oxford and support him during what proved to be a brilliant
University career, and the prelude of a strange spiritual odyssey.[1]

After his failure to take a good degree, Newman wisely re-
laxed his rigorous time-table; he later recalled that "minerology
and chemistry were his chief studies and the composition of music."
Meanwhile he had resolved to prepare himself for ordination in
the Church of England; this decision seems to have come to him
quietly; there had been thoughts of the law, but these may have
been more a reflection of his father's hopes than of his own choice.
A bold plan for the immediate future had been formed; he would

[1] It is a pity that so much notice has been taken of Francis Newman's
oddities. He was a man of considerable intellectual power. The two brothers
disagreed on fundamental issues, but they kept in touch and met from time to
time throughout their long lives. Francis Newman's *Early History of the late
Cardinal Newman* (1891) needs to be read with caution. Both supported their
more than eccentric brother Charles for many years before his death in 1884.

stand for an Oriel Fellowship, one of the most coveted distinctions at Oxford at that time. To those who knew him, it seemed a hopeless quest after the disappointment of his degree examination. He went forward with a strange feeling of assurance, and was successful. It was an achievement that startled and rejoiced his College, and must have restored his confidence in his own powers. So, at the age of twenty-one, he became a Fellow of Oriel; he later recorded that he had never wished anything better than "to live and die a Fellow of Oriel."

It was not an easy position to take up; he felt diffident in the presence of the other Fellows, all of whom had won high honours in the University; their social backgrounds were different from his.

In his *Apologia* Newman paid warm tributes to the members of Oriel who did so much to open his mind and guide his studies; however divergent their paths were to be in the future, he never forgot what he owed to them. He was impressionable, and eager to benefit from their wider knowledge and experience.

Of the older Fellows he mentions William James who had been strongly in favour of Newman's election. He "taught me the doctrine of Apostolical Succession, in the course of a walk, I think, round Christ Church meadow." Dr Edward Hawkins[1] "was the first who taught me to weigh my words, and to be cautious in my statements." He also lent the new Fellow Sumner's[2] *Treatise on Apostolical Preaching* "from which I was led to give up my remaining Calvinism and to receive the doctrine of Baptismal Regeneration."

There is one other principle, which I gained from Dr Hawkins, more directly bearing upon Catholicism, than any that I have mentioned; and that is the doctrine of Tradition . . . He lays down a proposition, self-evident as soon as stated, to those who have at all examined the structure of Scripture, viz. that the sacred text was never intended to teach doctrine, but

---

[1] Edward Hawkins (1789–1882), Fellow of Oriel, 1813; Provost, 1828–74.
[2] John Bird Sumner (1780–1862), Archbishop of Canterbury. His *Apostolical Preaching* was originally published anonymously (1815).

only to prove it, and that, if we would learn doctrine, we must have recourse to the formularies of the Church; for instance, to the Catechism, and to the Creeds. He considers, that, after learning from them the doctrines of Christianity, the inquirer must verify them by Scripture. This view, most true in its outline, most fruitful in its consequences, opened upon me a large field of thought.

Then there was the formidable Dr Richard Whately.[1]

While I was still awkward and timid in 1822, he took me by the hand, and acted towards me the part of a gentle and encouraging instructor. He, emphatically, opened my mind, and taught me to think and to use my reason.

Whately persuaded Newman to give closer attention to the subject of logic, with such effect that the younger scholar contributed to the writing of his preceptor's textbook on the subject which was published in 1826.

What he did for me in point of religious opinion, was, first, to teach me the existence of the Church, as a substantive body or corporation; next to fix in me those anti-Erastian views of Church polity, which were one of the most prominent features of the Tractarian movement.

During the few months that Whately was at Oriel in 1822 he seems to have used shock tactics in dealing with the young Newman; he quickly sensed his worth for he appointed him his vice-president when he returned to Oxford in 1825 to take charge of Alban Hall.

One other name must be mentioned—the thirty-year-old John Keble.[2] His reputation for holiness of life was such that Newman "felt abashed and unworthy of the honour done me" when they

[1] Richard Whately (1787–1863), Fellow of Oriel, 1811; Archbishop of Dublin, 1831–63.

[2] John Keble (1792–1866), Fellow of Oriel, 1811; Vicar of Hursley, 1836–66.

first met. It was, however, some little time before they became warm friends; Keble was not drawn to the new Fellow who was regarded as an Evangelical, and his long absences from Oxford hindered a closer knowledge at that period.

In his second year as a Fellow, Newman was joined by E. B. Pusey[1] and thus began an association and a friendship that meant much to both of them and to the Anglican Church. Pusey was away in Germany from 1825 to 1827; he married soon after his return and his home became a second home for Newman.

A further stage in his development was the reading of Butler's *Analogy of Religion* (1736). From this he derived two principles that underlay "a great portion of my teaching."

First, the very idea of analogy between the separate works of God leads to the conclusion that the system which is of less importance is economically or sacramentally connected with the more momentous system, and of this conclusion the theory, to which I was inclined as a boy, viz. the unreality of material phenomena, is an ultimate resolution. At this time I did not make the distinction between matter itself and its phenomena, which is so necessary and so obvious in discussing the subject. Secondly, Butler's doctrine that probability is the guide of life, led me, at least under the teaching to which a few years later I was introduced, to the question of the logical cogency of Faith, on which I have written so much.

This phase of Newman's development was brief; it was part of that conditioning to which he was submitted as a very young Fellow. His own originality of mind was reasserted though it meant a break from Whately's influence.

On 13 June 1824, Newman was ordained deacon, and became curate at St Clement's, Oxford. He was ordained priest a year later. He gave himself to his new duties with his customary thoroughness; he visited his parishioners systematically; he instituted Sunday afternoon sermons and started a Sunday School, and he busied himself with raising over £5,000 for building a new

[1] Edward Bouverie Pusey (1800–82), Regius Professor of Hebrew, 1828–82.

church. His letters to his mother and sisters at this period show
how absorbed he was in pastoral work.

He was also bursar of his college and proved a good man of
business with a nice taste in wine. In 1826 he was appointed a
tutor in his college; he regarded his new charge as of pastoral as
well as of academic importance—a view that was not then shared
by his colleagues; he resigned his curacy at St Clement's, and also
his position as vice-principal of Alban Hall.

Towards the end of 1827 he was taken ill while conducting an
examination, and he complained of "an inability to think or
recollect". He went down to Brighton to stay with his family, and,
while he was there, his youngest sister Mary, for whom he had a
deep affection, was taken suddenly ill and, within a few hours,
died. Newman believed that this shock following his own breakdown, forced him to consider more deeply his own religious beliefs, with the result that he finally drew back from the vague
liberalism[1] into which he had been drifting. The remaining traces
of Calvinism and Evangelism were dissolved.

In 1828, when Hawkins succeeded Copleston as Provost of
Oriel, Newman was appointed Vicar of St Mary's in place of
Hawkins. So he came to occupy the pulpit from which his in-
fluence was to radiate throughout the University and beyond.

It was at this period that his significant friendship with Hurrell
Froude matured. Froude, two years younger than Newman, became a Fellow of Oriel in 1826, but at first they did not come
closely together. There must have seemed little in common between them. Froude was an enthusiast for all outdoor activities—
riding, fishing and sailing. He belonged to a social setting that was
alien to Newman, but Froude's brilliant intellect, his burning
enthusiasm and his deep religious faith combined with great charm
of personality captured the affection of Newman. In later years,
Froude claimed that one of his most important services had been
to bring Newman and Keble into close association. Froude had

---

[1] "Liberalism" has here no political connotation. To quote Newman:
"Liberalism in religion is the doctrine that there is no positive truth in religion,
but that one creed is as good as another. . . . Revealed religion is not a truth,
but a sentiment and a taste; not an objective fact, not miraculous; and it is the
right of each individual to make it say just what strikes his fancy."

been Keble's pupil and was profoundly impressed, as so many others were, by his tutor's deep piety, his devotion to his duties as a country parson, and his great learning. Keble's *The Christian Year* was published in 1827, and it reflects the faith of its author; during the following years its increasing popularity did much to raise the tone of English Churchmanship. Keble must have been startled at some of his pupil's more extravagant views, for Froude tended to express his opinions in extreme forms.

Newman wrote of him:

His opinions arrested and influenced me, even when they did not gain my assent. He professed openly his admiration of the Church of Rome, and his hatred of the Reformers. He delighted in the notion of an hierarchical system, of sacerdotal power, and of full ecclesiastical liberty. He felt scorn of the maxim, "The Bible and the Bible only is the religion of Protestants;" and he gloried in accepting Tradition as a main instrument of religious teaching. He had a high severe idea of the intrinsic excellence of Virginity; and he considered the Blessed Virgin its great Pattern. He delighted in thinking of the Saints; he had a vivid appreciation of the idea of sanctity, its possibility and its heights; and he was more than inclined to believe a large amount of miraculous interference as occurring in the early and middle ages. He embraced the principle of penance and mortification. He had a deep devotion to the Real Presence, in which he had a firm faith. He was powerfully drawn to the Medieval Church, but not to the Primitive.

Froude's belief in "penance and mortification" was not just an idea; he subjected himself to rigorous self-examination and adopted ascetic practices that may well have contributed to his later breakdown in health; he was without the guidance of an experienced spiritual director, and so went to extremes that, when later they were revealed, excited some ridicule.

Another acquaintance of this period was Joseph Blanco White,[1]

[1] Joseph Blanco White (1775–1841), born at Seville; ordained priest (R.C.) 1800; left Spain, 1810; Anglican until 1835 when he became a Unitarian.

who had been trained in the seminaries of Spain and had aposta-
tized. He was admitted to the common room of Oriel during his
Anglican phase. He provided the nearest approach Newman had
to a direct knowledge of Roman Catholic practices before his own
conversion. Blanco White taught Hurrell Froude the use of the
breviary; with Newman he shared a love of music and they
frequently played their violins in company. Blanco White's influence must have strengthened any antipathy to Rome at that
period.

When Froude became a tutor at Oriel, he was in full agreement with Newman that his responsibility was as much pastoral
as academic. Robert Wilberforce,[1] another new tutor, joined
them in this attitude to the relationship between tutor and pupil.
Their intentions were frustrated by the new Provost, Edward
Hawkins. He did not approve of this more intimate association of
tutor and pupil; he therefore refrained from sending new pupils to
the three tutors. This decrease in his college work gave Newman
more time for his own studies.

He began to read the Fathers systematically. This marked an
important stage in his development. His new studies were focused
when he was asked to write a volume for a Theological Library on
the early Councils. He began with the first Council of Nicaea (325)
when Arianism was condemned. The result was not the book
originally planned but dealt with a more restricted field. *The
Arians of the Fourth Century* was finished in 1832 and published in
the following year. Its importance lies in the intensive study of an
early period of Church history with particular reference to heresy.
It confirmed Newman's opinion that "Antiquity was the true
exponent of the doctrines of Christianity", but for him this still
meant "the basis of the Church of England."

During these years Newman's influence was steadily growing
as his sermons at St Mary's drew more and more of the undergraduates to hear him. There are a number of accounts of the

[1] Robert Isaac Wilberforce (1802–57) was the second son of William
Wilberforce, the philanthropist; the third son was Samuel (1805–73), who
became Bishop of Oxford (1845) and later of Winchester; the youngest son
was Henry William (1807–73). Both Robert and Henry were ordained in the
Church of England, and both became Roman Catholics.

impression he made on his listeners. Gladstone, who was at Oxford during the years 1828 to 1831, wrote:

Now Dr Newman's manner in the pulpit was one about which, if you considered it in its separate parts, you would arrive at very unsatisfactory conclusions. There was not very much change in the inflexion of the voice; action there was none. His sermons were read, and his eyes were always bent on his book; and all that, you will say, is against efficiency in preaching. Yes, but you must take the man as a whole, and there was a stamp and a seal upon him; there was a solemn sweetness and music in the tone; there was a completeness in the figure, taken together with the tone and with the manner, which made even his delivery, such as I have described it, and though exclusively from written sermons, singularly attractive.

Dean Church, a listener of a somewhat later period, wrote:

Every sermon had a purpose and an end which no one could misunderstand. Singularly devoid of anything like excitement—calm, even, self-controlled—there was something in the preacher's resolute concentrated way of getting hold of a single defined object which reminded you of the rapid spring or unerring swoop of some strong-limbed or swift-winged creature on its quarry. Whatever you might think that he did with it, or even if it seemed to escape from him, you could have no doubt what he sought to do; there was no wavering, confused uncertain bungling in that powerful and steady hand.

When we think of Newman and St Mary's, his sermons at once come to mind; but, if we are to have a clear picture of him at this period, we must remember that St Mary's was a parish church, and Newman had all the responsibilities of a vicar. These he carried out fully and devotedly. Soon after his appointment he was considering how to meet the needs of Littlemore, an outlying part of his parish. He was not the scholarly recluse emerging from his study from time to time to preach a sermon or give a lecture; he was an active parish priest whose aim was the "gaining of souls to God."

By the time he had finished his book on the Arians, Newman was on the verge of another break-down. His friend Froude was also in ill-health and was showing signs of the consumption that was to bring his death; his father, Archdeacon Froude, decided that a winter spent abroad would be beneficial; they persuaded Newman to join them. They left Falmouth for the Mediterranean early in December 1832.

Newman's warm tributes in his *Apologia* to the guides and mentors of his youth may mislead the reader into thinking that his development was shaped by them more than by his own genius. It has been said that his "was one of the minds which mature slowly." This, too, seems to accept his own account at its face value without noting that he did not hesitate to take his own line when he disagreed with such seniors as Whately and Hawkins. It must be remembered that Newman was only twenty-one when he became a Fellow of Oriel—an age at which maturity of mind cannot be expected. Yet by the time he set off for the Mediterranean at the age of thirty-one, he had established a unique position for himself in Oxford, and had written a book that showed original research and thought. It was not that he matured slowly; indeed it can be argued that he developed rapidly from about 1824. It would be nearer the truth to say that he was cautious and prudent in forming opinions. His thoughts were stimulated, as with all of us, by discussions with friends, but his conclusions were always his own and were the result of much hard thinking in solitude. He moved from position to position carefully, making sure of the security of each step; he rarely revealed his full thoughts until he had reached conclusions that he felt were well-founded. This scrupulousness often annoyed his friends, especially those who were inclined to leap rather than walk; they felt at times that he was not open enough with them especially when they thought they knew the direction in which he was moving. They found it difficult to appreciate the refinement of thought and expression which was part of his nature. For him there were "two and two only absolute and luminously self-evident beings, myself and my Creator."

The Mediterranean voyage, as we shall see, was to do much to widen his outlook, but, it was in solitude that he found his strength.

CHAPTER III

NICHOLAS WISEMAN
1802–1830

NICHOLAS WISEMAN was born at Seville on 2 August 1802. Both his father, James Wiseman, and his mother were Irish. His grandfather had left Waterford to establish himself as a merchant in Spain and had prospered. One of the friends of the family at the beginning of the nineteenth century was a young Catholic priest, Joseph Blanco White, who was, for a time, to be intimate with Newman.

James Wiseman died in 1804, and in the following year his widow took her two sons and her daughter to Waterford. The family was left in comfortable circumstances. The two boys received some schooling at Waterford and became better acquainted with the English language. In 1810 they went as boarders to St Cuthbert's College, Ushaw, a few miles west of Durham. Their mother lived in Durham at one period to be near her sons; on one of his visits to her, Nicholas experienced the anti-papist feeling in England. An election was in progress, and the boy was hissed for being a Catholic.

Intimate family life ended for him at the age of eight. His affection for his mother and sister remained strong, but he had none of those happy memories of a boyhood at home which meant so much to Newman and Manning.

St Cuthbert's College was one of the two seminaries, with preparatory schools attached, which were founded in England after the seizure of Douai College during the French Revolution. Although the Relief Acts of 1778 and 1791 had freed Catholics from the most onerous of the penal laws, it was still necessary to be prudent in the setting up of schools and seminaries in England. The excesses of the Revolution brought much sympathy to the dispossessed French priests and to those English Catholics who had been imprisoned or exiled when their colleges had been seized. The southern seminary was attached to the academy at Old Hall Green in Hertfordshire, an out-of-the-way place that was little likely to attract attention. The northern seminary was established in 1794 at Crook Hall on the moors south-west of Durham; a new building on Ushaw Moor nearer Durham was completed in 1808. It had therefore been occupied for only two years when Nicholas Wiseman and his elder brother arrived.

The first president died in May 1810, and for the next year the college was under the vice-president, John Lingard. Although their association was neither long nor close, Wiseman always retained a feeling of gratitude to the great historian for his kindness and interest.

Ushaw continued the strict Douai tradition, with the exception that, as a concession to the northern climate, the hour of rising was six and not five; studies occupied some eight hours daily; the religious instruction was thorough; of other studies, Latin was the main subject. The first five years of a boy's schooldays were spent on the ordinary curriculum; at the end of that period he either returned home, or, if he had a vocation for the priesthood, he remained for six years for the courses in philosophy and theology.

Nicholas Wiseman applied himself to his studies, but it was not until his last year that he reached the first place in his class. He took no part in games, but preferred a book or other intellectual interests as his relaxation. He recalled his early attraction to Rome: "its history, its topography, its antiquities, had formed the bond of a little college society devoted to the queen of cities, while the dream of its longings had been the hope of one day seeing what could then only be known through hearsay tourists and fabulous plans."

In 1814 there arrived at the college a student who was to be closely linked with Wiseman's career. George Errington came of an old Catholic family of Yorkshire. The two boys struck up a warm friendship in spite of dissimilarities of temperament. It was mainly through Errington and other companions that Wiseman gained some knowledge of the long established Catholic families who had suffered so grievously for their religion since Elizabethan

C

times. The county of Durham was one of their strongholds, but it is not known how far the boys and students were brought into contact with them. Wiseman spent one long vacation at George Errington's home, and he may have made similar visits at other times. He was certainly in London in the summer of 1814 when Cardinal Consalvi arrived as the representative of Pope Pius VII; Napoleon was then in Elba and the Emperor of Russia and the King of Prussia came to England at the invitation of the Prince Regent. Consalvi acted with great discretion and had a friendly reception. Wiseman recalled "the fêtes, splendid but somewhat childish. . . . The writer retains them among his holiday reminiscences, for they took place in vacation time; and they belonged decidedly to the age of pavilions and pagodas." This visit by Consalvi was not without its effect in creating a more favourable attitude towards the papacy.

Such contacts as these, however, could not have given a boy much understanding of the peculiar position of Catholics in England at that period. They long retained the reticence, even secretiveness, that had been forced upon them for generations; they were deeply devout but undemonstrative in their religion, and their long severance from the main stream of Catholic life and thought made them suspicious of any outward display or public commitment that might draw attention to them. In quietness, they believed, lay their safety.

Writing in 1862, Wiseman said:

I belong to the old time and I have often felt hearty gratitude to Almighty God for having been withdrawn from England just at the age when opinions take hold of the mind so as to become obstinate and at the period when party spirit became highest amongst Catholics and I should have understood its sides sufficiently to have made a choice. Through my eight years of Ushaw my Spanish recollections remained uneffaced and vivid. I can recollect explaining to companions what a rosary was, few if any having seen one any more than a discipline or a hairshirt; while there was not a crucifix in the house except those on the altar. Before these impressions had been lost with the language to which they had been associated, I was mercifully sent to Rome. . . . I certainly had few English prejudices to overcome when I reached Rome.

At some time during his years at Ushaw—it is not known when—Wiseman had resolved, much to his mother's happiness, to enter the priesthood. It was a momentous decision. He was not, however, to complete his studies in England.

In 1818 the English College at Rome was again ready to receive students. It had been seized by the French in 1798; they had sold everything that could be sold, and had wantonly destroyed all they could, even breaking open the coffins and scattering the remains. The property had been recovered in 1802 under the concordat between the Pope and Napoleon, but the Pope's imprisonment from 1809 to 1814 had thrown all into confusion again. Then had come the problem of making the building habitable and of finding the resources for a fresh beginning. Robert Gradwell was appointed rector. He had begun his own training at Douai and had suffered two years' imprisonment in France; he completed his studies at Crook Hall and Ushaw. It was decided that ten students should be sent from England to form the nucleus of the college; five of these, including Wiseman, came from Ushaw. The following recommendation was sent on his behalf:

> This young man may truly be pronounced above all praise. His talents are unrivalled in Ushaw Cottage, his piety fervent, and solid, and his character as a Christian scholar quite without fault. He is of a good family, and though quite independent as to circumstances, has voluntarily devoted himself to the English mission.

The students left Liverpool on 2 October 1818 for Leghorn by sea; the voyage was stormy and all but disastrous; it took two months. The land journey from Leghorn to Rome also had its dangers in those disturbed times, but at last, on 18 December they heard the longed-for cry, "Ecco Roma!"

Wiseman's strong romantic feeling for the past almost overwhelmed him as he entered the English College where he was to

spend the next twenty years. "One felt at once at home; it was
nobody else's house; it was English ground, a part of fatherland, a
restored inheritance." One may smile at first at this young Irish-
man, born in Seville, putting so much stress on the word "English". It was, however, a deeply felt sentiment that was to colour
his life's work.

His thoughts went back over the centuries to the hostel for
pilgrims of Saxon and medieval times, which had been transformed by Gregory XIII in 1579 into a seminary for the training
of English priests, many of whom were to be martyred for the
True Faith.

Rome itself enthralled the young student, and, as the years
passed, so his knowledge of churches and antiquities increased,
and he had few greater pleasures in later years than in conducting
his students, friends and visitors about the city and drawing upon
the wealth of his information for their instruction. So too he delighted in the multitudinous details of church ceremonial and
ritual. At the end of his life he could say, "As people in the world
go to a ball for their recreation, so I have enjoyed a great function."
Rome won his complete devotion and absorbed him, yet, when
the call came he did not hesitate to return to the English mission.

On Christmas Eve, the rector took the students to be presented
to the Pope. "Our hearts beat with more than usual speed, and not
without some little flurry, as we ascended the great staircase of the
Quirinal Palace." To these young men, Pius VII was not only the
Holy Father, but one who had suffered imprisonment and
humiliation in defence of the Church.

> The friendly and almost national grasp of the hand, after
> due homage had been willingly paid, between the Head of the
> Catholic Church, venerable by his very age, and a youth who
> had nothing even to promise; the first exhortation on entering
> a course of study—its very inaugural discourse, from him he
> believed to be the fountain of spiritual wisdom on earth;—
> there surely formed a double tie, not to be broken, but rather
> strengthened by every subsequent experience.

The students at the English College attended lectures in philosophy, theology and canon law at the Roman College, now the Gregorian University. Here they mixed with students of many nationalities. Latin was the language of instruction and of converse. Wiseman proved a brilliant student. His earliest successes were in physico-mathematics and physico-chemistry, but he soon showed a facility in languages and, in particular, excelled in Oriental studies. In 1824, at the age of twenty-one, he was successful in the public disputation in theology. The attendant cardinals and professors were so impressed with the clarity of his exposition and his learning that the Doctorate of Divinity was conferred upon him *extra tempus*. This achievement, and the successes of his fellows, brought prestige to the re-established English College.

He was ordained priest in 1825, two months before Newman was ordained in the Anglican Church.

Freed from college discipline, Wiseman concentrated on Oriental languages, and was able to spend more time exploring Rome and the Campagna. Some of his most pleasant days were spent at the college summer villa at Monte Porzio in the Alban Hills above Frascati. In his last hours his thoughts went back to those early days. "I can see the colour of the chestnut trees, and Camaldoli and the top of Tusculum."

The publication of *Horæ Syriacæ* in 1827 gave him a distinctive place in the world of scholarship. In this book he contributed to the study of the Syriac versions of the Old Testament. As with most works of that kind, later study and research have superseded his pioneer work, but in its day it brought him recognition from scholars of other countries who had correspondence with him or visited him in Rome. In the same year he became vice-rector of the English College.

Outwardly all seemed to prosper with the young scholar; but inwardly he was to endure the onset of intellectual doubt. This seems to have been, in part, the result of his Old Testament studies. In later life he referred to his struggle against "subtle thoughts and venomous suggestions of a fiendlike infidelity" which he won by concentrating on his studies and by intense meditation. His advice to those who had similar periods of difficulty was that "during the actual struggle the simple submission of faith is the only remedy."

This period of desolation lasted several years; it was a lonely trial for he felt that there was no one who could possibly sympathize with him. One of the minor effects was that his love for Rome was temporarily eclipsed.

When we think of the Wiseman of his most influential period, with his vitality and boundless enthusiasm for all that concerned the Church, it is well to recall that, in his early twenties, he went through the trial of bitter dejection when the very foundations of his life seemed to be slipping from under him. Out of this crucial experience came much of his spiritual strength.

It was in 1827 that he was given a task that he rightly regarded as a turning point in his career, "dragging from the commerce with the dead to that of the living, one who would gladly have confined his time to the former; from books to men, from reading to speaking." Pope Leo XII had noted the increase in the numbers of English, Catholic and Protestant, who were settling in Rome since the restoration of peace; there were also many who spent the winter there or who came as visitors. He felt it was desirable that they should have opportunities of hearing sermons in their own language. When he put this suggestion to the rector of the English College, Dr Gradwell at once suggested that his young assistant should be the preacher, and Wiseman had to accept this charge. He had not hitherto preached publicly, and he faced his task with diffidence. "It would be impossible to describe," he wrote, "the anxiety, pain and trouble which this command cost for many years after."

The sermons were given in the small church of Gesù e Maria in the Corso. The Pope showed his special interest by sending part of his choir to the opening service. There are no records of Wiseman's early sermons, but as his confidence grew, so his reputation spread and English Protestants as well as Catholics were glad to hear him.

His initial mistrust of his powers does not correspond with the popular conception of Wiseman in his mature years. He had a naïve delight in his own range of information and in his command of languages, and many tales are told of his conversational powers; he was able to contribute something of value on many varied subjects. At times there may have been a suggestion of "What a clever boy am I!", but the fact was that he did know a great deal about a great many subjects; his knowledge of literature, of painting and sculpture, and of music was not that of a dilettante but was based on serious study and on genuine appreciation. In these days when a scholar is likely to be a specialist on a specialized section of a subject and can converse on that alone with any authority, it is difficult to believe that any one man could have talked intelligently on so many things as Wiseman was undoubtedly able to do; the evidence is convincing and it comes from many sources.

It should be remembered that he was living in a cosmopolitan city. When he became rector of the English College in 1828[1] (the year that took Newman to St Mary's) he was brought more and more into the society of Rome. There was a danger, perhaps, that the tall, handsome young rector might become too absorbed in social activities.

His sermons made him known to the influential English residents and visitors who sought his advice and enjoyed his conversation; scholars of other countries came to consult him on the problems of Old Testament languages. He was the natural host of priests from England. To all he gave his time and attention. It was in such meetings that he learned so much of the development of Catholic thought in France and Germany and the problems of the Catholic minority in England.

In 1830 George Spencer, son of Earl Spencer, came to the English College as a student. He was one of a small group of Cambridge converts such as Ambrose Phillipps and Kenelm Digby, who took an optimistic but unreal view of the possibilities of the re-conversion of England. Spencer, who took the name of Ignatius, told Wiseman that Syrian manuscripts were of no importance compared with England's need for priests. He may have infected Wiseman with his own too favourable opinion of the prospects of Catholicism at home; he certainly caused the young rector to turn his thoughts to the position of England.

[1] Dr Gradwell had left Rome to become coadjutor to the Vicar-Apostolic of the London District.

Meantime, Wiseman was occupied with his duties at the English College. George Errington became vice-rector, and it was on him that most of the day-to-day work fell. Wiseman had little aptitude for administration; he guided and encouraged the students, and once a week took them off to visit early Christian remains in Rome, or to the museums and galleries. They could have had no more enthusiastic or informed guide. During his early years as rector, his own intellectual difficulties still troubled him, and this may have made him reluctant to act as a spiritual director, but as his period of desolation passed, so he was able with renewed and greater confidence to help others in their difficulties.

For himself, his days as a scholar were numbered. In the summer of 1828 he noted in his diary, "When shall I once more be quietly at my books?" The answer was to be "Never". He occasionally took a day or two off from the College to prepare a lecture or a sermon, and the summer vacation at Monte Porzio was precious as a period of recuperation and meditation. But he was never again to take his seat in the Vatican Library as a scholar entirely devoted to research and study.

CHAPTER IV

HENRY EDWARD MANNING
1808–1837

HENRY EDWARD MANNING was born on 15 July 1808 at Copped
Hall, Totteridge, Hertfordshire. His father was William Manning,
M.P. for Evesham, of the prosperous West India merchant firm
of Manning and Anderdon, and a director of the Bank of England.
William Manning's mother was a Ryan, and his wife's grand-
mother was a Bosanquet; there were therefore Irish and Huguenot
strains in the family.

Henry Edward was the youngest son of a large family, and he
always treasured the happiest memories of his seven years as a
child at Totteridge. In the year of Waterloo, the family moved to
Combe Bank, Sundridge, near Sevenoaks in Kent. The rector was
Dr Christopher Wordsworth, the youngest brother of the poet,
and later Master of Trinity College, Cambridge; he was a tory
High Churchman of the old school. His two younger sons, Charles
and Christopher (both to be Anglican bishops), were of near age to
the youngest of the Mannings, and the three became playfellows.

After four years of preparatory schooling, Manning joined
his friend Charles Wordsworth at Harrow in 1822. The school
was not at that period notable for its scholarship; the headmaster,
Dr George Butler, set high standards of conduct and character
which had their influence on his pupils, but the instruction, both
in religion and classics, seems to have been uninspiring.

The older pupils read William Paley's *View of the Evidences of
Christianity* (1794), and Charles Leslie's *Short and Easy Method with
the Deists* (1698). "These two stuck by me," wrote Manning in
later years, "and did my head good. I took in the whole argument,
and I thank God that nothing has ever shaken it."

Manning distinguished himself at Harrow as a cricketer and as
a dandy.

31

It was while he was at Harrow that he began a long correspondence with his brother-in-law, John Anderdon, who had married the second of the Manning daughters. He was fourteen years older than Henry, and became the boy's confidant and mentor; many of his letters are concerned with the writing of correct English, not only as to style but as to the arrangement of ideas—a training that was the more helpful as Harrow was not concerned with such matters. So inadequate was the instruction there, it was necessary for Manning to go to a private tutor to be prepared for Oxford.

The idea of taking Orders in the Church of England was in his mind when he left school in 1826. He then wrote to Anderdon, "I cannot take Orders till twenty-three, and therefore have upwards of four years before me." He does not seem to have had any strong conviction on the matter; the suggestion was a family one. For nine months he worked hard at the classics and also learned some French and Italian, and wrote verses as a relaxation. On 2 April 1827 he matriculated at Balliol and went into residence that October. Francis Newman was then beginning his second year at the college, but the two men do not appear to have seen much of each other. Charles Wordsworth was in his third year. Manning was, in fact, rather above the usual age of undergraduates.

During the first half of his Oxford career, Manning took an active part in the social and sporting life of the University. He had a number of contemporaries who were to be distinguished in later life, such as Samuel Wilberforce and W. E. Gladstone, but his association with them was not then intimate. The Union was their meeting ground and it was in the debates that he formed his wish to make a career in Parliament. By this time the intention of taking Orders seems to have lost its hold on him. "It was at the Union," he said, "I learnt to think on my feet." He spoke fluently on a diversity of subjects and was able to hold the attention of a most critical audience; he was president in the Michaelmas term of 1829. By then his father's business affairs were in danger and he had to warn his son that there could no longer be the prospect of the financial independence that was essential for a political career. One result was that Manning applied himself to his reading with that concentration that was always at his command. He took a first in classics at the end of 1830.

He had no deep religious experience at Oxford. He continued the practices he had learned at home; he attended chapel regularly, read his Bible and such standard works as Butler's *Analogy*. He took little interest in the Church problems that were being discussed by Newman and his friends, but he thought seriously about moral questions and discussed these with his brother-in-law. An indication of how strongly he could feel is shown when, after a visit to the Opera in Paris in 1828, he decided never again to enter a theatre—a resolution he kept all his life.

He heard some of Newman's sermons at St Mary's, but they did not have the powerful effect on him that others experienced. The two men had little intercourse during Manning's Oxford days. Manning's spare-time reading was in political economy, particularly the works of Adam Smith and Ricardo, and he delighted in argument on the matters raised in such books.

It was during his last year at Oxford that he felt the first stirrings of a deeper sense of religion. This was in part due to the continued influence of his brother-in-law. Their correspondence, and no doubt their conversation, was more and more concerned with religion. John Anderdon was a Churchman of the seventeenth-century tradition, and he wrote what is still a standard life of the saintly Bishop Ken. In his letters to Manning, he laid special stress on devotion to the Holy Spirit, on the need for self-examination, and on the necessity for a visible and organized Church. They exchanged note-books in which each commented on the other's thoughts on spiritual matters. Thomas Ken's dying words indicate the position that John Anderdon accepted. "I die in the Holy, Catholic and Apostolic Faith, professed by the whole Church before the disunion of East and West. More particularly I die in the Communion of the Church of England as it stands distinguished from all Papal and Puritan innovations, and as it adheres to the doctrine of the Cross." The influence of John Anderdon on Henry Manning's religious development over a period of many years was considerable.

A second influence was of a different character. Anderdon was not an Evangelical nor a Calvinist, but Manning was also intimate with a strongly Evangelical family. He spent some of his vacations with a school and university friend, Robert Bevan, whose sister, Mrs Mortimer, as she became, was a prolific authoress of booklets for the guidance of the young; they were after the manner of Hannah More. At a time when Manning was feeling depressed at his father's financial failure, he was staying with the Bevans; the sister, in true Evangelical spirit, talked to him of the state of his soul. The three read the Bible together each morning and had much conversation, and, after that vacation, correspondence on religious subjects. Manning spoke of Miss Bevan as his "spiritual mother", since it was through her that his devotion to the Church was deepened and his thoughts were turned to its service. He did not accept completely the Evangelical teaching; he looked, as his brother-in-law had taught him, to the divines of the seventeenth century.

When he came down from Oxford at the end of 1830, Manning was still in a state of indecision as to his future course. He had the unhappy experience of accompanying his father on his appearance before a Commissioner of Bankruptcy. Combe Bank was sold and the once wealthy merchant and bank director spent the few remaining years of his life in retirement.

As an immediate step, Manning took a part-time clerkship in the Colonial Office; the desire for a political career had not yet been driven out by a more compelling call. His leisure was still spent in studying such subjects as Constitutional Law and Political Economy. He thought of trying for a Fellowship at Merton College, but, for that, a layman had small chance of success. His relatives were urging him to take Orders, but he could not be driven to such a serious decision. His conception of the duties of a clergyman was too high for him to accept such obligations on bread-and-butter terms. The thought of taking Orders had been in his mind, but only to be rejected as he had not yet experienced the irresistible call he felt was essential. It is not known how that call came but, looking back over many years, he wrote that the decision was "as purely a call from God as all that He has given me since. It was a call *ad veritatem et ad seipsum.*"

The whole course of his future life was to show the truth of that statement.

The seriousness with which he accepted his vocation is indicated by the unusual course he followed—unusual for that time. A university man of his academic distinction and of his social standing would probably have been accepted at once by any bishop. It was before the days of theological colleges; indeed, even an elementary knowledge of theology was not an essential qualification. Manning, however, was not prepared to take up his life's work on such easy terms. He wrote to his brother-in-law, "I do not think I can possibly enter upon a profession of such responsibility without a much more mature preparation . . . and I should feel myself highly culpable were I to press forward without more solid acquirements and deliberate study."

He again sought a Merton Fellowship and was successful. This gave him the means to devote himself to reading and study. The records show that he concentrated on the works of the Anglican Divines of the seventeenth century: here again may be traced the influence of John Anderdon.

He was ordained deacon on 23 December 1832 and preached his first sermon at Cuddesdon on Christmas Day. Early in the New Year he went as curate to the rector of Lavington-with-Graffham in West Sussex, an out-of-the-way agricultural parish. His rector was the Rev. John Sargent and he invited Manning to live with his family. Manning was ordained priest on 9 June 1833. There were four daughters at the rectory; the eldest had married Samuel Wilberforce. His brother Henry was courting the fourth daughter. John Sargent died in May 1833, and Manning was presented to the living. In November of that year he married Caroline, the third of the daughters.

From his arrival in Lavington, he gave himself completely to pastoral work. John Sargent, an Evangelical, had done much to foster the religious life of the parish. Manning came to know all the members of the parish, visiting them in their homes in health and sickness, and climbing the Downs to talk with the shepherds. There was much ignorance and superstition to be overcome, but his kindliness and his devotion to them won their affection. Daily morning prayers were instituted and attendances at Sunday services and at Communion increased. His sermons were suited to his congregation and were on moral themes and not on dogma. He introduced no novel usages to bewilder country folk; he wore a surplice but that was no longer as unusual as it had been in the previous generation. He shared Newman's indifference to what was popularly known as "ritualism"; both insisted on comeliness and decency without being fussy about vestments or ornaments.

His marriage gave him a perfect home life and he was absorbed in his duties as a pastor and was able to share his anxieties and his hopes with his wife. In after years he could look back with tenderness to "the little church under a green hill-side, where the morning and evening prayers, and the music of the English Bible for seventeen years became a part of my soul. Nothing is more beautiful in the natural order, and if there were no eternal world, I could have made it my home."

It would be misleading to apply to Manning at this period any such label as High Churchman, Low Churchman or Evangelical. Indeed, during his Anglican days, he belonged to no school or party. His opinions were formed out of his own study, meditation and prayer. He did not turn to any one leader for the solution of the problems he had to face. He exchanged opinions in correspondence or conversation with such friends as the Wilberforce brothers and S. F. Wood of Oriel, a close friend of Newman. It does not seem, however, that they radically influenced his views; these developed slowly, partly through his own reading and partly in response to events that called for practical decisions on the issues raised.

There was another side of these years that is significant. Although his early political ambitions had dropped from him, he remained acutely aware of the social problems of a rural community. Of the agricultural workers he wrote;

We have a people straitened by poverty—worn down by toil: they labour from the rising to the setting of the sun: and the human spirit will faint or break at last. It is to this unrelenting round of labour that the sourness so unnatural to our

English poor, but now too often seen, is chiefly to be ascribed
... Those who have lived, as it is our blessing to do, among the
agricultural poor, well know that, with some rudeness of
address, and with faults not to be denied, they are still a noble-
hearted race, whose sincerity, simplicity and patience we
should buy cheap at the cost of our refinements.

After four years of happy married life, Caroline Manning's
health rapidly declined. She died in the summer of 1837. Manning's
grief was deep, but he had so disciplined his emotions that only
those most intimate with him knew how profoundly he was
afflicted. In after years he was silent about those brief, happy years;
those around him were alien to the Lavington life. On his death-
bed, he handed to Herbert Vaughan a worn note-book; it contained the prayers and meditations that Caroline Manning had
written down. "Take precious care of it!" said the dying Cardinal.

CHAPTER V

NEWMAN IN ROME AND AFTER
1833–1839

THE details of the Mediterranean journey of the Froudes and Newman do not concern us here. Some aspects however call for notice.

From the time of leaving Falmouth at the end of 1832 until his return alone seven months later, Newman's poetic faculty was stimulated. The result was a series of poems later published in the volume *Lyra Apostolica*. He set little store by his verses. Writing to Frederic Rogers after the party had arrived in Rome in March 1833, he advised him, as a relaxation, to "attempt verses. One ought to make the most of one's talents, and may write useful lines (useful to others) without being a poet. Ten thousand obvious ideas become impressive when put into metrical shape." Hurrell Froude shared in this verse making. The topics were mainly religious, and those that were written before Newman went off to Sicily alone, probably reflect the subjects of their conversations. We would give much for a record of the many discussions between the two men, with, perhaps, Archdeacon Froude voicing the opinions of the older generation as against his son's radical views. Newman's long letters home are traveller's tales of places seen and of impressions received; he said little of his thoughts.

Two years after his return, Newman contributed to the *British Magazine* some dialogues under the title "Home Thoughts Abroad." Two Englishmen in Rome discuss their impressions. The Ambrose of these conversations suggests Hurrell Froude. He put forward the view that "there is no reason why the ancient unity of Christendom should not be revived among us, and Rome be again the ecclesiastical head of the whole Church." To this his companion replied:

You will be much better employed, surely, in speculating upon the means of building up our existing English Church, the Church of Andrewes and Laud, Ken and Butler, than attempting what, even in your judgment, is an inconsistency. Tell me, can you tolerate the practical idolatry, the virtual worship of the Virgin and the Saints, which is the offence of the Latin Church, and the degradation of moral truth and duty which follows from these?"

Ambrose replied:

The actual English Church has never adopted it: in spite of the learning of her divines, she has ranked herself among the Protestants, and the doctrine of the Via Media has slept in libraries.

With this idea of the "ancient unity of Christendom" in their minds, Newman and Froude had two conversations with Wiseman at the English College; they also heard him preach. Newman's reference in the *Apologia* to these meetings is not informative; he says nothing of their import, but, "when we took our leave of Monsignor Wiseman, he had courteously expressed a wish that we might make a second visit to Rome. I said with great gravity, 'We have a work to do in England.' "
Froude gave a friend a more detailed account.

It is really melancholy to think how little one has got for one's time and money. The only thing I can put my hand on as an acquisition is having formed an acquaintance with a man of some influence in Rome, Monsignor Wiseman, the head of the English College, who has enlightened Newman and me on the subject of our relations to the Church of Rome. We got introduced to him to find out whether they would take us in on any terms to which we could twist our consciences, and we found, to our dismay, that not one step could be gained without swallowing the Council of Trent[1] as a whole. We

[1] 1545–63. The decrees were published in 1564.

D

made our approaches to the subject as delicately as we could.
Our first notion was that terms of communion were within
certain limits under the control of the Pope, or that in case
he could not dispense solely, yet at any rate the acts of one
council might be rescinded by another—indeed, that in Charles
I's time it had been intended to negotiate a reconciliation on
the terms on which things stood before the Council of Trent.
But we found, to our horror, that the doctrine of the infallibility of the Church made the Acts of each successive Council
obligatory for ever, that what had once been decided could
never be meddled with again—in fact, that they were committed finally and irrevocably, and could not advance one step
to meet us, even though the Church of England should again
become what it was in Laud's time, or indeed what it may have
been up to the atrocious council, for Monsignor Wiseman
admitted that many things (e.g. the doctrine of the Mass)
which were final then had been indeterminate before. . . . We
mean to make as much as we can out of our acquaintance with
Monsignor Wiseman, who is really too nice a person to talk
nonsense about.

An echo of this conversation is heard in some lines in a letter
Newman wrote at the time to one of his sisters.

Oh that Rome were not Rome! but I seem to see as clear
as day that a union with her is *impossible*. She is a cruel Church
asking of us impossibilities, excommunicating us for disobedience, and now watching and exulting over our approaching downfall.

Wiseman's *non possumus* was indeed not only the right answer,
but it was the kindest he could give; had he shown the slightest
inclination to compromise, there might have followed unreal
discussions such as did come later in the century. Froude and
Newman were left without any shadow of a doubt of Rome's attitude.

Wiseman recorded, many years later, that this meeting marked an epoch in his life. "From that hour I watched with interest and love the Movement of which I then caught the first glimpse. My studies changed their course, the bent of my mind was altered, in the strong desire to co-operate in the new mercies of Providence."

At that date the Oxford Movement, as we think of it, had not yet begun; it may be that in their two conversations with Wiseman these Anglican clergymen had given him some intimation of what they believed their work was to be in England.

The Froudes and Newman parted company in Rome; there was no kind of discord between them, but Newman had an unexplained urge to revisit Sicily, and probably Archdeacon Froude realized that his son could not have stood the strain of such an expedition. It was with regret that they parted.

The earlier short visit to Sicily had made a deep impression on Newman—one that every visitor to that island must share. "It has been a day in my life to have seen Egesta", he had written home. He later thought that his journey was because "I wished to see what it was to be a solitary and a wanderer." He had in fact tried to find a companion, but his failure to do so had not deterred him from what was a venturesome journey for anyone to make alone in those times. Yet this staid Oxford don collected his equipment and supplies, and, against the advice of his friends, set off with an Italian servant for an island where law and order were little regarded. Was the impulse that drove him a need to think out for himself the impressions and ideas that had crowded upon him since he left England? For more than three months he had been in the stimulating—perhaps over-stimulating—company of Hurrell Froude, and had been subjected to a storm of ideas. Then there was also the disturbing impression made upon him by Rome. He had told Wiseman that they had work to do in England; but what was its nature? The experiences he had in Sicily were certainly momentous, even though, try as he later did, he could not define their significance with any satisfaction to himself.

When his misfortunes came on him, he thought they might be a judgment on his self-will in leaving the Froudes, and on the resentment he had felt before the voyage when he had been deprived of pupils by the Provost of Oriel. Thus, in his own words,

"the devil thinks his time is come. I was given over into his hands."
And later, "I could almost think the devil saw I am to be a means
of usefulness, and tried to destroy me." His recovery seemed to
him providential as if confirming his remark to Monsignor Wiseman, "We have a work to do in England."

For a month he was prostrated by an all-but fatal fever. The
first symptoms had shown themselves soon after landing in the
island, but he had struggled on until he collapsed at Castro Gio-
vanni. He had periods of delirium, and to the good folk who
cared for him, it seemed that he could not recover. "I said, 'I do
not think I shall [die]. I have not sinned against the light', or,
'God has still work for me to do.' I think the latter." As soon as
he could stand again, he slowly made his way to Palermo. It was
there that he composed some lines on the Catholic Church beginning:

> Oh that thy creed were sound!
> For thou dost soothe the heart, thou Church of Rome,
> By thy unwearied watch and varied round
> Of Service, in thy Saviour's holy home.

He was delayed at Palermo waiting for a ship, and, after they
had sailed, by a calm between Corsica and Sardinia. It was then
that he wrote his best known poem "The Pillar of the Cloud"
("Lead, Kindly Light"). It reveals a mood of resignation and
trust; it was as if the trials he had suffered had brought him renewed faith in the guidance of God.

> Keep thou my feet; I do not ask to see
> The distant scene—one step enough for me.

His opposition to the Roman Church became less severe
during his months in Italy and Sicily.

The sight of so many great places, venerable shrines, and
noble churches, much impressed my imagination. And my
heart was touched also. Making an expedition on foot across
some wild country in Sicily, at six in the morning, I came

upon a small church; I heard voices, and looked in. It was crowded, and the congregation was singing. Of course it was the mass, though I did not know it at the time. And, in my weary days at Palermo, I was not ungrateful for the comfort which I had received in frequenting churches; nor did I ever forget it. . . . Thus I had learned to have tender feelings towards her [Rome]; but still my reason was not affected at all. My judgment was against her, when viewed as an institution as truly as it had ever been.

He arrived in Oxford on 9 July 1833;[1] his friends were impressed by the new air of confidence he had and by the sense of urgency he expressed.

A few days after his return, he heard John Keble preach the Assize sermon at St Mary's, a sermon which Keble entitled "National Apostacy." The occasion of it was that Parliament had passed an Act suppressing ten bishoprics of the Protestant Church in Ireland. To Keble and his friends this was a monstrous intervention by the State in the affairs of the Church. In Newman's letters from the Mediterranean there are several references to his anxiety over the fate of the Bill then before Parliament; "that wicked spoliation Bill", and, "the atrocious Irish sacrilege Bill", as he termed it. It was not therefore surprising that he warmly welcomed Keble's outspoken denunciation; "I have ever considered and kept the day, as the start of the religious movement of 1833."[2]

This is not the place to attempt yet another account of the Oxford, or Tractarian, Movement. The idea of publishing and disseminating tracts was Newman's own; he had a dislike for Committees and Organized Associations. The first tract was published in September 1833. Most of the early ones were written by Newman, but he had the encouragement and help of John Keble, and, until his final breakdown in health, of Hurrell Froude. Their respective shares in the work were summed up by Dean Church. "Keble had given the inspiration, Froude had given the impulse;

[1] His brother Francis landed in England on the same day. He had returned from a mission to Baghdad on behalf of the newly formed Plymouth Brethren.

[2] Newman so referred to what is more usually called the Oxford, or Tractarian, Movement.

then Newman took up the work, and the impulse henceforward, and the direction, were his."

Dr Pusey brought powerful support in 1835 by a tract, or rather treatise, on Baptism; this was the first to be signed; he had written an earlier one, anonymously, on Fasting. His name was so well known that the term "Puseyism" came to be applied popularly to the movement itself.

A concise account of the principles of the tracts is found in a passage from the fourth of a series of lectures Newman gave in 1850 on *The Difficulties of Anglicans*.

> That idea, or first principle, was ecclesiastical liberty; the doctrine which it especially opposed was, in ecclesiastical language, the heresy of Erastus, and in political, the Royal Supremacy. The object of its attack was the Establishment, considered simply as such . . . the writers of the Apostolical party of 1833 were earnest and copious in their enforcement of the high doctrines of the faith, of dogmatism, of the sacramental principle, of the sacraments (as far as the Anglican Prayer Book admitted them), of ceremonial observances, of practical duties, and of the counsels of perfection. . . . Dogma would be maintained, sacraments would be administered, religious perfection would be venerated and attempted, if the Church were supreme in her spiritual power; dogma would be sacrificed to expedience, sacraments would be rationalized, perfection would be ridiculed if she was made the slave of the State . . . It was for this that the writers of whom I speak had recourse to Antiquity, insisted upon the Apostolical Succession, exalted the Episcopate, and appealed to the people, not only because these things were true and right, but in order to shake off the State; they introduced them, in the first instance, as means towards the inculcation of the idea of the Church, as constituent portions of the great idea, which, when it once should be received, was a match for the world.

The appointment of Dr R. D. Hampden as Regius Professor of Divinity gave the Tractarians a rallying cause. He had, they maintained, expressed unorthodox views in his Bampton lectures four years earlier, and now he was to be thrust by the Prime Minister into a key position in the University. Here was, they pointed out, a clear case of the State usurping the proper function of the Church. Little could, in fact, be done. Protests were ignored. It was however possible to register objection by depriving Dr Hampden of his right to share in the selection of University preachers. This proposal was carried in Convocation by 474 votes to 94. Amongst those who came up to Oxford to vote against Dr Hampden was Henry Manning. Not all of the 474 were Tractarians, but their initiative had shown that many were thinking along the same lines on the relations between Church and State.

The next important stage to be noted was the series of lectures given by Newman in 1837 on *The Prophetic Office of the Church viewed relative to Romanism and Popular Protestantism*. In these he developed the theory of the Via Media adumbrated in his talks with Hurrell Froude in Rome. The Anglican Church, he argued, had its own proper course to follow, between, on the one hand, Romanism, and on the other, Protestantism. In the Introduction to the published lectures he wrote:

Protestantism and Popery are real religions; no one can doubt about them; they have furnished the mould in which nations have been cast: but the *Via Media,* viewed as an integral system, has never had existence except on paper; it is known, not positively but negatively, in its differences from the rival creeds, not in its own properties; and can only be described as a third system, neither the one nor the other, but with something of each, cutting between them, and, as if with a critical fastidiousness, trifling with them both, and boasting to be nearer Antiquity than either.

These lectures, wrote Dean Church, made a "lasting mark on English theological thought." They attracted many listeners from all sections of the University. Other courses followed on such subjects as Justification, and, the Canon of Scripture. Amongst his listeners was a young Fellow of Balliol, William George Ward;

he came at first with reluctance, but he fell under the spell of
Newman and was to become one of his most outspoken and
embarrassing supporters.

At this period Newman was working at full stretch. His sermons and lectures called for careful preparation and writing based
on much reading; the Tracts were pouring out from the press—
over seventy had been published by 1836; he was Vicar of St
Mary's and had built a new church at Littlemore to which he gave
much time and care; he was editor of the *British Critic,* which had
become the organ of the Movement. Some opposition had been
roused; the Heads of the Colleges were lukewarm or antagonistic;
the cry "Popery" had not yet become shrill, but fears were expressed of the direction in which things were moving.

He found time for weekly tea-parties when undergraduates
and older men could meet for general talk or for more serious
discussion. One of the undergraduates, Aubrey de Vere, later
recalled those days.

> Early in the evening a singularly graceful figure in cap and
> gown glided into the room. The slight form and gracious
> address might have belonged either to a youthful ascetic of the
> middle ages or to a graceful high-bred lady of our own days.
> He was pale and thin almost to emaciation, swift of pace, but
> when not walking intensely still, with a voice sweet and
> pathetic, and so distinct that you could count each vowel and
> consonant in every word. When touching on subjects which
> interested him, he used gestures rapid and decisive, though not
> vehement.

Well could he later recall that "in the opening of 1839 my
position in the Anglican Church was at its height."

CHAPTER VI

WISEMAN AND ENGLAND
1831–1839

NICHOLAS WISEMAN was agent in Rome for the vicars-apostolic of England. It was noted in the opening chapter that this country was ruled as a missionary field by Rome; the difficult circumstances of the long years of the penal laws had made it impossible for a hierarchy of bishops to have effective authority as in countries where the Catholic Church was either supported or tolerated by the State. An inevitable result was that many Catholics in England were unaware of the nature of full episcopal authority. One of the problems the vicars-apostolic had to face was how best to restore that authority in keeping with the new situation created by the Relief and Emancipation Acts. The long, and sometimes bitter, disputes between them and leading and influential laymen in the years leading to those Acts had left scars that only time could heal.

A fresh problem was created by the flight to their homeland of English monks and nuns from monasteries and convents that had been spoliated in France and the Low Countries. The tradition of monasticism had been almost lost since the suppression of the sixteenth century. The wealthier Catholics generously helped these fugitives to re-establish themselves, but the vicars-apostolic had now to consider what authority they had over these monastic orders.

After having been suppressed for just over forty years by Rome, the Jesuits were re-established in 1814; during that period many who had been Jesuits in 1773 remained in informal association as secular priests. Their famous school at St Omers had found a refuge at Liège when driven out of France; they were again forced to move as the French armies advanced. They came to England and were established at Stonyhurst by Thomas Weld.

When the order was revived, it was inevitable that problems of relations with the vicars-apostolic should arise. French emigré priests, and the influx of Irish in search of work presented other problems. The French went, but the Irish remained, and were soon joined by many thousands of their countrymen.

This brief survey will show that the vicars-apostolic had a complicated task before them in the 1830's. James Yorke Bramston was Vicar-Apostolic of the London District, a position he held from 1827. We have already seen that Dr Gradwell was appointed coadjutor in 1828. His death five years later was a serious loss; his first-hand knowledge of the Curia might have prevented some of the misunderstandings between the vicars-apostolic and Rome. He was succeeded by Thomas Griffiths, the first bishop to be appointed who had received all his training in England. The Midland District had Thomas Walsh as its Vicar-Apostolic; he had been trained at St Omer; he was a far-sighted man and somewhat bolder in his plans than his colleagues. The Vicar-Apostolic of the Northern District was Thomas Smith who had succeeded in 1821. The most recently appointed was Peter Augustine Baines, a Benedictine of Ampleforth, who became Vicar-Apostolic of the Western District in 1829 after six years as bishop coadjutor; he was a man of bold ideas but of an imperious nature who created more problems than he solved.

These were the men for whom Wiseman acted as agent. His lack of personal acquaintance with them in the early years made his task difficult, and his own imperfect knowledge of the special problems of England was a further handicap. On their part, the want of first-hand experience of Roman ways caused some misunderstanding. Their practical difficulties were not fully appreciated; thus it was not an easy matter to arrange a conference of four vicars-apostolic living far apart. Their resources were limited and there was a pressing need for more and more churches and for priests to man them. The wealthier Catholics, such as the Earl of Shrewsbury, were most generous but they could not bear the whole burden.

Bishop Baines was the first of the vicars-apostolic with whom Wiseman made close acquaintanceship. They met when Bishop

Baines was in Italy for more than two years for the sake of his health; this was happily restored by 1829 when he had to return to take up his duties as vicar-apostolic. He had already had an acrimonious dispute with the Benedictines of Downside over his proposal to make that place a seminary. On his return, he bought Prior Park, Bath; he proposed to use this magnificent mansion as a school, a seminary, and, ultimately, as a Catholic University. His disputes with the Benedictines continued and neither side conducted itself with decorum. In 1832 Rome decided to send Wiseman to England in the hope that he could effect some kind of settlement. During his three months' stay, he was unable to reconcile the parties; indeed, tempers were so frayed that he could not get them to meet. On his return journey, he had a serious accident when his carriage was overturned near Turin, but he managed to reach the English College for High Mass on the Feast of St Thomas of Canterbury at which eleven Cardinals were present.

The years 1833 and 1834 were passed quietly as Wiseman's health was indifferent. His meeting with Froude and Newman in 1833 has already been recorded, and at the beginning 1834 Bishop Baines was again in Rome to discuss his problems with Propaganda. He and Wiseman saw much of each other. They had some characteristics in common. Both were fertile in large, even grandiose, projects for the future of the Church; both were delightful conversationalists; both were eloquent preachers. Bishop Baines, however, was a man of uncertain temper who could not brook opposition to his bold schemes. He found that Wiseman was sympathetic to these, and even went so far as to suggest to Propaganda that Wiseman should become his coadjutor. This proposal was put on one side; it was probably felt desirable that the bishop's own problems should first be cleared up. He discussed with Wiseman a plan he had in mind to create a Catholic University at Prior Park; he realized that his greatest handicap was the lack of priests of the standard of scholarship to command respect and give prestige to such an undertaking. He suggested that Wiseman should come to England to organize such a University, a proposal that had the approval of the Pope.

In August 1834 Wiseman wrote to Archbishop Whitfield of Baltimore:

> I go to England in Spring to undertake the establishment of a new Catholic University under the sanction of His Holiness, who has been pleased to express his approbation, with a kind reserve that I give up none of my situations in Rome till I see, after a year or two, whether I shall continue them. In the meantime a Pro-Rector will fill my situation, one every way qualified for the office, formerly Vice-Rector [Errington].

During August 1834 Wiseman gave a series of lectures in Cardinal Weld's apartments "On the Connexion between Science and Revealed Religion." These dealt with the comparative study of languages, the natural history of the human race, the natural sciences, early history, archaeology, and Oriental literature. Though much of the material of the lectures is now outdated, the main argument holds good: advances in human knowledge do not invalidate the Christian revelation. Had his warning, that we should not hastily assume that each new discovery calls for a revision of the Christian tradition, been heeded in the coming years of Darwinian and other hypotheses, much bitter controversy would have been avoided. He took the view that we should not swallow new ideas merely because they are new, but calmly wait until the dust has settled and a true judgment can be made.

The lectures were attended by many eminent ecclesiastics and scholars who were greatly impressed by the lecturer's learning and his grasp of his subject. His reputation was thus again advanced just before he left for England in the summer of 1835.

He stayed in London for a short time and got to know the vicar-apostolic, Dr Bramston, and his coadjutor, Thomas Griffiths. Then he went on to Prior Park, full, no doubt, of expectations of the work that might open there for him. He was, however, to be disappointed. Bishop Baines had persuaded an Italian priest, Dr Gentili of the Institute of Charity, to become religious superior and vice-regent at the college. He very quickly introduced more demonstrative devotions than those to which Catholics in England had been accustomed in their enforced seclusion. Wiseman fully approved of this policy; he felt that Catholics in England should now free themselves from old restraints and benefit from the same aids to piety that were practised on the Continent. To his dismay he found, however, that Bishop Baines had lost his earlier enthusiasm for his co-operation. There was no longer any suggestion of the coadjutorship. Moreover the bishop seems to have resented Wiseman's advice on the conduct of the college. Advice from a man of Wiseman's academic distinction and experience should surely have counted for something. So the two men parted after a month and Wiseman returned to London. This proved to be a change of programme that served the Church in England at that time more usefully than a premature attempt to found a University.

He set out on a tour of the country to get a closer knowledge of the Catholic position. His visits were mostly to the landed gentry—the representatives of those families that had suffered so much for the faith in past centuries; this was an aspect of their lives that Wiseman, with his strong sense of tradition, could deeply appreciate, but he also saw that these faithful Catholics, with their ingrained habit of reticence, could not be expected to lead a revival; they had little sympathy with, or understanding of, the movement of opinion within the Anglican Church, and were inclined to be suspicious of converts. He made a valued friend in Dr Walsh, the Vicar-Apostolic of the Midland District, who felt it desirable that Wiseman should remain in England, and suggested that he should become coadjutor for that District, but the Pope felt that the time had not yet come for Wiseman to leave Rome. The collapse of the Bishop Baines scheme in addition to the difficulties Rome was then having with the vicars-apostolic, probably underlined the need for prudence in dealing with these awkward and contentious English.

Wiseman returned to London late in November and undertook duty at the Sardinian Chapel while the chief chaplain was away. In addition to some sermons in Italian, Wiseman gave a course of lectures in English on Sunday afternoons in Advent. They very soon attracted large congregations which included many Protestants. His purpose was to put before them the truths of the Catholic faith. It is difficult for us to realize what an innovation this was in the religious life of that day. Here was a priest from Rome itself daring to proclaim a faith that had been proscribed for generations; he was not doing it in some secret meeting place, but was inviting anyone who chose to come and hear him. "The method," he said, "which I shall follow is what I would rather call demonstrative than controversial. It will consist in laying before you the grounds of our doctrines, rather than in endeavouring to overthrow those professed by others." His grasp of his subject, his learning and his eloquence impressed his hearers; those of Protestant allegiance may not have been convinced or even shaken, but, for the first time in their lives, they heard a plain exposition of the meaning of the Catholic faith.

Many priests rejoiced at this bold course, but some were hesitant and a few antagonistic. The London coadjutor was one of those who did not whole-heartedly support Wiseman's proceedings. There had been some coolness between them when Wiseman, perhaps a little tactlessly, had criticized the clergy for their want of energy and initiative. Thomas Griffiths not unnaturally resented this attitude; he knew, only too well, how bravely many priests, living on a pittance, were serving the Church. The vicarapostolic, Dr Bramston, at once saw the value of Wiseman's work, and he persuaded him to repeat the lectures during the following Lent at the large church at Moorfields. As garbled versions of these lectures were being printed, Wiseman decided to publish as quickly as possible an authorized edition. This appeared in 1836 under the title *Lectures on the Principal Doctrines and Practices of the Catholic Church*; this was frequently reprinted in London and Dublin, and translated into French.

Another matter occupying Wiseman's thoughts at this time was the proposal that a Catholic Review should be established that would compel the serious attention of educated people. His attack, as it may be termed, was directed at the public that read the *Edinburgh* and *Quarterly Reviews*. The original proposal was made by Michael J. Quinn and was supported by Dr Charles Russell of Maynooth; Wiseman enlisted the interest of Daniel O'Connell; so the *Dublin Review* appeared in May 1836. It would be difficult to exaggerate the influence of this review as the organ of Catholic scholarship and opinion. It could not be ignored by the other churches; in Wiseman, scholars found that they had someone who could meet them on their own ground. He contributed numerous learned articles himself and enlisted the support of other scholars and men of science and letters. The articles, in the manner of the day, were in the form of reviews of books, but the books were excuses for discussions and expositions on the subjects suggested. There were occasional general articles on, for example, German and French Catholic Literature; these brought to the notice of English readers important work that was going on in countries where there was a Catholic revival. The range was wide—religion, literature, politics and science, all came under consideration.

Wiseman's year in England had been most productive; it is true that the original purpose of his stay had been frustrated, but, although he could be easily cast down at failure or opposition, he could as quickly recover his buoyancy. His lectures in London, his sermons at many centres, and the *Dublin Review* were achievements of first importance.

He lost a good friend in Dr Bramston in July 1836. Thomas Griffiths, who then became Vicar-Apostolic of the London District, was not so strong a supporter of Wiseman's plans. One obstacle to understanding was that the vicar-apostolic had not been out of England and had, therefore, no direct knowledge of Catholic practices in more favoured countries; he made his first visit to Rome in 1837. This want of full sympathy between them was a handicap to development. Wiseman certainly did not appreciate at that time the difficulties of Catholic life and pastoral work in England, yet, it would not be absurd to say, had he realized the true position, he could not have achieved the great work that was his contribution to the Church. By his very boldness of conception, he was able to bring the Catholics of England back into the main stream.

It would be tedious and little to our purpose to detail here the course of the vexatious negotiations and misunderstandings between the vicars-apostolic and Rome, during the three years that followed Wiseman's return to the English College. One of the lesser difficulties must be noted. He believed that much good could be done by establishing in England one of the religious communities, such as the Passionists, who could give retreats for the clergy and missions for the laity. The proposal was not well received; the introduction of foreigners would, it was felt (not without reason) be unpopular, and some of the older priests disliked the unfamiliar idea of retreats. Unfortunately Wiseman put his suggestion direct to the Pope without consulting the vicars-apostolic or Propaganda; the Pope, however, being wiser, decided that the matter must be dealt with in the usual manner. Wiseman's action naturally annoyed the vicars-apostolic, and by April 1839 they had lost confidence in him and resolved that it would be better to have an agent "unconnected with the English College, and not employed in any other office."

Meanwhile Wiseman was devoting himself to his work as rector of the English College. He seems to have gone into society less frequently, and his courses of lectures were for his students. He arranged for the annual retreat in 1837 to be conducted by the Jesuits; this had not only a beneficial effect on the students, but on Wiseman himself. He then formed resolutions for deepening his own spiritual life and for his conduct of affairs that marked an important stage in his development. He drew up a *Journal of Meditations for the whole year* as a guide to his students.

At this period he received many English visitors, some eminent and others on the way to eminence. Macaulay called at the college in November 1838. He noted, "We found the principal, Dr Wiseman, a young ecclesiastic full of health and vigour—much such a ruddy, strapping divine as I remember Whewell eighteen years ago—in purple vestments standing in the cloister." Soon afterwards, W. E. Gladstone and Henry Manning came to the College. In later life Gladstone recalled a return visit Wiseman made to his rooms.

> Mr Gladstone, full of the prospects of the Oxford Movement, maintained in the course of conversation, that the movement would tend, for the time at least, to keep people from the

Roman Church, by satisfying within the Anglican pale growing Catholic aspirations. Wiseman, rejoicing equally at the
movement, was quite prepared to endorse this view. Mr
Gladstone appears to have been struck by Wiseman's sympathy with the spread of Catholic ideas, irrespective of immediate gains to the Catholic body and the Apostolic See. In
point of fact Wiseman's confidence that the Church of England could not be the ultimate goal of the Tractarian movement was absolute. And yet, if the movement was to secure
any large band of adherents it must necessarily, in the first
instance, take form on Newman's *via media*. He welcomed it
as restoring to the Church of England great Catholic principles
which must, with men of active minds, eventually lead to a
sense of the duty of that Catholic unity which is their correla-
tive.

Wiseman and his vice-rector, George Errington, gave much
thought to the future of the Catholic Church in England. They
both saw that the urgent need was the training of zealous and
educated priests. Wiseman was in England again during the second
half of 1839; he saw much of Bishop Walsh and of the college at
Oscott which had been rebuilt according to the ideas of the convert Augustus Welby Pugin, who was also at work on the designs
for St Chad's Cathedral at Birmingham. Wiseman preached at the
opening of the new church at Derby; this too had been designed
by Pugin. There were indeed many signs of a forward movement.
Bishop Griffiths had come to take a more sympathetic view of
Wiseman's activities, and asked him to deliver another series of
lectures in London in 1840. In spite of their different approaches to
the problems of the Church, the two men respected each other and
recognized the services each could render in his own sphere. Some
of the older priests, such as the historian John Lingard, still clung
to the old quiet ways and regarded innovations with suspicion.
The answer to one question—the restoration of the hierarchy
—was to bring Wiseman to England permanently in 1840. It has
already been noted that as vicars-apostolic, the bishops in England
did not exercise full authority; they were bishops *in partibus*. With

E

the passing of the Emancipation Act in 1829, the desirability of the establishment of the hierarchy became evident; as we have seen a number of fresh problems called for attention, and there was much delay in referring these to Rome. The matter was long under discussion. One view expressed in Rome was that the English were quarrelsome and therefore not yet ready for hierarchical control! We need not here follow all the details. In September 1839, the Pope decided to postpone the hierarchy question, and, as a temporary measure, to double the number of vicariates. The negotiations were protracted, but by the early summer of 1840 the scheme was completed. Included in the arrangements was the appointment of Wiseman as coadjutor to Bishop Walsh, and as president of Oscott College. He was consecrated at the English College as Bishop of Melipotamus on 8 June 1840.

CHAPTER VII

MANNING AT LAVINGTON AND IN ROME
1837–1840

AFTER his wife's death, Manning found solace in his parish duties and in a continuation of his reading of the Early Fathers. He recalled in later years that, as he paced his study, the very titles of their works forced him to consider that "these are the witnesses of the mind of the Church at all times. How far am I in harmony with them?" His was not, however, a strongly speculative mind, nor had he a trained historical judgment. The actual problems of the day had to be faced, and he turned his thoughts to the consideration of policy in dealing with them. He had the outlook of the statesman, who, while adhering to considered principles, has to deal with affairs of the moment.

Two problems in particular seem to have occupied his mind at this period—the unity of the Church, and, the right relations between Church and State. On the second of these, he had a voluminous correspondence with W. E. Gladstone, and the two enjoyed a close friendship at this period. Gladstone was working on his book *The State in its Relations with the Church* which was published at the end of 1838. In his book Gladstone considered also the unity of the Church, a matter to which Macaulay referred in his well-known review.

What wide differences of opinion respecting the operation of the sacraments are held by bishops, doctors, presbyters of the Church of England, all men who have conscientiously declared their assent to her articles, all men who are, according to Mr Gladstone, ordained hereditary witnesses of the truth, all men whose voices make up what, he tells us, is the voice of true and reasonable authority! Here, again, the Church has not unity.

Both problems are aspects of one question: wherein lies authority in spiritual matters?

In a sermon on "The Rule of Faith" preached in 1838, Manning argued that for the Protestant the Rule of Faith was the private judgment of the individual; for the Catholic, the teaching of the living Church, and, for the Anglican, Scripture supported by the teaching of Antiquity. He defended the notion of the Anglican *Via Media*. This summary account serves to show that he had moved some way from the Evangelical position, and he was approaching the teaching of the Tractarians. He had for several years professed belief in the Apostolical Succession of the Anglican hierarchy. In a sermon preached in 1835 he asked, "Our commission to witness for Christ hangs on this question, Are the Bishops of our Church the successors in lineal descent of the Lord's Apostles?" His hearers were left in no doubt of the preacher's conviction that the answer was "Yes".

Moreover he regarded the Anglican Church as Catholic; this is shown in two articles he wrote in *The British Magazine* at the end of 1836. He signed them "A Catholic Priest". He had been reading Wiseman's Moorfields lectures. Manning's objection is stated in the following sentence:

> The assumption of the exclusive right to the name "Catholic" for the Church of Rome, and the confounding of the Church of England with other Protestant bodies, was on the part of Dr Wiseman an unworthy controversial artifice.

It may well be that the reading of Wiseman's lectures gave Manning his first comprehensive account of the Roman Catholic claims to authority.

These lectures also drew comments from Newman in *The British Critic*. His point of view shocked some of his adherents, for he claimed that, as a result of such propaganda as these lectures, "Dissenters and irregulars" might be converted to Rome, and that would be a matter for rejoicing. "Romanism", he wrote, "has great truths in it, which we of this day have almost forgotten, and its preachers will recall numbers of Churchmen and Dissenters to an acknowledgment of them." He was so sure of the validity of Anglican claims that he had no fears that Wiseman would influence Churchmen to look to Rome.

So, for the first time, the three men came together in the field of controversy.

In view of these expressed opinions, it is not surprising that Manning was regarded as a Tractarian. He himself refused to accept the label, and, while the reading of the Tracts had its part in the development of his ideas, he did not identify himself intimately with the movement of 1833. His attention was drawn to the Tracts by an old friend, an Oriel man, Samuel Wood, one of Newman's fervent disciples. With Newman himself, Manning had little personal intercourse; for several years from 1838 they were in correspondence. Manning contributed one or two articles to *The British Critic* then under Newman's editorship, and he offered to do a translation for Pusey's *Library of the Fathers*.

William Otter was appointed Bishop of Chichester in 1836. He had been the friend of Thomas Malthus author of the *Essay on Population*. It may be that Manning knew Malthus and Otter in the days when he was interested in the Political Economy Club of which they were both members. Bishop Otter does not seem to have held strong opinions on the religious controversies of the day. He had been the first principal of King's College, London, and his interest in education was continued when he became a bishop. His work is summed up in *The Dictionary of National Biography* in the following words:

> The chief acts of his episcopate were the establishment (1838) of the diocesan association for building churches and schools, and for augmenting the incomes of poor livings and curacies; the foundation . . . of the theological college; the setting on foot of a training school for masters; the institution of a weekly celebration in the cathedral (1839), and the revival of rural chapters.

All this was achieved during the four years of his life at Chichester. Whatever their differences on Church questions may have been (the bishop preferred peace to controversy) Manning soon found himself working enthusiastically in the causes that William Otter had at heart. Indeed it may be conjectured that Manning was permanently influenced by having his energies directed into practical channels in this way; the inclination to be up and doing was there, but it was William Otter who gave him the opportunity to test his ability in handling men and in promoting desirable reforms.

Manning became Rural Dean in 1837, and at a meeting of his colleagues he suggested they should discuss the proposition that "all Church matters ought to be administered by the Church alone." He was very soon, however, occupied with educational schemes. Gladstone, Samuel Wood and others were opposed to the proposal that the State should become responsible for secular education leaving religious instruction to the churches. Manning preached a sermon on "National Education" on behalf of the Chichester Central Schools in 1838. He argued that the Church itself should be responsible for education, and that the reading of the Bible in schools "without note or comment" was not sufficient. In practical affairs of this kind, Manning was not content to criticize; he formulated the policy he thought desirable; he stressed the importance of training teachers to meet the growing needs of the middle class, and he wanted to see Cathedrals become the power-houses for educational developments. Here he was in harmony with the views of his bishop and with those of such friends as Samuel Wood.

Manning strongly opposed the proposals of the Ecclesiastical Commission to redistribute the incomes of bishops and to create new sees. In an open letter to his bishop (1838), he declared against the interference of Parliament in Church affairs. "The next Patriarch of the English Church will be Parliament, and on its vote will hang our orders, mission, discipline, and faith." He backed his argument with some doubtful history. The decisive evidence of his conclusion did not come until 1927 when Parliament rejected a Revision of the Prayer Book recommended by the Convocations.

Bishop Otter's scheme for a Theological College at Chichester was warmly supported by Manning and his friends, some of whom hoped that he would be the first principal. The bishop selected Charles Marriott of Oriel, one of Newman's disciples; evidently the bishop was not hostile to the Tractarians. He appointed Manning to be secretary of the Diocesan Board of the National Society for Promoting the Education of the Poor.

The strain of his wife's death and his increasing activity in Church affairs led to a breakdown in Manning's health. He was a man who gave himself completely to whatever he took in hand, and his absorption in the subject on which he was at any given time engaged was so intense that he sometimes lost his sense of proportion; that subject, whatever it might be, became, for the time, the only subject that mattered. By such concentrated attention he achieved much, but he was apt to judge harshly those who could not follow his example.

To recover his health he left England towards the end of 1838 to spend the winter in Rome. There he found Gladstone, and the two friends spent much of their time together; they listened to sermons and visited the churches. It will be recalled that Newman had avoided church services while in Italy. The meeting with Wiseman has already been noted; it took place on 29 December, Gladstone's twenty-ninth birthday; Manning was in his thirtieth year. On St Agnes' Day, 21 January, Wiseman took Manning to see the blessing of the lambs. In his diary he noted:

> Wiseman told me that the controversy about the Anglican succession turned on the fact of the Lambeth Register. Lingard affirmative, a Dominican (*sic*) of Downside negative. Temper bad; therefore Lingard broke off.

Presumably Wiseman did not know that his visitor was the "Catholic Priest" who had criticized him two years earlier.

Other entries in his diary show that he was thinking out the positions of the Anglican and the Roman Churches, but his notes make it clear that he was not drawing nearer to Rome at that period; there were many things of which he was critical, and some that he found distasteful.

He was an indefatigable sightseer, and he also mixed with the members of the English colony; he met John Sterling, whose biography was written by Thomas Carlyle. Sterling gave his impression of Manning in a letter to a friend.

> He is one of the most finished and compact specimens of his school of manhood and of theology that I have ever fallen in with, and it was amusing to see how by faultless self-command, dialectic acuteness, coherent system, readiness of expression, and a perfect union of earnestness and gentleness, he always seemed to put in the wrong the gentlemen of the so-called Evangelical class, who muster strong here, and whom he frequently met with. . . . I conceive him to be, in his own place and generation, one of the most practically efficient and energetic men I have ever known.

Restored to health, Manning returned to Lavington; the anniversary of his wife's death renewed his sense of loss; he devoted himself even more wholeheartedly to his rustic parishioners; his work for education was gradually drawing him into a larger field of activity, and he was becoming known as an effective preacher. He was aided by a fine presence and a pleasant delivery, but he did not cultivate the art of the orator; his reliance was on expressing his message as simply and clearly as he could. His published sermons of his Anglican period are, in point of style, misleading. Those published separately from 1838 onwards were delivered on special occasions, and were elaborated for publication. His first volume of collected sermons was published in 1842.[1] Unfortunately he allowed his brother-in-law, John Anderdon, to revise the text; the result was a pseudo-seventeenth-century style that makes for artificiality. Manning never did achieve a distinctive style, and this may have been due to his long tutelage. It was his custom to send proofs of his writings to those whose opinions he valued;

[1] Other volumes were published in 1846, 1847, and 1850. It is interesting to note that the first three volumes were published by James Burns, and the last by Wm Pickering. By 1850 Burns had become a Catholic, and it was to help his new publishing business that Newman gave him *Loss and Gain*.

Newman and Keble helped him in this way. On one proof Newman wrote, "I have nothing to find fault with, but a few grammatical and other points which I have marked" (1838); this suggests that comments on style were invited as well as on matter.

His recollections in old age give his considered views on preaching.

> If I know myself, I can say that I have carefully and conscientiously prepared the matter of all my preaching, but never the form, or style, or manner . . . I have tried to say what I had to say in the fewest and simplest words, and my great comfort has been to watch altar-boys, and see them listen without moving, and to know that servants and poor people had understood what I said.

Two incidents are of interest.

> A very simple but devout person asked me why in my first volume of sermons I had said so little about the Holy Ghost. I was not aware of it; but I found it to be true. I at once resolved that I would make a reparation every day of my life to the Holy Ghost. This I have never failed to do to this day. To this I owe the light and faith which brought me into the true fold.

> I was walking in the fields at Lavington one afternoon, and it came to my mind that the Apostles going forth *a latere Jesu* must have always preached in His name, making Him and it their subject, and keeping up their consciousness of their personal relation to Him, and His to them. This made me believe that we ought also to do the same; and I have ever since endeavoured to choose the matter and to dispose the manner so to make Him the beginning and the ending, the chief person and main idea, of all preaching.

It was clear that this greatly gifted man could not long remain in his country parish; the opportunity for more extended work soon came to him.

CHAPTER VIII

NEWMAN AND LITTLEMORE
1839–1845

In the spring of 1839 my position in the Anglican Church was at its height.

From the end of 1841, I was on my death-bed, as regards my membership of the Anglican Church.

Littlemore, October 8th, 1845. I am this night expecting Father Dominic, the Passionist. . . . I mean to ask of him admission into the One Fold of Christ.

Those three sentences, the first of which has already been quoted, mark the stages of Newman's course to Rome. He gave us "the history of my religious opinions" in his *Apologia*(1864–5); he there tells us, as openly and plainly as any man has ever revealed his inmost self, how he came to leave the Anglican Church which meant so much to him, to submit himself to the Roman Catholic Church. The more contemporary records are studied, and there is a vast amount of material, the more must Newman's candour be appreciated.

Here it is not possible to do more than make a bold sketch map of Newman's journey; much ancillary detail must be omitted, but the chief landmarks can be indicated.

In the Long Vacation of 1839, Newman began to study the history of the Monophysites.

It was during this course of reading that for the first time a doubt came upon me of the tenableness of Anglicanism. . . . My stronghold was Antiquity; now here, in the middle of the fifth century, I found, as it seemed to me, Christendom of the

64

sixteenth and the nineteenth centuries reflected. I saw my face in that mirror, and I was a Monophysite.

While he was engaged in this study, a friend drew his attention to an article by Wiseman in the *Dublin Review* of August; in discussing Anglican Claims, the writer drew a parallel with the position of the Donatists of the fourth century, and he quoted "the palmary words of St Augustine". "Quapropter securus judicat orbis terrarum bonos non esse qui se dividunt ab arbe terrarum in quacumque parte orbis terrarum" (For the whole [Christian] world judges with assurance that they are not good men who separate themselves from all the world in any part of the world).

At first this pronouncement on the significance of schism focused Newman's attention on an aspect of the Anglican position that was startling in its clarity.

I had seen the shadow of a hand upon the wall. It was clear that I had a good deal to learn on the question of the Churches, and that perhaps some new light was coming upon me. He who has seen a ghost, cannot be as if he had never seen it. The heavens had opened and closed again. The thought for the moment had been, "The Church of Rome will be found right after all;" and then it had vanished. My old convictions remained as before.

Here must be noted the entry of a man who was to cause much distress to Newman, and in later years to ruin the chances of accord between him and Manning. William George Ward was eleven years Newman's junior; he became a Fellow of Balliol in 1834. He was a man of acute intellect but a doctrinaire who ruthlessly followed an argument to its logical conclusion. His exuberant personality concealed serious limitations; his knowledge outside his chosen field was curiously defective; he had, for example, no interest in history or in the natural world. Things for him were either black or white; he was not sensitive to half-tones;

he could not understand, still less imaginatively share, the hesitations and infirmities of others; those who disagreed with him
were anathema. It would be difficult to find a nature more at
variance with the temperament of the man he chose as leader.
Newman's sensitiveness to shades of thought; his deep insight into
the working of men's minds; his scrupulous fairness to opponents;
his refusal to dominate—all these were far removed from Ward's
ultra-dogmatism.

He was one of those "eager, acute, resolute minds . . . who
knew nothing about the *Via Media* but had heard much of Rome",
as Newman described some of his younger followers. He recognized their true concern for religion and their fearlessness; but he
had no wish to be their kind of leader or prophet; indeed he had
no wish to be a leader at all. The impact of this younger and more
impetuous group came at the period when Newman "had seen
the shadow of a hand upon the wall"—a period when his greatest
need was for "peace and silence", so that he could consider his new
problem in all its aspects. There were "practical abuses and excesses" in the Roman Church that made him wince, and for a
time he concentrated his thought on "the political conduct, the
controversial bearing, and the social methods and manifestations
of Rome" rather than on questions of doctrine or authority. This,
however, was to postpone, not to face, the main issue.

He spent more and more of his time at Littlemore, and as early
as October 1840 he considered resigning from St Mary's, but was
dissuaded by Keble. He did give up the editorship of *The British
Critic,* and the new editor, Thomas Mozley, who had married
Harriet Newman, found zealous (sometimes over zealous) contributors in W. G. Ward and his friends.

Meantime these enthusiasts embarrassed Newman by urging
that he should go further and faster than he was prepared to
go; they wanted *ex cathedra* pronouncements that would settle
things once and for all. Newman's attitude puzzled them. As he
wrote:

> With an anxious presentment on my mind of the upshot of
> the whole inquiry, which it was almost impossible for me to

conceal from men who saw me day by day, who heard my familiar conversation, who came perhaps for the express purpose of pumping me, and having a categorical *yes* or *no* to their questions,—how could I expect to say anything about my actual, positive, present belief, which would be sustaining or consoling to such persons as were haunted by doubts of their own? Nay, how could I, with satisfaction to myself, analyze my own mind, and say what I held and what I did not hold? or how could I say with what limitations, shades of difference, or degrees of belief, I still held that body of Anglican opinions which I had openly professed and taught? how could I deny or assert this point or that, without injustice to the new light, in which the whole evidence for those old opinions presented itself to my mind?

One of Newman's later articles in *The British Critic* was "On the Catholicity of the English Church." It argued that "the Church of England was nothing else than a continuation in this country (as the Church of Rome might be in France or Spain) of that one Church of which in old times Athanasius and Augustine were members." This raised the question of whether the Catholic faith of "old times" was to be found in the XXXIX Articles of the Prayer Book. To this problem Newman now set his mind.

The outcome was Tract 90, published in February 1841; the purpose was "merely to show that, while our Prayer Book is acknowledged on all hands to be of Catholic origin, our Articles also, the offspring of an uncatholic age, are, through God's good providence, to say the least, not uncatholic, and may be subscribed by those who aim at being Catholic in heart and doctrine."

In this way Newman hoped to quieten the younger men and to make them content to remain where they were; some were already looking to Rome, and it was not long before occasional conversions took place. He had not expected that his Tract would cause more contention than its predecessors, but he recognized that its reception would have a decisive influence on his own position.

Though my Tract was an experiment, it was, as I said at the time, "no *feeler*"; the event showed this; for, when my principle was not granted, I did not draw back, but gave up. I would not hold office in a Church which would not allow my sense of the Articles.

A few months after the publication of the Tract, Dr Charles Russell of Maynooth was moved to send Newman a comment on his treatment of transubstantiation (Article 28). It was done in such a kindly way that Newman replied and the two men began a correspondence. He later wrote of Dr Russell:

> He had, perhaps, more to do with my conversion than any one else. He called upon me, in passing through Oxford in the summer of 1841, and I think I took him over some of the buildings of the University. He called again another summer, on his way from Dublin to London. I do not recollect that he said a word on the subject of religion on either occasion. He sent me at different times several letters; he was always gentle, mild, unobtrusive, uncontroversial. He let me alone.

The last sentence is significant. Newman had refused to meet Father Ignatius Spencer in Oxford, and he also declined overtures from Ambrose Phillipps. Any suggestion of negotiations was repugnant to Newman. He wanted to be "let alone". He did, however, receive Wiseman at Oriel in July 1841, but there is no record of their conversation.

Newman was now engaged on a translation of Athanasius, and this took him back to his earlier work on the Arians. The "ghost" raised by Wiseman's article on the Donatists returned.

> I saw clearly, that in the history of Arianism, the pure Arians were the Protestants, the semi-Arians were the Anglicans, and that Rome now was what it was then.

This renewed disturbance of mind coincided with the condemnation of Tract 90 by the bishops. "The bishops one after another began to charge against me. It was a formal, determinate movement." To one who had such a high opinion of the office of a bishop, this attack was decisive. The Heads of Houses had protested against the Tract, and there had been other strong criticisms, but these, in Newman's eyes, did not carry the same authority as an episcopal censure.

Then followed the strange episode of the Jerusalem bishopric. By an agreement sponsored by the British and Prussian governments, a bishopric was created which was to be held alternately by an Anglican and a Lutheran. Newman commented:

> Now here, at the very time that the Anglican Bishops were directing their censure upon me for avowing an approach to the Catholic Church not closer than I believed the Anglican formularies would allow, they were on the other hand, fraternizing, by their act or by their sufferance, with Protestant bodies, and allowing them to put themselves under an Anglican Bishop, without any renunciation of their errors or regard to their due reception of baptism and confirmation.

Other indications of mounting opposition to the Tractarians were to follow. Even the election of a Professor of Poetry in 1842 was decided by the fact that one candidate was a Tractarian and the other an Evangelical. Then came the high-handed suspension from preaching of Dr Pusey because a sermon of his on "The Holy Eucharist" was considered to be contrary to Anglican teaching.

By this time Newman had settled at Littlemore where a few younger men joined him in a regulated life of prayer and study. He resigned from St Mary's in September 1843, and preached his last sermon as an Anglican on the 25th of that month. At the same time he published a retractation of former attacks on the Roman Church.

A few close friends knew his mind; he did not attempt to conceal from them his travail of spirit; they could only await the outcome with trepidation, mingled with the hope that even yet they might be spared an irreparable loss. Some wrote to him to express the anxiety caused by rumours. In reply to such a letter from Manning, Newman wrote on 16 November 1844:

As far as I know myself, my one great distress is the per-
plexity, unsettlement, alarm, scepticism, which I am causing
to so many, known and unknown, who have wished well to
me. . . . My one paramount reason for contemplating a change
is my deep, unvarying conviction that our Church is in schism
and my salvation depends on my joining the Church of Rome.
. . . I have no visions whatever of hope, no schemes of action, in
any other sphere more suited to me; I have no existing sympathies with Roman Catholics; I hardly ever, even abroad, was
at one of their services; I know none of them; I do not like
what I hear of them. And then, how much I am giving up in
so many ways, and to me sacrifices irreparable, not only from
my age, when people hate changing, but from my especial love
of old associations and the pleasures of memory. Nor am I
conscious of any feeling, enthusiastic or heroic, of pleasure in
the sacrifice; I have nothing to support me here. What keeps
me yet is what has kept me long—a fear that I am under a
delusion; but the conviction remains firm under all circumstances, in all frames of mind.

He was not, however, to be allowed the peace and quiet he so
greatly needed. In February 1845 W. G. Ward's book *Ideal of a
Christian Church* was condemned by Convocation at Oxford and
he was deprived of his degrees. It was an astonishing book to come
from one who was in Anglican Orders. Thus he declared that
Rome was "that quarter where my own eyes are always first
directed when in search of spiritual wisdom." The authorities
were determined to condemn Ward, but they were as anxious in
so doing to involve the man who, as they imagined, was really
responsible for Ward's provocative opinions. A vote of censure on
Tract 90 was vetoed by the proctors. Pusey wrote, "So, on
scarcely nine days' notice it is proposed to condemn Tract 90. It
is monstrous. Such headlong persecution never can prosper in the
end. . . . Newman has successively given up the Tracts, an influential pulpit, sermons, a most deep and healthful influence over
young men, his residence in Oxford . . . and now he has been
doing nothing but editing St Athanasius's great defence of the

faith, he is to be pursued even to his retreat at Littlemore and condemned there."

With the fear in his mind, as he had written to Manning, that he might be deceiving himself:

> At the end of 1844, I came to the resolution of writing an Essay on Doctrinal Development; and then, if, at the end of it, my convictions in favour of the Roman Church were not weaker, of taking the necessary steps for admission to her fold.

He worked hard at the book during 1845; it took more out of him than any previous work of his. His companions at Littlemore noticed how he seemed to grow frailer as his labour went forward. It was never finished. He at length reached the stage at which conviction ousted all doubts and hesitations. He broke off his writing.

> *Littlemore, October 8th, 1845.* I am this night expecting Father Dominic, the Passionist. . . . I mean to ask of him admission into the One Fold of Christ.

F

CHAPTER IX

WISEMAN AT OSCOTT
1840–1845

THE arrival of Wiseman at Oscott in September 1840 was to prove a notable event in the advance of the Catholic Church in England. It must not, however, be seen in isolation. Ever since the Relief and Emancipation Acts, the freed Church had been gaining ground but with the circumspection born of three centuries of oppression and sufferance. A fresh impetus came from converts who submitted to the Church before the influence of the Tractarian Movement was felt; the names of Ambrose Phillipps, George Spencer, Frederick Lucas, Henry Bagshawe, Chisholm Anstey and of Augustus Welby Pugin (only one of whom became a priest) sufficiently indicate the strengthening of the Catholic life of the country. Some of them, notably Ambrose Phillipps, took too sanguine a view of the prospects of the Church; they, to some extent, helped to form Wiseman's early expectations of widespread conversions. When the Catholic tendencies of Tractarianism became evident, these hopes were raised. The old Catholics were not so optimistic, and indeed some were inclined to be suspicious of newcomers.

It is against this background that we must set the life and work of Wiseman in England. He had the advantage of bringing to his task the prestige he had gained in Rome; he could take a bolder view than was possible for those who had spent their lives on the mission, or for those who represented the established Catholic families with the traditions of penal times. The vicars-apostolic were devout pastors but the restrictions under which they had been forced to work had inevitably made them cautious; moreover, their knowledge of the self-denying lives of their priests made them quick to resent any suggestion that these faithful journeymen of the Church were suddenly out-dated.

72

The situation called for great tact and forbearance; tempers were sorely tried at times; on the one hand were some who clung to the old ways and frowned upon new men and new methods; on the other were the more vociferous of the converts who failed to appreciate the deep-seated piety of those whose families had kept the Faith over the centuries. It is not easy to see how such difficulties could have been overcome by anyone whose training and work had been limited to England. Herein lay the importance of Wiseman's position; it was to be his mission to bring the Church in England safely through this transitional period.

These and other problems could not be seen in their fullness in 1840, and Wiseman had no exceptional authority; he was coadjutor to Bishop Thomas Walsh of the new Central District, and president of Oscott College, near Birmingham. The reception he had at Oscott must have pleased him; the full ceremonial for the entry of a newly appointed bishop to his diocese was carried out with due solemnity. He described his early impressions in a letter to Dr Lingard who was far from sharing Wiseman's hopes for the conversion of England.

I find everything to my hand that I could desire for furthering my views—a magnificent College, with a still more magnificent library; professors some already most able, the rest qualifying themselves to raise our education to the highest standard; a united and zealous clergy; a fine opening at Birmingham for every Catholic institution. These are certainly great advantages, which conjointly with a central position, I could hardly have found elsewhere. As to my own pursuits, if worthy of a thought or mention, I think I shall have quite as much time as I had at Rome as soon as I have got things here as I expect and wish, and have organized what seems to me to have been neglected till now, proper regulation of the official transaction of ecclesiastical affairs. Till now the Bishop's writing desks seem to have been the only chancery and archivium of the districts; and the whole episcopal regimen seems to have led a sort of nomadic life, wandering about in stage coaches or gigs from place to place.

This quotation is evidence that he had much to learn about English conditions. The vicars-apostolic had neither the means nor the men to maintain what Wiseman described as "episcopal chanceries . . . by which everything is properly filed and preserved." Much had to be achieved, and much was achieved, with slender resources. A glimpse of how things had to be done was recorded by the popular Anglican preacher W. H. Brookfield; he wrote of having seen the Vicar-Apostolic of London (Dr Griffiths) "get out of an omnibus in Piccadilly, seize his carpet bag, and trudge straight home with it to Golden Square."

Wiseman's first move in organizing diocesan business received a set-back. He wanted the services of William Thompson, a former student of his in Rome, but was refused. This trifling occurrence is worth noting because it illustrates a characteristic of Wiseman that has its importance in understanding his personality. This refusal depressed him; he was quickly cast down at any check to his plans; he as quickly recovered his buoyancy, but momentarily he was inclined to give way to despondency. Life had indeed been kind to him; his brilliant career at Rome and his earlier successes in England had not yet been tempered by disappointment or failure.

He made some changes in the staff of the college; one of the Cambridge converts, Henry Logan, became vice-president, and George Errington was brought from Rome to be prefect of studies. The routine work of the college was left in their hands. Father George (Ignatius) Spencer was already there as spiritual director to the boys.

Canon Bernard Smith, one of the earlier Oxford converts, has given us an interesting account of Wiseman in his Oscott days.

As Fellow of Magdalen I had known Routh and many of the most distinguished Oxford men of the time, including Newman, Pusey and Keble. But excepting Newman (whose gifts were different) I had never come across anyone who gave me nearly so much the impression of a *great* man as Dr Wiseman— a man with great gifts, great designs and a truly large heart. He was, however, emphatically a great Bishop rather than a great President. His distinction gave *prestige* to Oscott, and drew many eminent men to the place; but the minutiæ of college discipline and *routine* did not interest him. He left such things to others. . . . But as a Bishop, constantly visiting various parts of the diocese, giving retreats to the clergy, urging them to great zeal and raising their tone, he was indeed an acquisition to the Church in England.

The building of new churches, no longer disguised as warehouses, was a sign of the forward movement amongst Catholics. The munificence of the Earl of Shrewsbury and the genius of Pugin were at the service of the Church, and Wiseman's presence at the laying of a foundation stone or at the opening added distinction to the occasion. Not the least of his achievements was that, in spite of his love of Palladian architecture, he came to terms with Pugin's Gothic monomania. Pugin was, indeed, one of the links with Tractarian Oxford, and Wiseman was anxious to strengthen any such link and, if possible, establish personal relations. Precipitate action would have been harmful. Fortunately Wiseman sensed this danger and, for a time, he was content to receive reports from such intermediaries as Pugin and Ambrose Phillipps. The latter was persistent in his efforts to reach an understanding with the Oxford men. He deprecated the publication of some of Wiseman's articles in the *Dublin Review* in a volume entitled *High Church Claims* (1841). He kept up a correspondence with J. R. Bloxam and Bernard Smith, both of Magdalen, who were former curates to Newman; the first did not leave the Anglican Church; Bernard Smith's memories of Wiseman at Oscott have just been quoted.

These letters were shown to Newman, and Ambrose Phillipps also wrote to him direct. A less persistent or obtuse man than Phillipps would have been discouraged by Newman's plain-speaking. A few sentences will indicate his attitude.

I must ask your leave to repeat on this occasion most distinctly that I cannot be a party to any agitation; but mean to remain quiet in my own place, and to do all I can to make others take the same course.

If your friends wish to put a gulf between themselves and us let them make converts.

Some months since, I ventured to say in a letter to Mr Bloxam, which was sent to you, that I felt it a painful duty to keep aloof from all Roman Catholics, however much to be respected personally, who came with the intention of opening negotiations for the union of the Churches.

This correspondence was carried on in the period immediately following the publication of Tract 90 early in 1841. When Newman published his Letter to Dr Jelf in explanation of the Tract, Wiseman thought it opportune to print his own comments in "A Letter respectfully addressed to the Rev. J. H. Newman". This thirty-two paged pamphlet went through four editions in that year. Wiseman wrote "not as presuming upon the passing acquaintance I made with you some years ago in Rome", but from an "earnest anxiety to convince" such a sincere inquirer. In his Letter to Dr Jelf, Newman had reiterated his objection to the prominence given in Roman Catholic practice "as a popular system" to devotion to Our Lady and the Saints, to the veneration of relics and to the granting of Indulgences. These, he argued, went beyond the Decrees of the Council of Trent. To this Wiseman replied:

Bear with me if I speak too prominently in my own name, because I have some right to come forward as a witness in this matter. I have resided for two-and-twenty years in Rome, intimately connected with its theological education. For five years I attended the Roman schools in the Roman College, where all the clergy of the city were obliged to be educated. I went through the entire theological course and publicly maintained it in a Thesis. Since then I have been always engaged in teaching theology in our national College, and for some years have held the office of professor in the Roman University. I ought, therefore, to be tolerably well acquainted with the doctrines of the Roman schools.

He then went on to show that the devotions and practices to which Newman objected formed but a small part of the authoritative teaching of the Church. He concluded:

> If there was ever a time when you did not see many of our doctrines as you now view them; when you utterly rejected all comprecation with, as much as prayers to, saints; all honour, without reserve, to images and relics; when you did not practise prayers for the departed, nor turned from the congregation for your service; when you did not consider bodily mortification necessary, or the Breviary so beautiful; when, in fine, you were more remote from us in practice and feeling than your writings now show you to be, why not suspect that a further approximation may yet remain; that further discoveries of truth, in what today seems erroneous, may be reserved for tomorrow, and that you may be laying up for yourself the pain and regret of having beforehand branded with approbrious and afflicting names that which you will discover to be good and holy?

Newman did not reply to this published letter, but left that task to William Palmer of Worcester College, who opened his argument by calling in question Wiseman's episcopal Orders!

Throughout 1841, Wiseman, encouraged by Ambrose Phillipps, was hopeful of a speedy accession to the Church of the Tractarians. He was deeply concerned not only for the souls to be saved, but for the influence for good they could have within the Church. The following extract from a letter to Ambrose Phillipps reveals Wiseman's attitude at this time.

> There is one point which has always struck me as important to *us,* though it would not easily strike *them.* It is that *our* reformation is in *their* hands. . . . Our ecclesiastical education has

been necessarily very imperfect, from the necessity of placing
our clergy as soon as possible into active operation from dearth
of priests. Still more the succession of men contemplative,
ascetic, and devoted to God, who abound in Catholic countries
(as in Rome) has been lost among us. . . . Let us have an influx
of new blood; let us have but even a small number of such men
as write in the Tracts, so imbued with the spirit of the early
Church, so desirous to revive the image of the ancient Fathers
—men who have learnt to teach from St Augustine, to preach
from St Chrysostom, and to feel from St Bernard: let even a
few such men, with the high clerical feeling which I believe
them to possess, enter fully into the spirit of the Catholic religion, and we shall speedily be reformed, and England quickly
converted. I am ready to acknowledge that, in all things, except the happiness of possessing the truth, and being in communion with God's true Church, and enjoying the advantage
and blessings that flow thence, we are their inferiors. It is not
to you that I say this for the first time. I have long said it to
those about me—that if the Oxford Divines entered the
Church, we must be ready to fall into the shade and take up
our position in the back ground. I will gladly say to any of
them "Me oportet minui." I will willingly yield to them place
and honour, if God's service require it. I will be a co-operator
under the greater zeal and learning and abilities of a new leader.
Depend upon it, they do not know their own strength.

That passage calls for careful consideration. It explains much
in Wiseman's subsequent conduct towards the converts; his hopes
were not realized to the full, but he did all he could to bring them
to fruition. His attitude was not intelligible to many Catholics,
nor indeed to the vicars-apostolic. Dr Griffiths of London pointed
out that "scarcely shall we find in history a body of schismatics
returning with sincerity to the obedience of the faith." Dr Lingard
doubted the candour of the Tractarians. Joseph Rathbone, priest
at Cowes, published a pamphlet in 1841 entitled, "Are the Pusey-
ites Sincere?", and answered his own question with an emphatic
"No."

Wiseman wrote to Newman in May 1841 to protest against an article in *The Tablet*, written from Oxford, attacking Daniel O'Connell. He wrote to Phillipps, "With yours I received a most distressing letter from Newman, which has thrown me on my back and painfully dispirited me." In his reply Newman satisfied Wiseman as to O'Connell.

He then goes on [reported Wiseman] to express his regret that I should have attempted to vindicate the invocations to the B.V. used in the Church—and augurs it as a bad omen that we do not give them up. Now really, if his expectation was that the Church, or that we, should give up our tender and confident devotion towards the Holy Mother of God, or that the least of her pastors would join (on his private judgment) with Mr Palmer in condemning expressions sanctioned and approved by her Pontiffs, how high indeed must his demands of condescension be before we can hope for reunion!

In July, Wiseman wrote, "I think Mr Newman is a timid man, and one who looks forward to reunion as a mere contingency."

Renewed hopes came when Tractarians began to visit Oscott. They included Bloxam, W. G. Ward, Oakeley, Bernard Smith and R. W. Sibthorpe. All but the first were later to become Catholics. Sibthorpe, on a sudden impulse, asked to be received at once; it was not perhaps surprising that he relapsed two years later—a set-back that so depressed Wiseman that he took to his bed. Encouraging as these personal contacts were, the forward movement that Wiseman expected did not come; a thin stream of converts was not the longed-for flood.

In May 1842, Newman wrote to John Keble:

As to the "Dublin", poor Dr Wiseman is dying to get us, and this makes him write in an anxious, forced, rhetorical way, being naturally not a little pompous in manner, though I believe it is principally manner.

At times Wiseman must have asked himself if his hopes were baseless. Newman's silence during his long agony which seemed to the onlooker so unduly protracted, tested the patience and affection of his friends, but, it equally troubled those who prayed for his conversion. An occasional sign brought renewed hope. His retraction of some of his censures on Rome, his resignation from St Mary's in September 1843, his seclusion at Littlemore, the outcry against Ward in 1844 and the renewed attack on Tract 90, seemed to bring the crisis nearer. Newman's close companions J. D. Dalgairns, Ambrose St John and Richard Stanton were unable to wait for their leader.

Wiseman was anxious to avoid doing anything that would harass Newman, yet, the tension was almost unbearable. For nearly five years Oscott had waited, and in spite of set-backs and the embarrassing comments of some Catholics, Wiseman still believed that the Church would triumph.

Towards the end of June 1845, he asked Bernard Smith, then studying theology at Oscott, to go to Littlemore to see if he could gather any news. Newman received him rather coldly and soon left him, but the others were eager to hear about Oscott and of what kind of folk Catholics were. Newman appeared at dinner time; Bernard Smith noticed that he was wearing grey trousers— it meant that Newman considered himself to be a layman. On his return to Oscott, Smith assured Wiseman that the great decision could not be far off. "What did he say to make you so confident?" "He hardly spoke." Then Bernard Smith explained the significance of the grey trousers. Wiseman was incredulous. "I knew you would think nothing of it," said Smith, "but I know the man. He will come, and come soon." Even so, three months passed before Newman was received.

On 31 October 1845 John Henry Newman went to Oscott to be confirmed by Bishop Wiseman. He was accompanied by John Walker, a Fellow of Brasenose College, and by Ambrose St John, who was to be his closest and most faithful confidant. To them came Bishop Wiseman, Bernard Smith and George Spencer. All were embarrassed; there was some laborious conversation then "a message which shortly announced that a boy was waiting to go to Confession to the Bishop gave Wiseman an excuse for retiring, which he accepted with significant alacrity."

Newman and Wiseman were never completely at ease with each other; each recognized the fine qualities of the other, and there was no sign of discord. They had one trait in common; a sensitiveness that made adversity more than normally disheartening, and each was to suffer many rebuffs.

CHAPTER X

THE RESTORATION OF THE HIERARCHY
1840–1850

IT will be convenient here to interpose a brief account of the restoration to England of a Hierarchy to replace the rule of vicars-apostolic that had lasted since 1688.

Within a decade of the passing of the Emancipation Act (1829) it was clear that the increasing strength and renewed vigour of the Catholic Church in England was putting a great strain on the vicars-apostolic with their vast districts. It is important to appreciate the enormous amount of work they had to do in days when travelling was slow (as we should think) and the centres of Catholic life widely scattered. Moreover, as was noted in the previous chapter, they had neither the means nor the men to employ suitable staffs for themselves; nor had they those many communities that are so much a part of Catholic life today, to support the secular priests in charitable and other works.

Rome did not fully understand the circumstances in which the vicars-apostolic laboured, nor did Wiseman himself until he came to live in England and share their responsibilities. Regular visits to Rome would have meant serious interruptions of other pressing duties.[1] It was not easy to arrange a meeting of all the vicars-apostolic and this led to delays in replying to requests from Rome —delays that were misinterpreted. Only men of utter devotion could have achieved as much as they did.

In 1838 the four vicars-apostolic submitted to Rome proposals for making their task less exacting. The decision in 1840 to double the number of districts has already been noted. Five years later the vicars-apostolic favoured a proposal for the restoration of the Hierarchy, but the death of Pope Gregory XVI postponed the

[1] When Sir Robert Peel was summoned to England in 1834 it took him twelve days from Rome to London, travelling as expeditiously as possible.

matter. Cardinal Mastai Ferretti succeeded as Pius IX and so began a reign that for thirty-two years was to mean so much to the Church.

The vicars-apostolic decided in 1847 to send Bishop Wiseman and Bishop Sharples to Rome to put before the Pope the increasing urgency of restoring the Hierarchy and so bring England under the normal system of order in its Catholic affairs. The Pope was hesitant; there had been some mischievous criticism of the vicars-apostolic that disturbed him. Cardinal Acton, who had died in June 1847, had left a reasoned case against the restoration. Wiseman and Sharples were able to reassure the Pope, but two events caused some delay in pursuing the matter. Dr Griffiths of the London District died in August, and, in an unusually short time, Wiseman was appointed to succeed him as pro-vicar-apostolic; this curious title was chosen as a kind of stop-gap arrangement. The second event was that Wiseman was sent back to England on a diplomatic mission.

It is not necessary here to describe the political situation; suffice it to say that the Austrians were threatening the Papal States, and the Pope was determined to avoid an armed clash. It was known that the English Government, with Lord Palmerston as Foreign Secretary, was sending Lord Minto to Italy to see what could be done to maintain peace. The Pope was anxious to gain the moral support of Great Britain, but as there were no diplomatic relations, it was difficult to open consultations. Wiseman put the case with his usual lucidity to Palmerston who decided that Minto should go to Rome, not as an accredited minister—that being impossible as the law stood—"but as an authentic organ of the British Government." Palmerston was able to restrain Austria, but the "authentic organ" was not a useful instrument.

The vicars-apostolic soon began their consideration of the scheme that had been drawn up in Rome; they had been asked to divide the country into twelve dioceses. Several problems at once arose—geographical boundaries, titles, the legal safeguarding of ecclesiastical property, and, the right person to be archbishop. The bishops felt that they needed someone in Rome who could explain their problems. At first they hoped that Dr Grant, rector

of the English College, would come to England to learn their
views, but he felt unable to leave Rome at that period. The vicars-
apostolic therefore chose one of themselves, William Bernard
Ullathorne, O.S.B., of the Western District.

Here we meet for the first time in these pages one of the most
attractive and influential personalities of the Church in England
during the nineteenth century. His relations with Wiseman, and
more particularly with Newman and Manning were so important
that some account of him must be given.

A descendant of St Thomas More, he came of an old Catholic
family of Yorkshire. As a boy he had gone to sea; the
call to the Church had come to him, and he entered the Benedictine
monastery at Downside in 1823. His lack of a sound early schooling
was a handicap, but he studied diligently and was all his life a
reader of the Early Fathers. He was ordained priest in 1831 and in
the next year volunteered for the Australian mission. He did a
great work during his ten years there, and his revelations of the
horrors of the transportation system helped to bring about its
abolition. On his return he was appointed to Coventry and was
building up a vigorous Catholic community when he was called
to be Vicar-Apostolic of the Western District in 1846. It was with
reluctance that he accepted episcopal office; he had previously
declined an Australian bishopric.

He was a man of deep piety and utterly fearless and forthright;
this plain speaking came from one who had seen mankind in the
raw, but his dreadful experiences had not soured him, nor had
they robbed him of his youthful appearance even in middle age.
His warm-hearted nature made him greatly beloved. After a preliminary skirmish, to be noted later, he and Newman formed a
strong friendship; he was not on such happy terms with Manning,
to whom he is said to have remarked on one occasion, "I was a
Bishop when you were an 'eretic." Manning valued Ullathorne's
vigorous commonsense and frequently sought his advice. Ullathorne was trusted by the old Catholics for he was one of them,
but he was also the friend of the converts; in this way he became,
as it were, a bridge between the old and the new generations from
neither of which would he stand any nonsense.

Earlier visits to Rome in connexion with his work in Australia and with problems in his District, had made him well-liked; there was no vestige of self-seeking; he knew his own mind and was shrewd in negotiation. When therefore he went to Rome on behalf of the vicars-apostolic he was able to put their views forcefully and to counteract the harmful criticisms that had influenced the Pope and the Cardinals.

We need not go into all the details. Ullathorne's guidance was welcomed, but he could not persuade Propaganda to drop the proposal that Bishop Walsh, in spite of his serious state of health and his own protestations, should be transferred to London as the first archbishop. There was some doubt as to the expediency of appointing Wiseman; he was still under fifty, and there were strong opponents to his appointment; it was hinted that he was too much under the influence of the aristocracy, that he was too rash in his financial commitments, and that he showed too much favour to the converts.

Here it may be remarked that much harm was done, and continued to be done, at Rome by disgruntled chatterers who managed to secure a hearing in official circles; had the vicars-apostolic been able to keep in closer touch with the authorities, this kind of misrepresentation would have been avoided. The arrival of Ullathorne with his robust speaking made all the difference, and at once progress was made.

It was decided that when Dr Walsh left the Central District, Ullathorne would take his place. He returned to England at the end of July, and was formally received in St Chad's Cathedral, Birmingham, on 30 August. Meantime, Dr Walsh had moved to London; he died six months later at the age of seventy-two.

The plans for the restoration of the Hierarchy were delayed by political events in Rome. A revolutionary uprising forced the Pope to seek refuge in Gaeta on 22 November where he remained until the French had driven out Mazzini and Garibaldi. The Pope re-entered Rome on 12 April 1850. A month later Wiseman received a letter from the Cardinal Secretary of State to tell him that the Pope proposed raising him to the Cardinalate. This would mean that Wiseman would have to leave England to reside in Rome. In July he wrote to Dr Russell of Maynooth:

> The truth, then, is that I leave England (for ever) next month. In September the Consistory is to be held which binds me in golden fetters for life, and cuts off all my hopes, all my aspirations, all my life's wish to labour for England's conversion in England, in the midst of the strife with heresy, and the triumphs of the Church. I have written as plainly and as strongly as one can about oneself; but a peremptory answer had come that I am wanted at Rome, and that a successor will be provided.

He left England on 16 August and reached Rome on 5 September. By that time some leading Catholics had expressed their dismay at his withdrawal from England. There was also the problem of finding someone to take Dr Walsh's place in London; there was no obvious choice for what was to become the leading position in the Catholic Church in England. After reconsidering the matter, the Pope decided that Wiseman should return to England as Cardinal-Archbishop of Westminster. On 29 September 1850 the Papal Brief was issued restoring the Hierarchy, and on 3 October Wiseman received the Red Hat, and shortly afterwards the Pallium as the sign of his new jurisdiction.

On 7 October he sent to England the manuscript of his first Pastoral; four days later, in high spirits, he set out on his return journey. The Pastoral was couched in that exuberant language that was an expression of one side of Wiseman's personality. The publication of the Papal Brief, with its formal phrasing, was not likely to cause much disturbance, but this triumphant paean created a storm of vilification. The Prime Minister himself, Lord John Russell—who must have long known of the proposed restoration—led the hue and cry. It is an old story now.

Parturiunt montes, nascetur ridiculus mus—the Ecclesiastical Titles Act,[1] which imposed a fine of £100 on any person assuming

[1] The Act was repealed without any outcry by Gladstone's first government in 1871. In the previous year Manning had been prosecuted for using the title of Archbishop of Westminster, but the case was lost as the plaintiff had not obtained the necessary consent of the Attorney-General.

a title to a "pretended" see, with deprivation of legal status. The Bill was opposed by Gladstone in one of his finest orations, and also by John Bright—an Anglican and a Quaker. One sentence from the latter's speech should have made any government reconsider its proposals. "The noble lord has drawn up an indictment against eight millions of his countrymen."

By the time this foolish measure became law, the storm had died down. This was in some degree due to Wiseman's vigorous response. The first warning of the tempest came to him in Vienna on 3 November as he was making his way leisurely across Europe. He at once hastened his journey after sending off a letter of protest and explanation to the Prime Minister. At home there was consternation; had England reverted to the mood of the Gordon Riots? Many influential Catholics were in favour of advising Wiseman not to come to England for the present, and a message was sent to intercept him in Brussels; he had no hesitation in continuing his journey and he arrived in London unexpectedly on 11 November. No doubt during those days of incessant travel he had thought out the main lines of his policy, but Ullathorne too had been aware of the need. He, with the help of his convert friend Edgar Estcourt, collected material that might prove useful, such as previous statements made by the Prime Minister and other statesmen on religious toleration. Wiseman had these notes by him when he sat down to write his *Appeal to the English People*; this thirty-one paged pamphlet was completed within four days, and was published in full in five London daily papers. Within a few days 30,000 copies of the pamphlet had been sold. It was a magnificent piece of work that commanded the serious attention of all but the most bigoted fanatics. What had seemed to be a *débâcle* was turned into a powerful vindication.

Newman wrote of Wiseman at the time, "He is made for this world, and he rises with the occasion. Highly as I put his gifts, I was not prepared for such a display of vigour, power, and judgment, and sustained energy as the last two months have brought. I heard a dear friend of his say that the news of the opposition would kill him. How he has been out! It is the event of the time. In my own remembrance, there has been nothing like it."

There was one shadow over the scene. Some of the old Catholics (perhaps in an I-told-you-so mood), such as Lord Beaumont and the Duke of Norfolk,[1] were opposed to the restoration of the Hierarchy; that was an arguable matter; but they did not hesitate to voice their opposition to Wiseman at a time when he was faced with a nation-wide attack. Henry Manning, down at Lavington, noted this want of loyalty in a small section of the old Catholics.

[1] This was the thirteenth duke. He died in 1856. He had supported the Ecclesiastical Titles Bill.

CHAPTER XI

ARCHDEACON MANNING
1840–1851

BISHOP OTTER of Chichester died in August 1840; his successor was P. N. Shuttleworth, a most determined opponent of the Tractarians; nevertheless, he appointed Manning to be archdeacon within a few months. The new bishop died two years later, and was followed by Ashurst Gilbert, Principal of Brasenose; he was a High Churchman but not a ritualist. He was the last of the four Anglican bishops under whom Manning served. Bishop Otter had brought him out of his Lavington seclusion, and the two later bishops gave him further opportunities for using his considerable gifts.

As with all work he undertook, Manning applied himself zealously to his duties as archdeacon. The clergy soon found that he was determined to carry out his functions to the full; some may have resented this unwonted intrusion, as it seemed to them, and churchwardens were not always eager to give the information for which they were asked; this was inevitable after a period of torpor. By the end of his decade of office, Manning had won the respect and esteem of the clergy of the diocese. His tact and fine manners helped him to carry through his plans, but, above all, it was his selfless devotion to his duties that brought men to accept his guidance.

One of his early engagements after his appointment was to speak at a meeting in London in aid of the Colonial Bishoprics Fund to establish dioceses in British territories. In later years Gladstone recalled Manning's "striking and most powerful speech", and referred to him as one "whose whole mind and whole heart were then given to the service of the Church of England." Shortly afterwards he was again an effective speaker at a Mansion House meeting in support of the Society for the Propagation of the Gospel.

His work as archdeacon can be studied in the Visitation Charges he delivered; seven of these were published between 1840 and 1850. The topics were, at first, mainly of parish interest; later he dealt with more general subjects and with national questions raised by Bills before Parliament. In the first group may be noted as typical—state of the fabric of the parish church, lack of free seats, pews, voluntary oblations and parish clerks. The second group concerned such subjects as the Ecclesiastical Courts Bill, the Parochial Settlement Bill, training for Holy Orders, the Church abroad, marriage within prohibited degrees, Relief of Persons in Holy Orders Bill, and, the schools. A leading theme of his criticism of proposed legislation was that the State must not encroach upon the province of the Church. In one Charge (1846) in which he dealt with the horrors of the Australian penal settlements, he used the outspoken revelations of Ullathorne.

While we can in this way get a conspectus of the practical problems that occupied Manning's attention, it is more difficult to follow his religious development. Had he not written his *Apologia*, it would still be possible to write a history of Newman's religious opinions based on his own publications, his correspondence and the many contemporary records. Manning's progress from the Anglican to the Roman Church cannot be charted in detail; we have to move from landmark to landmark without knowing the intermediate steps. The nearest guide we have is given in letters to Robert Wilberforce during the period 1848 to 1851.

The difficulty of tracing the movement of his mind is in part due to his need for some event to crystallize his thoughts. This is not to suggest that his conclusions were purely empirical. Our difficulty is increased by his habit in old age of discounting early influences that, in fact, were stronger than he was later prepared to admit.

In 1842 he published his most important book as an Anglican, *The Unity of the Church,* a defence of the position of the Church of England. As with much that Manning wrote, the reader sets off in high hopes, only to be disappointed at the outcome which is sometimes commonplace. He may also be disconcerted by Manning's imperfect knowledge of the history of the Church. He seemed unable to think a subject right through; with considerable skill he could assemble a catena of quotations from the authorities, but would fail to raise a satisfying structure on that basis. Gladstone, to whom the book was dedicated, made the comment in later years that "in parts, it is somewhat wanting in depth and solidity." Manning's most effective writings were such short compositions as his Charges, and articles in Reviews, especially where he was handling matters of fact. He was better at assertion than at argument.

We can note some of the landmarks in his progress. In 1842 he declined to take sides in the contest for the election of a Professor of Poetry at Oxford—an Evangelical *v.* Tractarian affair, thereby annoying and mystifying the followers of Newman. An event in the following year must have dismayed still more those who regarded Manning as in sympathy with the Tractarians. On Guy Fawkes Day he preached before the University at St Mary's. It was a strongly anti-Roman sermon. He rejoiced at the frustration of the Powder Plot, "conceived, planned, and brought to the eve of perpetration, by members of the Roman Communion", and in the events of 1688 he saw a special providence defeating "the secular dominion of Rome. . . . The reign of princes alien from the English Church has been twice brought to an end with a speed truly significant; foreign armaments ignominiously baffled: conspiracies at home laid bare: insinuation of secret emissaries detected and expelled: the whole line of the House of Stuart repelled by steady and uniform defeats." It is a curious perversion of history; did the preacher forget that Dutch William's troops were two thirds alien? Did he forget that William and Mary were both descendants of the first of our Stuart kings? Did he overlook the wording of the coronation oath of 1689—to uphold "the Protestant Reformed Religion established by law"—so inconsonant with his own view of the Anglican Church? Did he forget the loyalty of Charles I to that Church? Blind spots such as these make it difficult to follow the workings of Manning's mind.

He went out to Littlemore on the day following this sermon. Newman avoided seeing him; a message of "Not at Home" was delivered by James Anthony Froude, the future apologist of

Henry VIII. Manning himself felt qualms about that sermon; in
his diary he noted seven reasons in its justification; these are
specious as there was no obligation to preach in such terms, nor
indeed to preach at all. A comment made by Keble in after years
suggests a possible explanation of Manning's strange behaviour.
"I always feared what would become of Manning when I heard
of his violent Fifth of November sermon. Exaggerations of this
kind provoke a Nemesis, and it did not surprise me so much as it
pained me to hear that he had become a Roman Catholic."

Two months later, Manning wrote to Newman in the hope
that their intercourse had not been irreparably broken. Newman
replied in a cordial manner; the incident was overlooked but it
must have puzzled Newman. He added a note of warning as to
his own position.

> It is no pleasure to me to differ from friends, no comfort to
> be estranged from them, no satisfaction or boast to have said
> things which I must unsay. Surely I will remain where I am as
> long as I can. I think it right to do so. If my misgivings are
> from above I shall be carried on in spite of my resistance. I
> cannot regret in time to come having struggled to remain
> where I found myself placed. And, believe me, the circum-
> stance of such men as yourself being contented to remain is the
> strongest argument in favour of my own remaining.

Manning sent this letter to Gladstone, whose reply included
these words:

> Is he aware of the immense consequence that may hang
> upon his movements? His letters do not show it. If he is not,
> either now or at some future time he ought to have his eyes
> opened.

Late in 1843 the preachership of Lincoln's Inn was vacant, and
Manning allowed his name to be proposed, but he was not
appointed. He had hoped to have a London pulpit at his command;
he could then advocate at the centre the Church policy that was

at that period much on his mind. He wanted to see the Church freed of Parliamentary control in all spiritual affairs; his suggestion was that provincial synods should be established with the Archbishop of Canterbury as supreme spiritual head. Gladstone saw no hope of this in face of the inevitable opposition of the bishops. As we shall see, this problem of the control of the Church was to play an increasingly important part in Manning's development.

Manning kept in touch with Newman by occasional letters, and it was in reply to one of these that Newman wrote the passage previously quoted, "What keeps me yet is what has kept me long —a fear that I am under a delusion."

By 1844, with Gladstone's encouragement, Manning was hearing confessions, and using a stone altar. When it was proposed in 1845 to condemn W. G. Ward's book, Manning was at first inclined to hold aloof, but Gladstone persuaded him to go to Oxford; both voted against the condemnation of the book and the degradation of its author. Manning and Ward met for the first time on this occasion in Dr Pusey's rooms. When Ward began to jest about his reversion to the status of an undergraduate, the archdeacon rebuked him. "The situation seems to me, Mr Ward, to be one of the utmost gravity. It is indeed a serious crisis. Let us not at such a time give way to a spirit of levity or hilarity."

Samuel Wilberforce was made Bishop of Oxford in that same year; he had been Sub-almoner to the Queen, and Manning was offered the position. This would have brought him into influential circles, and have led to greater preferment. Many recognized by this time that Archdeacon Manning was of episcopal timber; had they foreseen that his great friend Gladstone was to be four times Prime Minister, they would have been even more certain of the future. In his diary Manning minutely examined his conscience on the problem of accepting or refusing this appointment; finally, he refused it, one of his reasons being "the highest obligation I have is to my flock, and the highest season of it is Easter", when his duties as Sub-almoner would have taken him away. This scrupulous weighing of the reasons for and against an action was but one expression of the deep seriousness that characterized his sense of vocation.

His Charge of 1845 dealt, in part, with the proposal to remove the adjudication of divorce cases from the Ecclesiastical to the Civil Courts. "To this purely secular court," he wrote, "is transferred the primary and entire jurisdiction now exercised by the Church in matters of marriage and divorce. . . . If divorce be a question between individuals in their lay character, in what is marriage holy?" He sent a copy of the Charge to Dr Pusey, who commented, "Is there quite enough love of the Roman Church? However you do put forth strongly that we are sick, and what you say of chastenings must do good. I desiderate more love for Rome. When the battle with infidelity and rebellion comes, we must be on the same side." Manning sent this letter to Gladstone who expressed the fear that Pusey was becoming too favourable to Rome. Manning wrote to Pusey, "The Church of Rome for three hundred years desired our extinction. It is now undermining us."

Newman's submission in October 1845 was followed by that of many who looked to him for guidance. John Morley in his *Life of Gladstone,* records how the statesman and his friend felt at that time.

> More than once I have heard Mr Gladstone tell the story how about this time he sought from Manning an answer to the question that sorely perplexed him: what was the common bond of union that led men of intellect so different, of characters so opposite, of such various circumstance, to come to the same conclusion. Manning's answer was slow and deliberate; "Their common bond is their want of truth." "I was surprised beyond measure," Mr Gladstone would proceed, "and startled at his judgment."

Newman's *Essay on the Development of Christian Doctrine* was published in November 1845. (It was in the following month that Manning refused the Sub-almonership.) A number of letters passed between Manning and Gladstone about Newman's book; both felt that it called for an answer. In a letter in 1847 Manning wrote, "When Newman's book was published, Gladstone urged me to answer it. I declined pledging myself; but it forced me again into the same two subjects (Unity and Infallibility) to which I have continued to give all the thought and reading I can."

The book greatly disturbed him, and his references to it in his letters show how much it was on his mind; indeed, it can be said with some assurance that this book gave the first serious jolt to Manning's Anglicanism. A few quotations from his diary for 1846 show how his assurance had been shaken.

May 15. Tho' not therefore Roman, I cease to be Anglican.
July 12. I feel less able to say that Rome is wrong.
August 2. Now I see that St Peter has a Primacy among the Apostles. That the Church of Rome inherits what St Peter had among Apostles. That the Church of Rome is therefore heir of Infallibility.

In that month he wrote to Gladstone, "I have a fear, amounting to belief, that the Church of England must split asunder." Gladstone so firmly maintained his confidence in the Anglican position that from then onwards he no longer received Manning's full confidence; he turned to his brother-in-law, Robert Wilberforce, who was moving in the same direction.

Manning fell gravely ill early in 1847; the exact nature of his sickness is not known, but it may be hazarded that it was a serious breakdown due to his unrelaxing labours aggravated by his spiritual and mental incertitude. During the months that he was ill, he reviewed his past life, and made a strict examination of his spiritual state; the full record he made is a distressing document; he was all but overwhelmed with remorse and self-reproach, and this conflict had to be endured without the guidance of a spiritual director. There are some parallels with the self-revelations of Hurrell Froude. This period was the crisis of Manning's religious development.

When he was sufficiently well to travel, he set off for Belgium. His detailed diary shows that he spent much of his time visiting churches and seminaries and gathering information from priests. He attended many services and was deeply impressed by what he saw, especially by the rite of Exposition and Benediction of the

Blessed Sacrament. He continued his journey down the Rhine
into Switzerland, but he felt so ill again that he hastened home.
With his sister and her husband he left again for the Continent;
they travelled through to Nice, and, by way of Genoa and Leghorn, to Rome where they arrived on 27 November. Manning
was in Rome for five months.

His diary is a factual record of things seen, with sketches and
plans, and of information gathered. The impression given is that
he was intent on learning all he could of the Roman Church, not
so much of its doctrines as of its ritual, organization and practices.
He got into touch with priests and the directors of institutions and
questioned them closely on administration and on the significance
of what he saw. The precarious political situation was discussed
on many occasions; it will be recalled that the Pope fled to Gaeta
only six months after Manning left Italy.

He met Newman and Ambrose St John in Rome but recorded
nothing of what passed between them. Newman did not at first
recognize him so ill did he look.

Manning was presented to the Pope on 9 April 1848, and had
a private audience on 11 May. The Pope expressed some surprise
at the practices of the Anglican Church. Manning afterwards
recalled "the pain I felt at seeing how unknown we were to the
Vicar of Jesus Christ. It made me feel our isolation", a feeling
deepened by the ignorance shown by even scholarly priests of the
Anglican Church.

On his way home he spent some days at Assisi and then at
Milan where he saw the relics of St Charles Borromeo.

Archdeacon Manning returned to his work in the summer of
1848, with restored physical health and with a considerable
knowledge of the Roman Catholic system. His approach to the
Church had been very different from the course followed by
Newman who had avoided contacts, as far as possible, with
Catholics and their practices. When he entered the Church he had
no direct knowledge of Catholic worship; he knew it solely from
the Breviary and the Missal. Manning, on the other hand, had
spent six months in visiting churches and institutions and in
gathering information about them.

His Charge of 1848 referred to the appointment of Dr Hampden to be Bishop of Hereford. This had created a storm at the beginning of the year, for the preferment was being given to one whose orthodoxy had been questioned by the University eleven years earlier. Manning was in Italy at the time so had no opportunity of taking part in the protest, but, in a letter to Robert Wilberforce, he described it as "the most dangerous conflict we have ever had." Yet, in his Charge he accepted the *fait accompli*, as "Dr Hampden has up to this moment never been condemned by any tribunal of the Church."

He was soon called upon to take a leading part in defending the religious autonomy of the Church Schools against the threat of government interference. In 1839 the Church had secured, as it believed, the management of its schools, but in 1846 some suggestions of the Committee of the Council of Education (the forerunner of the Board) seemed to encroach on the Church authority. Manning at once took up the cause. His was the most influential speech at a meeting of the National Society in June 1849, and he dealt with the same subject in his Charge of that year. He drew a distinction between the instruction of individual scholars and the moral and religious superintendence of the school; he claimed that the latter was the province of the Church and must not be subjected to state interference. Once more the problem of State and Church was pressing itself upon him.

At this period he was following with acute anxiety the course of an ecclesiastical case that was to prove his dividing line. A sixty-year-old clergyman, G. C. Gorham, was in November 1847 presented by the Lord Chancellor to a living in the diocese of Exeter. The bishop—the litigious Henry Phillpotts—insisted on satisfying himself of Gorham's orthodoxy before instituting him. He was examined during seven days, at the end of which the bishop declared that he was unsound on the question of baptismal regeneration, and could not therefore hold the living. Gorham took the matter up in the Ecclesiastical Court which supported the bishop; an appeal to the Judicial Committee of the Privy Council resulted in a reversal of that decision. The bishop tried to bring the matter before the civil courts, but was told that the

Judicial Committee was the final authority. It was not until June 1850 that the case was settled over the bishop's head.

To Manning, as to many High Churchmen and Tractarians, this overriding of a bishop's authority by a committee of laymen —the members of which were not necessarily Churchmen—was an outrage. The essentially Erastian nature of the Established Church was clearly demonstrated. Manning took action at once: with a group of twelve friends he published in *The Times* a series of resolutions on the subject of baptismal regeneration. Both Pusey and Keble signed the declaration, but Gladstone abstained.[1]

The clergy of Chichester were called together by Manning to consider "the interference of civil authority in questions of doctrine." Manning felt it necessary to explain why he had condoned the appointment of Dr Hampden. "I did not defend Dr Hampden, but the Church of England."

His next move was to circulate to the Anglican clergy a declaration signed by himself and Archdeacon Robert Wilberforce and Dr W. H. Mill;[2] they asked for signatures to this protest against the supremacy of the Crown in spiritual matters. Out of some 20,000 clergymen, only 1,800 were willing to affix their signatures. This poor response was a set-back for Manning; he had hoped for a strong support that would carry weight, and the lack of it convinced him that the clergy were indifferent to these questions. He then published a moderately worded pamphlet, *The Appellate Jurisdiction of the Crown in Matters Spiritual*. This too evoked little support. He spoke also at a meeting convened in London on 23 July 1850 to protest against the Gorham decision. But again the call to action brought little support, and the Archbishop of Canterbury made it clear that he would not move in the matter.

The failure of these several attempts to mobilize opinion in the Anglican Church at length convinced Manning that he was beating the air; the Church as a whole was content with the existing position.

Meantime friends, as well as many others, were submitting to

---

[1] Six of the signatories became Roman Catholics.
[2] Professor of Hebrew at Cambridge.

the Roman Catholic Church—such men as Edward Bellasis, William Dodsworth, T. W. Allies, Henry Wilberforce, and Manning's own curate, C. J. Laprimaudaye.

In June 1850 he wrote to Robert Wilberforce, "Logically I am convinced that the One, Holy, Visible, Infallible Church is that which has its circuit in all the world, and its centre accidentally in Rome. But I mistrust my conclusion." About the same date, Gladstone wrote to Manning, "With my whole soul I am convinced that if the Roman system is incapable of being powerfully modified in spirit, it never can be the instrument of the work of God among us; the faults and virtues of England are alike against it." Gladstone was not aware of how close Manning was drawing to Rome; it was therefore a shock to him in September to get a letter from Bishop Samuel Wilberforce from Lavington to say that Manning "has left on my mind the full conviction that he *is* lost to us." The letter concludes with a glimpse of what the struggle was costing. "Few can understand what his and my brother's [Robert's] present state is. I believe you can; the broken sleep, the heavy waking before the sorrow has shaped itself with returning consciousness into a definite form; the vast spreading dimensions of fear for others which it excites, the clouding over of all the future."

The outcry against the restoration of the Catholic Hierarchy brought Manning face to face with the kind of immediate situation which he needed as a stimulus to decision. He was asked to convene a clergy meeting at Chichester so that their protest against the Papal Aggression could be registered. He warned the bishop that he could not support such a protest and would prefer to resign at once. The bishop persuaded him to preside at the meeting. He did so and refrained from expressing his own views. After the business had finished, he made it clear that he was no longer in heart with the clergy of the diocese.

He left Lavington at the end of November 1850. His nephew, W. H. Anderdon, son of Manning's preceptor, had just been received into the Church.

During the few months that followed in London, he found his friend Hope-Scott to be in full accord with him. There were some discussions with friends and relatives and much correspondence, Gladstone vainly hoping that the decisive step might yet be avoided.

On 5 April 1851 Manning saw Wiseman[1] and on the following day was received by Father Brownbill, S.J., at Farm Street. James Hope-Scott was received later that day.

[1] *Dublin Review*, Jan. 1919.

CHAPTER XII

THE ORATORIANS

THE way of a convert is never easy; he leaves the well-known and well-loved paths, and, with trepidation, ventures into a strange land; it may mean discord with friends and relatives. Such trials are experienced today, but a century ago there was an added bitterness of feeling, often gross misrepresentation, and an ostracism it is hard to appreciate now that most people are indifferent to religion, and a declaration of faith is more likely to be regarded as an eccentricity than as a betrayal.

When Newman, Manning and their friends left the Anglican Church they were cutting themselves off from a past that was crowded with precious memories; friendships were broken, though some, after a lapse of years, were put together again. They moved into what was the unknown and half-feared society of "a few scattered worshippers." It was not surprising that some, as if in self-defence, went to extremes and showed little discrimination in the outward expression of their new-found faith, and were, in consequence, frowned upon by those whose forebears had remained true to the old religion during generations of proscription.

That the reception of the converts so quickly allayed their fears and deepened their understanding of the Church, was in large measure due to Wiseman; amongst his great services must be counted the generous welcome and sympathetic support he gave to the many who found their way to Oscott during the crucial period of Newman's reception. Wiseman moved to London in 1847, but he was followed at Birmingham by another great bishop, Ullathorne, in whom the converts found an understanding friend, less exuberant and sanguine, but steadfast.

The majority of the unmarried Anglican clergymen who were converted had a sense of vocation for the priesthood; Wiseman encouraged them, and, in spite of some hostile criticism, ordained them after what would now be considered inadequate preparation; but, in the circumstances of the time, he was justified and was rarely disappointed. The eccentric Sibthorpe baffled everyone in turn! Wiseman recognized that many of these converts had scholastic attainments beyond those of most seminary priests, and he ardently desired to raise the intellectual standards of the Catholic priesthood in England. Convert married clergymen were a special problem; many on becoming Catholics gave up their means of livelihood, and some were in sight of destitution; Wiseman was deeply distressed by their plight and he did all he could himself and through others to see them through their difficulties.

But what of Newman? He always refused to regard himself as a leader in the Anglican Church, but that was the position others gave him; his intellectual eminence, his influential writings, his power as a preacher and his distinguished position at Oxford set him apart. How could he fit into the pattern of the Catholic Church? Wiseman showed soundness of judgment by not trying to hasten a decision; the long period of waiting for Newman's accession must have warned Wiseman that Newman could not be urged beyond his will. The first step was well-advised. Over a period of three months, Newman paid visits to the Catholic seminaries, to the bishops and to some of the leading Catholic laymen. Wherever he went, he was received with the warmest kindness, and he came back greatly enheartened with this first extensive introduction to his new world. Ushaw College and its president, Dr Newsham, impressed him but he was not so pleased with what he saw in other seminaries; he sensed the intellectual mediocrity of which Wiseman was well aware, and both knew that in the years to come the Church would need men of outstanding ability and learning. Such a tour must have been a great strain on a nature that was shy and reserved.

At the end of January 1846 he wrote:

Of my friends of a dozen years ago whom have I now? and what did I know of my present friends a dozen years ago? Why, they were at school, or they were freshmen looking up to me, if they knew my name, as some immense and un-approachable don; and now they know nothing, can know nothing of my earlier life; things which to me are as yesterday are to them as dreams of the past. . . . And yet I am very happy with them, and can truly say with St Paul, "I have all and abound"—and, moreover, I have with them, what I never can have had with others, Catholic hopes and beliefs—Catholic objects.

His *Development of Christian Doctrine* had now been published in the form in which it had been written; he had submitted the manuscript to Wiseman who decided that it would be best to leave it just as it had come from the author's hand.

Wiseman offered Old Oscott (once the home of Bishop Milner) as a residence to the Oxford converts until more definite plans could be made. Newman reported in November "What we wanted, he [Wiseman] said, was this—a body of men educated above the common run not for ordinary missionary purposes but for extraordinary—principally for two objects, first to meet the growing Germanism and infidelity of the times by literature; next to be preachers."

This meant giving up Littlemore; Newman had stayed there between his visits, and on 22 February 1846 he left it for good and settled with his eight companions at Old Oscott which they re-named Maryvale. They led a regular life under rules approved by Wiseman. There must have been many discussions on their future. They could, of course, be secular priests acting under the direction of their bishop, or, they could join one of the existing orders. The Dominicans (the Order of Preachers) seemed to meet their needs; but the Order was in a depressed state and did not regain vigour until the revival of Thomism under Leo XIII. There was much to attract them in the Society of Jesus, but they felt that under the Jesuit system they would not have the freedom of writing and preaching that seemed to be their best form of service to the Church. For a time, they considered the possibility of making Maryvale a school of divinity attached to Oscott. They do not appear to have discussed the Benedictines, though Newman in his later writings showed how deeply he could appreciate their spirit. Nothing, however, should be settled, in Newman's opinion, until they had been to Rome and could see for themselves something of the working of the various communities. They carried with them a suggestion from Wiseman that they might find their field as Oratorians, as sons of St Philip Neri.

Newman, with Ambrose St John as his companion, left England early in September 1856; they were away for fifteen months. Their journey was leisurely enough for them to see something of the Church in France; this, it will be recalled, was Newman's first close contact with the Church on the Continent. They spent several happy weeks in Milan, and what they learned there of the Dominicans and Jesuits did not seem to meet their desires. Newman wrote, "I do not think we have got a bit further than this in our reflections and conclusions, to think that Dr Wiseman was right in saying we might be Oratorians."

Newman himself was deeply impressed—as indeed are all converts—by the matter-of-fact fashion, as it may be termed, in which Catholics use their churches: "a sort of world, everyone going about his own business, but that business is a religious one. . . . what everyone is used to—everyone at his own work, and leaving everyone else to his."

At Rome, where they arrived towards the end of October, they had a most friendly reception and every care was taken for their comfort. Their letters to Maryvale reflected their happiness, and at times showed a playful spirit.

They attended lectures at the Collegio di Propaganda; to Newman, at the age of forty-five, it must have been a trial to be the fellow pupil of young seminarists, but he accepted this experience as part of his preparation for the priesthood. They had their first audience with the Pope, Pius IX, on 23 November, and he was most cordial in his welcome. Ten days later, Newman, strongly against his wish (he was still only in minor orders), preached at the funeral service of a niece of Lady Shrewsbury. In his sermon he made some pointed remarks on the irreverent behaviour of English Protestants when sight-seeing in Roman churches; the Protestants in the congregation were offended, and their Catholic friends were equally irritated. George Talbot, who at first said he liked the sermon, spread a report that the Pope disapproved of the line Newman had taken.

This introduces a name that will recur in these pages. George Talbot, born 1816, fifth son of Lord Talbot of Malahide, was received into the Church by Wiseman in 1842, and, by Wiseman's influence, was given a position in the Curia; he became a Canon of St Peter's and a Chamberlain to Pius IX whose confidence he gained, though it may be doubted if he had the influence over that shrewd Pope that he liked others to believe he exercised. Talbot, undoubtedly, had for some years the confidence of Wiseman and of the bishops, but he could have had little first-hand knowledge of the state of Catholic affairs in England. As the years passed, so Talbot's character deteriorated; his self-conceit in his assumed role of *éminence grise* smothered whatever soundness of judgment may have been his in his earlier Catholic days. He had not the mental equipment to appreciate Newman, but, unhappily, he became the confidant of Manning.

Newman's rudimentary Italian was an inadequate means for communicating his ideas; the theologians at Rome could not read his works in English. He translated into Latin some of the discussions in the notes to his translation of St Athanasius; these *Dissertiunculae* helped to bring a better understanding especially with Father Perrone, S.J. (later Cardinal), then one of the leading theologians. But a cloud drifted over from America where the Unitarians used the *Development of Christian Doctrine* to support their claim that the doctrine of the Trinity was not primitive; the book was also adversely reviewed in a Catholic publication. Reports of these opinions created doubts of Newman's soundness; misunderstandings were apparently resolved but they left their mark and were to affect Newman's relations with Rome. It was unfortunate that he had no *amicus curiae* there; no doubt had he visited Rome more frequently his position would have been strengthened; as a Catholic he was there in 1847 and 1856; twenty-three years passed before his final visit at the age of seventy-eight to receive the Cardinal's hat.

It was partly on account of these difficulties that he gave up the idea of using Maryvale as a centre of instruction, but he was more influenced by the evident lack at Rome of vigorous thinking on theological problems. Wiseman himself admitted that things were at a low ebb; there was, to use a favourite word of Newman's, no "view"—by this he meant an intellectual basis on which could be built up a coherent philosophy and theology. He was shocked when a Jesuit father (Perrone?) told him that Aristotle and St Thomas Aquinas "are out of favour here and throughout Italy," and went on to say that the professors taught "Odds and ends— whatever seems to them best. . . . They have no philosophy. Facts are the great things, and nothing else. Exegesis but not doctrine." What was true of Rome, was indeed true, at that period, of Catholic scholarship in most countries. A great revival was on its way, but there were few signs of it in 1847. This decline was in part due to the disturbed political conditions following the French Revolution; more problems were already gathering to keep Europe in a ferment for a generation.

Newman and St John at length came back to Wiseman's suggestion that they should be Oratorians. The breadth of the work of an Oratory—lecturing, disputation, preaching, service in hospitals, work with the young, music—was attractive. Newman was influenced by the desire for a community life that had been in his thoughts for many years. Some twenty years earlier he had dreamed that Oriel College might be reconstituted on the lines of Adam de Brome's foundation as a small society of resident Fellows freed from the work of tutoring, not unlike the present constitution of All Souls' College. Pusey had a similar notion when three or four graduates lived with him for the study of theology; Newman followed this example in 1837 when he took a house for a similar purpose, but the two or three who occupied this Coenobitium, as he termed it, found that they were at once labelled as Tractarians and frowned upon by the University authorities. Littlemore was an expression of the same idea. The Oratory of St Philip Neri had something in common with these earlier endeavours, and it was not surprising that Newman and his companions decided to become Oratorians. He thus found the right setting for his future work.

The Pope warmly approved this decision and arranged for their novitiate under an Oratorian at Santa Croce. Newman and St John were joined by five companions from Maryvale. They themselves had been ordained priests on 30 May 1847; their companions were ordained six months later. Wiseman's visit to Rome in July fortified them, but he had to cut short his stay for his semi-diplomatic mission to London. Ullathorne was also in Rome in connexion with the proposed restoration of the Hierarchy; he too warmly approved the institution of the Oratory in England. So, whatever faint doubts there may have been of Newman in Rome, he began his work as Superior of the Oratory with the strong encouragement of the Pope, of his own bishop, and of that bishop's successor in Birmingham.

During the autumn of 1847, Newman wrote his first work of fiction, *Loss and Gain,* in answer to a "wantonly and preposterously fanciful" novel called *From Oxford to Rome* by an American authoress. A friend who visited him at that time found him at work on the story and chuckling to himself as he wrote it. He explained that one reason for such rapid composition was that he wanted to help James Burns, the former High Church publisher, who, as a convert, was having difficulty in continuing his business. *Loss and Gain* is a tale of the later period of Tractarianism at Oxford, but "no friend of mine, no one connected in any way with the Movement, entered into the composition of any one of its characters." The book, however, could not avoid being a reflection of his own experiences and feelings; the love of Oxford pervades the book, and at the end there is a fine tribute to Father Dominic: "On the Apennines, near Viterbo, there dwelt a shepherd-boy...."

The Oratory was formally opened at Maryvale on 2 February 1848; the original community under Newman consisted of five priests, a novice and three lay brothers. Within a few weeks they were joined by Father F. W. Faber, who, after six years as an Anglican clergyman, had been received into the Church three years earlier. He had formed a community, commonly called Wilfredians, of friends and former parishioners who had followed him after his conversion.

Faber was a man of deep piety, of great charm and of varied accomplishments; he had a strong regard for Newman who recognized Faber's great qualities, but they were not in complete harmony. Faber wanted to introduce the popular devotions used on the Continent; he felt that, once they were known and accepted, they would bring renewed vigour to the Church in England. In this he was supported by the younger men who had followed him. Newman was in no sense opposed to such devotions; the point of difference was the rate and manner of their introduction; the English temperament, he felt, should be taken into account. An early instance of this concerned a series of Lives of the Saints on which Faber had been engaged before entering the Oratory. The incident was not in itself of great moment, but it displays an aspect of Newman's temperament that needs to be kept in mind when considering his later difficulties. He encouraged the scheme; he had himself started a series of lives of English Saints during the later Littlemore days. Faber did not produce new biographies; they were translations of continental hagiologies written exuberantly and credulously. Newman himself was, at this period, ready, almost eager, to believe such miracles as the liquefaction of the blood of St Januarius at Naples, and the presence at Loretto of the house from Nazareth of Our Lady. Faber's lives were not welcomed by some of the older Catholics; they felt that there was need for more restraint and discrimination if such books were to appeal to English readers. One rather virulent attack was published in a Catholic magazine. Newman sought the advice of his bishop. In his letter Ullathorne showed that his sympathies were with those who disliked these continental extravagances. He wrote, "By proposing more than the Church proposes even of the wonders of God and His Saints . . . we may lay burdens greater than can be borne by a weak faith." He promised to publish a reproof of the extreme language used by the reviewer. There was some delay in this appearing in print, and Newman decided to suspend publication of the series in deference to the "strong feeling against it of a portion of the Catholic Community in England." Ullathorne was annoyed; his reproof when published did, in fact, produce a full apology from the reviewer. The bishop felt that Newman had acted precipitately and had been too easily offended. A passage from the bishop's letter is typical of that forthrightness that contributed to the warm friendship that developed between the two men.

> I love you so much, and yet I feel so anxious for the spirit recently, I think, indicated, a little, to say the least. . . . I know that your lives have been lives of warfare and contest, and that you have had painfully to controvert the authorities under which you have been brought up. We have not had that trial. Habits still cling in hidden ways, and will come back unknown to us, in this poor restless nature of ours. Our habits have made us habitually and instinctively subject to the most delicate intimations from those personal authorities, in which we see the voice of God in our regard.
> Believe me, that a little of human nature is to be found fermenting in this sensitiveness. I write with pain, for it is difficult for us to see . . . any of the more delicate shades of pride, and more especially of intellectual pride, until it is beginning to move from us by the impulse of an act of humility. Forgive my freedom. Hitherto from delicacy and respect I have withheld from pointing out to your charity a source from which some part of this uneasiness has sprung, whatever external occasion may have given it opportunity.

This was a shrewd comment on one element in Newman's nature. He had earlier shown a like susceptibility when, on taking up his office as bishop, Ullathorne had written for information on the Papal Brief setting up the Oratory. It was a courteous request for information, but it ruffled Newman. Had he had a slightly tougher skin, he would have spared himself much vexation in the years to come—but he would not have been Newman!

He sent this correspondence to Wiseman; Newman felt that Ullathorne had judged him without really knowing him; at the same time he reported that the offending reviewer had accepted an invitation to come and see them at the Oratory.

Referring to this incident nearly twenty years later, Newman paid tribute to the "wise prelate" and his advice. "If at that time I

was betrayed into any acts which were of a more extreme character than I should approve now, the responsibility of course is my
own, but the impulse came, not from the old Catholics or
superiors, but from men whom I loved and trusted, who were
younger than myself."

When Wiseman left Birmingham in the autumn of 1847, he
hoped that the Oratory could be transferred to London, but Newman felt that as the Pope had named Birmingham as the place of
the Oratory, no change should be made. This difficulty could, no
doubt, have been overcome had Newman been willing; his reluctance to move may have been due to a slight constraint in his
relations with Wiseman, not that there was any disagreement on
matters of first importance, but Wiseman was not an easy man
to work with; he too was over-sensitive, but he was also un-
predictable. Newman suggested that a branch of the Oratory
might be established in London, and this proved a most fruitful
project.

Premises were taken in King William Street, Strand, and
Father Faber with five of the younger Oratorians took up their
work early in 1849. Faber was now able to put into practice the
full Roman methods of devotion; for him, there could be no half-
way house; many, especially amongst established Catholics, regarded his enthusiasm with misgivings. Newman warned him,
"Be very much on your guard against extravagances." The work
prospered, and the Brompton Oratory is Faber's monument.

Before Faber left Birmingham, the Oratory had found a new
home in Alcester Street, and it was there that Newman preached
the *Discourses addressed to Mixed Congregations* which proved so
effective; their publication at the end of 1849 brought them to a
wider audience, and their reception must have encouraged Newman since a series of Lenten sermons he had preached a
year earlier in London at Wiseman's request had attracted only
small congregations—"a blunder and a failure", was Newman's
verdict.

A few months after the Oratorians had settled in Alcester
Street, there occurred an episode recalled by Ullathorne in later
years, in a letter to Newman.

When the cholera raged so dreadfully at Bilston, and the two priests of the town were no longer equal to the number of cases to which they were hurried day and night, I asked you to lend me two fathers to supply the place of other priests whom I wished to send as further aid. But you and Father St John preferred to take the place of danger which I had destined for others, and remained at Bilston till the worst was over.

It is said that this readiness to undertake hazardous service amongst the poorest people did much to break down the wall of reserve between Newman and the older Catholics. There may have been some danger at first of the Oratory becoming an enclave, but the work done by the fathers at the mission in Alcester Street, in the schools, in the workhouse and in the gaol, soon removed that danger.

The decision on the Gorham Case in March 1850 led, as has been noted in the previous chapter, to a crisis in the position of those Tractarians and their sympathizers who remained in the Anglican community. Faber and other friends urged Newman to use this opportunity to discuss the position of the Established Church, but he was reluctant to do so as he had no wish to get involved in public controversy, but at length he was persuaded to give a series of lectures in London on "Certain Difficulties felt by Anglicans in submitting to the Catholic Church." They attracted large audiences of Catholics and non-Catholics. One of the latter, R. H. Hutton, who was a young man at that time, wrote in later years:

I shall never forget the impression which his voice and manner, which opened upon me for the first time in these lectures, made on me. Never did a voice seem better adapted to persuade without irritating. Singularly sweet, perfectly free from any dictatorial note, and yet rich in all the cadences proper to the expression of pathos, of wonder, and of ridicule, there was still nothing in it that any one could properly describe as insinuating, for its simplicity, and frankness, and freedom from the half-smothered notes which express indirect purpose, was as remarkable as its sweetness, freshness, and its gentle distinctness.

The same observer gives us another glimpse of the lecturer. In the eighth lecture occurs this passage:

> Take a mere beggar-woman, lazy, ragged, and filthy, and not over-scrupulous of truth—(I do not say she had arrived at perfection)—but if she is chaste, and sober and cheerful, and goes to her religious duties (and I am supposing not at all an impossible case), she will, in the eyes of the Church, have a prospect of heaven, which is quite closed and refused to the State's pattern-man, the just, the upright, the generous, the honourable, the conscientious, if he be all this, not from a supernatural power—(I do not determine whether this is likely to be the fact, but I am contrasting views and principles)—not from a supernatural power, but from mere natural virtue.

Hutton noted that when Newman reached the words "not over-scrupulous of truth", "he was here so overcome by his own deep sense of humour that he laughed behind his MS, then crossed himself, and I think said a Pater Noster to himself before resuming."

Wiseman was one of the most appreciative of Newman's listeners, "swaying to and fro, his ruddy face beaming with delight", and it was probably at his suggestion that Rome conferred on Newman the honorary degree of Doctor of Divinity. Within a few months Wiseman was recalled to Rome to receive the Cardinal's hat and to return as Archbishop of Westminster. The anti-papist hysteria that swept the country has been described; when it died down, Newman decided to give a series of lectures in Birmingham on *The Present Position of Catholics in England*. Manning was present at the first of the lectures.

The fifth lecture contained a reference to the immoral life of Dr Giacinto Achilli who was touring the country scandalizing the Church he had forsaken. Newman based his account on an article (republished as a pamphlet) by Wiseman printed a year earlier in the *Dublin Review*. This disclosure had gone unchallenged, but in November 1851, Achilli took proceedings against Newman for libel. Newman was undismayed as he assumed that Wiseman would have the documentary evidence on which he had based his own attack, but when the Cardinal was appealed to, he was unable to find the papers until it was too late. Meanwhile it had been necessary to send to Italy to get the evidence and to bring over witnesses. The course of the long drawn-out proceedings need not be given here. *The Times* referred to them as "indecorous in their nature, unsatisfactory in their result, and little calculated to increase the respect of the people for the administration of justice." Newman was fined £100, but the costs came to £12,000. At the instigation of Wiseman, this sum was speedily raised by Catholics.

It is not hard to imagine the strain of all this publicity and slander on a nature as sensitive as Newman's, but during the whole period he was engaged on work of the highest importance—the establishment of a Catholic University in Ireland; and it was during these wearying months that he gave the lectures "On the Scope and Nature of University Education", which in their published form were dedicated to "his many friends and benefactors" who had come to his aid in his time of anxiety.

In the following year, Wiseman also had to appear in the Courts; he was sued for libel by a priest who had been removed for his ineffectual ministry. He attacked Wiseman in a French journal. Wiseman replied in a masterly statement that was both a description and a defence of what had been achieved by the Church in England. A reference to the priest gave the occasion for the prosecution. At the first trial the plaintiff was non-suited. On appeal the verdict went against Wiseman who was ordered to pay £1,000 damages. A higher court set aside the excessive damages. A third trial was avoided by a compromise.

At first public opinion was against Wiseman, but, as in the Achilli case, the prejudiced verdict in the second trial brought more sympathy than obloquy.

CHAPTER XIII

NEW WAYS

WISEMAN had many perplexing problems to face when he became Archbishop of Westminster. They were not created by his
predecessors who had served the Church in England faithfully
and well and had brought it safely through the hard years of proscription. His problems were the outcome of new conditions.

The immediate situation created by his pastoral on the restoration of the Hierarchy was met, as we have seen, boldly and effectively; the anti-papist fires soon died down, though they have not
died out completely. There were even signs of a reaction; they
were evident after the Achilli trial when many who had no sympathy with Catholicism felt uneasy at the prejudice shown. There
were, however, Catholics who remained critical of Wiseman; he
was, they felt, the man who had started the blaze. During his first
decade in England he had had to face opposition from some of the
older generation, and his Flaminian Gate pastoral did nothing to
win their support; some felt that it confirmed their gloomiest
apprehensions.

This initial trouble was transient; other problems were of a
more stubborn character. Dominating all was the need to blend
the varied elements into one united Catholic community—of
reconciling the old and the new generations, of assimilating the
converts, and of bringing the Church in England back into the
main stream of Catholic life.

Catholics in England, priests and laity alike, had now to learn
by experience the nature of the office of bishop; the bishops themselves had to work out their relations with their Metropolitan, for
at that time there were twelve sees suffragan to Westminster; as
more and more religious communities were established in the
country, so their relations with the episcopacy had to be regulated.
Then there were the converts, particularly those who had been

Anglican clergymen, to be established. The Irish, mostly Catholics, had poured in during the famine years; it has been estimated that 170,000 had come to England during the decade before 1851; most of them were poor and illiterate; a steadier influx continued throughout the century and created special problems in industrial areas. Churches and schools were needed in all parts of the country; it was a large undertaking to catch up with deprivations of several centuries. All dioceses suffered from a shortage of priests. Moreover, the Catholic community was poor; even the munificence of its few wealthy members could not meet a tithe of the need.

These, and many minor problems, confronted the Hierarchy in 1850; a review of the succeeding half century would show how magnificent was the response to the need. It was the work of a great multitude of men and women, priests and laity, who dedicated their lives to the service of the Church; to lead them and inspire them they had first, Wiseman, and then, Manning.

Wiseman had wide vision and bold ideas; he encouraged all who were eager to promote the welfare of the Church. He did not concern himself with the detailed carrying out of a plan; he launched the ship and left the crew to work out the problems of duties and responsibilities, but, the ship was launched. In spite of some grumblings and criticisms and minor mutinies, the Church moved forward.

We have seen how successfully he dealt with the Anglican converts during his first ten years in England. He was quick to recognize the value of the contribution they could make, and he ensured, as far as he could, that they had the opportunities for making it. In doing this he upset those who would have preferred a more cautious policy and a longer period of conditioning. Certainly he took a bold course, for instance, when, in 1851, he appointed W. G. Ward to lecture in Moral Philosophy at St Edmund's, and, in the following year made him Professor of Dogmatic Theology. The choice of a layman, a convert of five years' standing, for such key positions in the training of future priests, shocked many Catholics. Ward's intellectual power—though exercised on a narrow front—undoubtedly strengthened the work at St Edmund's, and his pupils were to bear testimony to the thoroughness of his teaching and to the stimulus they received from him. There was never any serious question of his academic suitability; criticism was directed at the anomaly of a convert layman, however learned, teaching theology in a seminary.

Wiseman felt the desirability, once the violence of the anti-papist agitation had sobered down, of making the Catholic Church more widely known to the public; every effort was, of course, directed towards the conversion of those outside the Church, and this work was fruitful, but it was also necessary to let people see that Catholics were not a race apart, living as it were in an immaterial ghetto. Personal contacts with the public were essential if Catholics were gradually to be brought back into the national life.

It was with this in mind that Wiseman used his gifts as a popular lecturer—it was an age of lectures of all kinds as there were few other ways of spreading general knowledge or opinions. In discussing a coming engagement at Leeds early in 1853, he explained his intentions.

1st. My idea in consenting to attend was this: Let us show the Protestants that we can give the public as good an intellectual treat as they can, and prove as great an interest in the improvement of the people as they display. Now for this we should court their attendance as freely as possible, and show that we are willing and not afraid to have them to listen to us. . . .

2nd. I have consequently understood that the burthen of the evening will fall on myself, and that the object of the meeting would principally be to enable me to address the people out of church on purely scientific or literary subjects, such as would give information and recreation. In this manner the object described in No. 1 will be accomplished, the work of showing that the Catholic Church does not fear science and does not discourage it.

3rd. On the other hand we must avoid mere crude and unprepared speeches, offhand talk, and slipshod eloquence, which will suit a tea party, but not such an assembly as I should wish this to be.

At first his lectures were given in Catholic churches and halls and were on religious topics; later he received many invitations from Protestants who had heard him, to lecture in public halls on a variety of subjects, such as, Education of the Poor, Perception of Natural Beauty, a National Gallery of Paintings, the Crimean War, Recollections of the Last Four Popes, Self-Culture. No one today would dare to lecture—sometimes for two hours—on such an assortment of topics; yet contemporary reports agree that Wiseman interested and stimulated his listeners out of the stores of his well-informed mind.

One who could recall hearing both Wiseman and Manning drew the following contrast between them.

> Cardinal Wiseman's public speaking had two special characteristics; he appeared to be full of his subject, and he was in close sympathy with his audience, and had the art of winning their sympathy. Both his voice and his manner were sympathetic. His presence was extremely impressive, but very different from the no less impressive presence of his successor, Cardinal Manning. I should say that Manning suggested the ascetic Apostle, whose words and thoughts were in a region above the hearer; while Wiseman's presence was that of the great prelate or Prince of the Church, and his discourse though less highly finished than Manning's, showed greater eagerness on his part to enter into the minds and tastes of his hearers and persuade them. A certain *bonhomie* accompanied the dignity of his manner, which was absent in Cardinal Manning's case. His discourses were remarkable for abundance of poetic imagery. At his best he was very fluent and brilliant.

This policy of going out to the people undoubtedly did something to break down prejudice—a first step to understanding. No doubt many went to his lectures out of curiosity; even so, a Cardinal became for them a real person and not a dim figure in a history book. All this helped to remove the barrier of ignorance between the public and the Church. It was the beginning of a long process that is still not complete.

The first Provincial Synod was held at Oscott in July 1852. It was indeed a memorable occasion; for the first time for three centuries the leaders of the Catholic Church in England could meet together and legislate for their own community without fear of proscription. (No one took the Ecclesiastical Titles Act to heart.)

There is an unfinished painting by James Doyle at Oscott of the Synod in session. It shows Wiseman seated in front of the altar with the bishops on either side of him. Amongst the priests behind the bishops are Newman and Manning sitting side by side. Both preached before the Synod. Manning's sermon "Help nearest when Need greatest" must have been listened to with some curiosity by the bishops to most of whom he was a stranger, a Catholic of only fourteen months. They must have been surprised that Wiseman should have chosen a neophyte for such an occasion. Newman preached two days later. He too was a convert but had found his place as Superior of the Oratory. His sermon "The Second Spring" has become a classic; to read it today is to recapture in some measure the emotions of that gathering: "it is the first Synod of a new Hierarchy; it is the resurrection of the Church." Ullathorne noted how Wiseman was reduced to tears as he listened to Newman's words.

> A second temple rises on the ruins of the old. Canterbury has gone its way, and York is gone, and Durham is gone, and Winchester is gone. It was sore to part with them. We clung to the vision of past greatness, and would not believe it could come to nought; but the Church in England has died, and the Church lives again. Westminster and Nottingham, Beverley and Hexham, Northampton and Shrewsbury, if the world lasts, shall be names as musical to the ear, as stirring to the heart, as the glories we have lost; and Saints shall rise out of them, if God so will, and Doctors once again shall give the law to Israel, and Preachers call to penance and to justice, as at the beginning.

His hearers were so overcome by the deep feelings roused by

his sermon, that, as they crowded round him afterwards, Newman became so agitated that he had to be rescued by Manning.

Much necessary business was carried through at this first Synod, but there was more yet to be done before the new order of things could work smoothly; the concord of that first Synod was not to be achieved again during Wiseman's lifetime. The bishops had cause for complaint. Wiseman was inclined to assert a degree of authority that was not his; to overrule legitimate opposition and to resent criticism. His power as Metropolitan and as sole Archbishop in the country was not absolute. All bishops, under the Pope, have equal authority and jurisdiction. Wiseman's position, even as Cardinal, did not give him supremacy over the other bishops; he was their natural head in the eyes of the government and the nation, but, though it was his business to call the bishops together, in giving advice the only advantage he had came from his position as a Prince of the Church in close touch with Rome; his fellow bishops naturally gave due weight to his opinions, but he could not impose his will on them. His failure to appreciate the limitations of his authority was, unhappily, to lead to serious disagreements.

Wiseman spent the winter of 1853 in Rome. On what we should regard as the interminable journeys there and back, he found relaxation in writing a story of fourth-century Rome. A projected Popular Catholic Library had his approval and he suggested that "a series of tales illustrative of the condition of the Church in different periods" would be attractive, such as "The Church of the Catacombs", and "The Church of the Basilicas". He was persuaded to write the first himself; the result was *Fabiola,* written, as he said, "in the roadside inn, in the halt of travel, in strange houses, in every variety of situation and circumstances— sometimes trying ones." The book was published late in 1854. Newman wrote, "It is impossible, I think, for anyone to read it without finding himself more or less in the times of which it treats, and drawn in devotion to the great actors who have ennobled them. I trust we shall have 'The Church of the Basilicas' from the same pen, for I do not know any other which can do it."

Fabiola had an astonishing success and was soon translated into a dozen languages; and, as Bernard Wall notes in his *Report on the Vatican* (1956), it "has become as national to Italian life as olive oil and pasta." The book has lost its appeal in this country; this is due in part to its rather lush style, but mainly because the leading characters and incidents are not convincing. Interest can still be found in the author's considerable knowledge of fourth-century Rome.

It may have been the reading of *Fabiola* that prompted Newman to finish a story of Proconsular Africa of the third century. Little is known of the composition of *Callista* beyond Newman's statement that some portions were written in 1848, and then laid aside until July 1855; it was published anonymously in 1856, but the authorship was soon recognized. It did not win the same contemporary popularity as *Fabiola*, though *Callista* was translated into several languages, but it shows greater insight of character. R. H. Hutton gave it extravagant praise when he wrote that to him *Callista* was "the most perfect and singular in spiritual beauty" of all Newman's works.

Wiseman had hoped to go some way towards solving the problem of the lack of priests especially in the poorer districts by the establishment of religious communities such as were part of the Catholic life of other countries. With his encouragement Redemptorists, Passionists, Marists and Oratorians were established as well as a number of Orders of Nuns. The work he hoped they would do included preaching, the care of young boys and girls who had left school, confessors to convents, retreats to the clergy, Advent and Lent courses of sermons, and special missions. His hopes were not fulfilled, and in a long letter to Faber in October 1852 he lamented his failure. The Rules of the Orders did not allow them to carry out all the work he wanted. (It is curious that he had not known this when he encouraged their establishment.) Faber at once responded to this appeal by offering to extend the work of the London branch of the Oratory. Newman, however, as Superior, did not approve of the suggestion that they should, at that time, undertake fresh responsibilities. Faber therefore applied direct to Propaganda in Rome for permission to relax the Rule so that Wiseman's needs could be met.

Quite rightly Newman was annoyed at this independent action in an attempt to by-pass his proper authority. He decided that he himself must go to Rome to get the matter straightened out; he and St John arrived there at the beginning of 1856. They were twice received in audience by the Pope, who, Newman wrote, "treated us as if we were the only people in the world he had to care for." Pius IX agreed that Newman had been improperly treated. When however they saw Cardinal Barnabo, the Prefect of Propaganda, their reception was less cordial. Newman had decided that it would be better to separate the two Oratories as was usual in Italy so that each should be autonomous. Barnabo rejected this suggestion. Six months later two of the Oratorians in London went out to Rome with the same suggestion; Wiseman had written supporting the proposal and George Talbot also spoke in its favour; this time Barnabo gave his approval and the London Oratory became a separate Congregation.

It was natural that Newman felt that he had been treated with scant consideration by Wiseman and Faber. Wiseman throughout seems to have acted with Faber, and there is no record of any consultation with Newman. As there was certainly no malice in Wiseman or Faber, the explanation may be that it was another of those muddles into which Wiseman drifted through his lack of business-like methods. This may seem strange in view of the letter to Lingard quoted in chapter nine in which Wiseman talked of "the proper regulation of the official transaction of ecclesiastical affairs." It was an ideal that he certainly never realized himself; his failure to put his hand on the Achilli papers when they were urgently needed was but one example of his lack of method. On his behalf it should be remembered that he could not afford a large enough secretariat when he was overwhelmed with business; his own frequent journeyings, including absences in Rome, added to the difficulties; moreover Newman was at this time more often in Dublin than in Birmingham. Unhappily Newman was apt to fret over annoying incidents of this kind and to see ill will where thoughtlessness was the explanation. Certainly he felt grieved by what had happened and his relations with Wiseman and Faber suffered.

One passage in Wiseman's letter to Faber on the work of the Orders has special importance in view of the troubles to which it was to lead.

In his search for "a body of priests in community, ready to undertake any spiritual work which the Bishop cut out for them", he mentioned the Oblates of St Charles. His letter continues:

It has appeared to me that Providence has now given me an opportunity of gathering together such a band. Mr Manning, I think, understands my wishes and feelings, and is ready to assist me; several will, I hope, join him, and I hope also some old and good priests. We shall be able to work together, because there will be no exemptions from episcopal direction, and none of the jealousy on one side, and the delicacy on the other, of interference and suggestion.

CHAPTER XIV

THE OBLATES OF ST CHARLES

ON 5 April 1851, Wiseman wrote to George Talbot:

> Archdeacon Manning has just been with me; he will be received tomorrow morning by Father Brownbill, and James Hope in a day or two. Badeley will, no doubt, follow immediately, and I shall begin to hope for Gladstone. . . . Ex-Archdeacon Manning will, no doubt, study for the Church, and I think ought to be rapidly promoted—he is most learned, as you know. At any rate, I will give him the tonsure as soon as possible, that he may not lapse into *Esq*.[1]

Wiseman wrote again on 14 April to say that Manning's "wish is to remain near me and study rapidly, so as to help many who are hanging on him and will follow him." When he told his correspondent that he intended to ordain Manning on Trinity Sunday, Talbot wrote in alarm, "Can it be true that you are going to ordain Manning priest on Trinity Sunday? If you do they will open their eyes in Rome."

Manning himself would have preferred to spend a year in Rome before ordination, but Wiseman kept to his intention and the ordination was on 14 June; two days later, after some instruction from Faber, Manning celebrated his first Mass in the Jesuit church, Farm Street.

After the ordination Wiseman said:

> I look upon you as one of the first-fruits of the restoration of the Hierarchy by our Holy Father Pius IX. Go forth, my son, and bring your brethren and fellow-countrymen by

---

[1] *Dublin Review*, Jan. 1919. Edward Badeley followed Manning's example, but there was no ground for expecting Gladstone to do so.

thousands and by tens of thousands into the one true fold of Christ.

Manning's labours to convert others were to be abundantly fruitful in the years to come, but Wiseman had again pitched his expectations too high. It is natural to ask what it was in Manning that made such an immediate and lasting appeal to the Cardinal, and to wonder why his ordination as priest should have been so unusually expedited. Did Wiseman recognize the presence of qualities that he himself lacked, such as administrative ability? He would know, of course, that Manning had shown that ability to a marked degree as an Anglican archdeacon, but that cannot be the whole story. Manning's expressed wish "to remain near me" was in keeping with Wiseman's desire to have priests at his disposal for special missions. Whatever the explanation, the two men found themselves in full accord, and they remained so throughout their close association. In attempting to assess Manning's character, this complete submission to his superior must be considered; he, in his turn, expected the same obedience from his subordinates.

He set out for Rome early in November 1851. With him were his younger brother Charles with his wife (already a Catholic) and their children. Manning received his brother and the children into the Church six months later.[1] Another travelling companion was Monsignor George Talbot who had been on a visit to England.

Manning had an audience with the Pope on 29 November. Wiseman had prepared the way, and the Holy Father expressed a wish that Manning should enter the Accademia dei Nobili Ecclesiastici, commonly regarded as the "nursery of Cardinals." He spent two winters in Rome studying theology, as Newman had done, with much younger students; each year he returned to England for several months during the Roman hot weather. Wiseman was impatient to get him back in 1853 but the Pope refused his consent until 1854. At the end of his course—a few months over one year in actual attendance—the Pope conferred on Manning the degree of Doctor of Divinity.

[1] His eldest brother, Frederick, was never reconciled to Manning's conversion, and broke off relations.

His first sermon as a Catholic was preached in a Westminster church on 10 July 1852, and, during his visit to England that year, he gave four lectures at St George's, Southwark, on "The Grounds of Faith", in which he followed the course of reasoning that had led him to submit to the Church; the argument was on the lines of Newman's statement that for him there had come a time when the only possible alternatives were Catholicism or rationalism. The lectures were published soon afterwards and went through many editions; they were translated into French and Italian.

Of this book and of others that were to follow through the years, a sympathetic Anglican critic (the Rev. A. W. Hutton) has written:

> As being the writings of a man who is always in the pulpit, they weary more than they convince. They deserve no doubt respect and praise; many striking passages could be culled from them; there are apt references and quotations, and there are vigorously-drawn conclusions from premisses not equally well established; but a reader cannot for ever sit patiently and be lectured as a catechumen; and it is the prevalence of assertion over every other kind of proposition that must always render these volumes unreadable to the great mass of men.

The fact that none of his many volumes, with the possible exception of *The Eternal Priesthood*, is now in circulation, tends to support this Anglican estimate. This, however, is in no way to belittle their value in their own day as part of the presentation of the claims of the Church and of its doctrines. Several of his larger volumes (he published many sermons in pamphlet form) went through two or more editions and were translated into other languages. They therefore spoke to their times. His pen was used most effectively for immediate purposes; it is the fate of much writing of this kind, once it has served its generation, to lose its appeal when the particular need has passed. We can see this happening with the more controversial writings of an author of the literary quality of G. K. Chesterton; they are losing their point because the grounds of dispute have changed, but this is not to underestimate their worth when they were written.

It was at the Accademia that Manning came to know Herbert Vaughan who was one of the students. There was a difference in age of twenty-four years, but a friendship developed that was to be lifelong.

Attendance at theological lectures did not occupy many hours of the day; Manning, in his thorough fashion, got to know many of the leading members of the Curia and made himself familiar with the workings of the various Congregations. As Wiseman had done, the Pope sensed that here was a priest of outstanding ability and of complete devotion to the Holy See. In a letter to Robert Wilberforce, 19 May 1854, Manning wrote:

> I tell you privately that I had free access at any moment to the Pope, who treated me as a father treats a son, with an affection and playfulness of kindness, as well as with a confidence greater than I ever had from an Anglican bishop. And Cardinal Antonelli, I know well, had the same access to, saw often, always agreed with, and whensoever we had to speak on matters which I had to do with, he was with me.

In the spring of 1853 Manning gave a series of addresses in Rome; his reputation as a preacher and as a leading convert drew large congregations of English, both Catholic and Protestant. He continued this practice in later years, and, on one occasion, had John Bright as a listener who commented that Manning "was a good speaker, if you don't listen to what he says." The Quaker statesman was not an unbiased critic of the matter of the discourse, but he was a good judge of oratory.

When he returned to England in 1854, Manning was given the use of a confessional in the Farm Street Church by the Jesuits; many were brought by him to submit to the Church, and his influence also grew through his sermons for he was in constant demand as a preacher. He followed Wiseman's example in avoiding controversy in the pulpit or on the platform but preached Catholic doctrine in a direct and persuasive fashion that brought understanding to many Protestants who later came to him for instruction.

During these unattached years he made a number of visits to St Edmund's College; he thus came to know W. G. Ward more intimately and the two men found they had similar outlooks on Catholic affairs in England. Both were impatient at the inflexibility of some of the hereditary Catholics; both believed that the quickening spirit must come from Rome; both from the beginning of their Catholic lives were ultramontanists. They shared this devotion to Rome with Wiseman. From 1855, Manning had another reason for visiting St Edmund's; in that year Herbert Vaughan became vice-president of the seminary.

Wiseman found Manning's services of increasing value. When the Crimean War—"an unwise war", as Newman termed it—broke out in 1854, the need for more Catholic chaplains with the army became urgent. Wiseman disliked carrying out negotiations with government departments as this was unknown territory to him; he was glad to leave such matters to Manning who, with his social background and earlier experience, knew the right people to approach and how to deal with them. The main responsibility for the appointment of Catholic chaplains was borne, however, by the Bishop of Southwark, Thomas Grant, himself a soldier's son.

The Crimean War involved Manning in Florence Nightingale's plans for sending out nurses. He had met her when she was in Rome in the winter of 1847–8, with Sidney Herbert and Mary Stanley (sister of Dean Stanley). Florence Nightingale was deeply interested in the work of the Dames du Sacré-Cœur, Trinità dei Monti, and with the Mother Superior she discussed her religious problems, for, like Manning at that period, she was in a state of spiritual unrest. Then began a friendship that led to their association during the Crimean War. When the desperate need for nurses was heard, Sidney Herbert, Secretary of State for War, appealed to Florence Nightingale.

The story of her great work is too well known to be retold here; Manning had a small share in the work, again as Wiseman's representative, in safeguarding the position of the Catholic nurses.

Bishop Grant of Southwark had already sent five Sisters of Mercy from Bermondsey under Mother Mary Clare, their Superior, before the Government had officially arranged for Miss Nightingale to take charge; these five waited at Paris for the main party, including five more Sisters from Bermondsey, as soon as they learned that Miss Nightingale was acting with Government authority.

Manning sent a note to Florence Nightingale on the eve of her departure.

> God will keep you. And my prayer for you will be that your one object of Worship, Pattern of Imitation, and Source of consolation and strength may be the Sacred Heart of our Divine Lord. Always yours for our Lord's sake,
>
> Henry E. Manning.

Among the ladies who helped in selecting the nurses was Mary Stanley. Under Manning's guidance she was approaching the Church. A second party was formed under her with Mother Francis Bridgman of Kinsale in charge of the Catholic Sisters. Manning collected funds to cover some of the expenses, and was in touch with Sidney Herbert and government officials as well as keeping the Catholic authorities fully informed. It was a task that called for delicate negotiations and careful handling. When Florence Nightingale expressed her annoyance at the unexpected arrival of Mary Stanley's party with the added worry of sectarian discord that arose, the difficulties were resolved by the strong common sense of Mother Mary Clare. Before she returned home, Mary Stanley was received into the Catholic Church.

After the war, Florence Nightingale and Manning carried on a long correspondence on the problems of religious faith, but she felt unable to make the great decision; in later years she found she had more in common with Dr Jowett of Balliol than with Dr Manning of Westminster.

The Jesuits found it of practical inconvenience for Manning to continue using Farm Street Church; the use of a confessional there could only be a temporary arrangement until Manning could be given some definite charge, but Wiseman presumably felt that he could not yet attach this distinguished convert to one of the missions as an assistant. One possibility was that Manning himself should establish a new mission, and this he proceeded to do. Early in 1846, with the help of his former Lavington curate, C. H. Laprimaudaye, he bought some property in Palace Street; this was the foundation of the present church of St Peter and St Edward.

Wiseman appointed him Diocesan Inspector of Schools later in 1846. This brought Manning back to work of the kind he had done so well at Chichester; there was no need for him to adjust his views on education for he had always held the Catholic opinion that the religious life of a school is the sole concern of the Church, and is paramount.

Wiseman had not yet given up the hope he had expressed in his letter to Faber that Manning would form some kind of community which would place its members at the service of the bishop for "multifarious missionary work". Manning was, as he himself admitted, "slow about it but not from unwillingness or disobedience but from doubt of myself." The purchase of the Palace Street property seems to have been made as an alternative should he find it impossible to form a community.

The suggestion that the Congregation of the Oblates of St Charles would be suitable had been made in 1853 by Wiseman, but, as has been noted, the Pope wished Manning to remain in Rome. When Archbishop Charles Borromeo went to Milan in 1565 he saw the need for the reform of the clergy in keeping with the decrees of the Council of Trent in which he had taken a prominent part. To this end he formed a Congregation of secular priests without special vows, at first known as Oblates of St Ambrose, as part, as it were, of his own household; they could be sent at his will to carry out whatever work he desired whether as missionaries or as organizers of seminaries. Manning studied the original Rule drawn up by St Charles and adapted it to English conditions. Wiseman approved the draft Rule.

With his nephew, Father William Manning, he left for Rome in November 1856; they stayed in Milan to study the work of the

Oblates in the city of their foundation. Manning found that they
were in charge of a parish and of four seminaries, and also had a
house for missions and retreats. Many of the diocesan officials were
Oblates. At Rome he received the approbation of the Pope and
of Cardinal Barnabo, the Prefect of Propaganda.

Manning had, however, to suffer one grievous personal loss
while in Rome. After long deliberation, Robert Wilberforce
submitted to the Catholic Church and was received in November
1854. He had that year published an *Inquiry into the Principles of
Church Authority*, which brought him to the threshold of the
Church. Manning had hoped and prayed that this close friend of his
would follow him, and their correspondence was an important
factor in Robert Wilberforce's decision. He went to Rome in 1855
and entered the Accademia and was shortly to have been ordained
priest when, early in 1856, he was seized by a fatal illness. Manning
wrote, "I had looked to him as the friend and helper of the rest of
my life, as he had been through the years of trial which hitherto
had united us so closely. I had been counting up what gifts and
means he had of doing work for the Church in England." Robert
Wilberforce was a learned theologian in a sense that could not be
used of Newman or Manning; had he lived he might have had a
moderating influence on Manning, who, from 1856, accepted the
more intractable views of W. G. Ward.

The Rule of the Oblates as drawn up by Manning was approved
in Rome. In a letter to Wiseman he explained that he had provided:

1. That they [the Oblates] should be closely united to the
bishop, and be as it were his familia.
2. That they should have just as much internal constitution
as to raise and preserve their spirit and theological standard,
and consolidate both.
3. That they should be completely mixed among the
clergy of the diocese.

There was one important variation from the original Rule of
the Milan Congregation. The Superior of the London Congrega-

tion was given more control over the stationing of the Oblates than was customary. Though working in co-operation with the bishop, the Superior had the last word. This unusual provision was the cause of subsequent discord.

On Whit Sunday 1857 the Oblates of St Charles met for the first time in a rented house in Bayswater, and they took over the partly-built church of St Mary of the Angels.

When Newman's *Sermons Preached on Various Occasions* was published that year, it bore the following dedication:

My dear Dr Manning,

On this day, when you are celebrating the opening of your new Church and Mission at Bayswater, I am led to hope, since I cannot give you my presence on so happy an occasion, that you will accept from me this small Volume instead, as my act of devotion to the great St Charles, St Philip's friend, and your Patron, and as some sort of memorial of the friendship which there has been between us for nearly thirty years.

I am, my dear Dr Manning,
Ever yours affectionately,
John H. Newman,
Of the Oratory.

So far there were no signs of tension between these two leading converts.

The original community of Oblates numbered seven. Robert Wilberforce would have been one, and a second, C. J. Laprimaudaye, died within the first year.

During the eight years that Manning was the active Superior of the Oblates, he had many trials to endure, but they were fruitful years; conversions were numerous; schools were established; mission work was carried on; churches and convents were built. The accession of Herbert Vaughan (vice-president of St Edmund's) and of three of his colleagues at the college, proved a source of weakness.

Manning returned to England not only as Superior of the Oblates of St Charles, but as Provost of the Westminster Chapter.

While he was in Rome he received a letter from Wiseman. Canon Robert Whitty had entered the Society of Jesus and this left a vacancy on the Westminster Chapter of which he was Provost. Wiseman wrote:

> I particularly entreat you that should the Holy Father name you Canon you will not decline. There are many reasons for it. It will be the first time the Holy Father will have exercised the prerogative of nomination and I wish the precedent to be given. It will be most gratifying to the Chapter. It will be most acceptable to every class of Catholics. It will prove that the Oblates are not a distinct Order, but true secular priests.

Wiseman's references to the Chapter and to "every class of Catholics" suggests that he was losing touch with opinion in the Church in England.

To Manning's surprise, the Pope appointed him Provost as well as Canon. George Talbot claimed that this was done at his suggestion. Some of the members of the Chapter were startled at such an appointment, and from the outset of his new duties Manning had to face opposition. Nor were some of the older Catholics too pleased at this sudden promotion of a convert.

The story of the disputes and disagreements of the next six years make sad reading, but they cannot be passed over. There is, however, the danger of letting them take too large a place in our picture of the life of the Church in England during that period. All the time, it must be remembered, the true work of the Church went forward; converts were made, institutions established and churches and schools built; priests pursued their calling, built up the Catholic community, and set patterns of holiness and humility that strengthened countless numbers of the faithful in their day-to-day lives, undisturbed by the contentions in high places.

CHAPTER XV

THE CATHOLIC UNIVERSITY

IN April 1851, Dr Robert Whitty, Provost of Westminster, suggested to Archbishop Paul Cullen of Armagh that he should invite Newman to Ireland to give a course of lectures on education and to advise on the establishment of a Catholic University. This was the beginning for Newman of seven years devoted to a task that brought much vexation and disappointment. It meant long absences from the Oratory and nearly sixty journeys between Birmingham and Dublin.

Those who have only an indifferent knowledge of the facts may think that the attempt to set up a Catholic University in Ireland was a failure and that the only lasting good that came out of it was the volume of lectures *The Idea of a University*. There was certainly failure to establish a permanent University, and after thirty years it became University College under the Royal University of Ireland. Yet, that is not the whole story. A recent appreciation[1] puts the matter in better perspective.

In the Catholic University as he planned, organized and launched it, in spite of its poverty, its inchoateness, its pitifully small numbers, and the regrettable mistakes and misunderstandings that hampered its progress, Newman left in Ireland a living exemplar of the noble idea which he had sketched in immortal prose, the idea of a university courageously treading every field of human knowledge, and valuing that knowledge not merely as the revelation of the wealth of the universe, not merely as the revelation of the deepest thoughts and loftiest aspirations of the human mind, but most of all as the revelation

[1] *Newman's University* by Fergal McGrath, S.J. (1951), p. 509: an essential study of the subject based on material not previously available.

of that which gives it all value and meaning, the ultimate Truth and Good.

The proximate reason for the creation of such a University was the establishment in 1845 of the non-sectarian Queen's Colleges by the government. In these no religious tests were to be applied, and any religious instruction had to be provided outside the curriculum by the Churches at their expense. The term "God-less Colleges" was soon adopted by the opponents of the scheme. The Catholic Hierarchy in Ireland considered the situation and decided that they could not encourage Catholics to share with Protestants an education that was divorced from religion. This opinion was upheld in Rome, but Propaganda, with the approval of Pius IX, went further. A simple condemnation of the government scheme was not sufficient; why should not a Catholic University be established in Ireland? The success of the Catholic University of Louvain, founded under the patronage of Gregory XVI in 1834, was an encouraging precedent. Such a University could have a far wider field than Ireland alone; the English-speaking Catholics on both sides of the Atlantic had no University of their own faith to which they could send their sons.

This larger prospect was in the minds of the Irish bishops when they appealed to Catholics in England and in North America. So it was that the English bishops at the first Synod in 1852—at which, it will be recalled, Newman preached—declared of the University, "Its advantages to us will be incalculable," and Wiseman, preaching at St George's, commended the proposal to all Catholics. Certainly Newman himself regarded the University not as an Irish Foundation for Ireland, but as the "Catholic University to spread," as he wrote, "religion, science and learning wherever the English language is spoken." With this wider vision in mind, he suggested that Wiseman should become chancellor but here he came up against the Irish fear of English domination (even though Wiseman was Irish), and Archbishop Cullen was given that position.

Newman was formally appointed rector in November 1851. A month previously he had invited Manning to become vice-

POPE PIUS IX

JOHN HENRY NEWMAN IN 1845

Reproduction the same size as original see p. vii. (No. 2)

JOHN HENRY, CARDINAL NEWMAN IN 1879

NICHOLAS WISEMAN ABOUT 1838

NICHOLAS, CARDINAL WISEMAN IN 1858

HENRY EDWARD MANNING IN 1844

HENRY EDWARD, CARDINAL MANNING in 1889

FIRST PROVINCIAL SYNOD OF WESTMINSTER, 1852

rector. Manning replied that his chief difficulty was "the desire and I may say resolution I have not to incline to any one work more than another till I have been in Rome. . . . But your words are too weighty with me to be passed by; and I will both think of them, and ask others who can guide me better than I can myself. I need not say that old affections and many debts draw me strongly towards you." Ultimately he declined the position.

Newman opened the campaign, as it may be called, by delivering five of his lectures "On the Scope and Nature of University Education," during May and June 1852, at a time when he was facing the Achilli prosecution.

He thought of himself as being seconded by the Oratory for what was to him a special mission; a few years should see the enterprise established and then he could return to Birmingham. At one stage it was suggested that an Oratory should be set up in Dublin, but this came to nothing.

The initial enthusiasm for a Catholic University was soon damped by the divisions of opinion in the Irish Hierarchy and by the resultant delays in getting things done. Archbishop Murray of Dublin had been lukewarm to the project as he favoured negotiations with the government in the hope of gaining concessions; on his death in February 1852, he was succeeded in Dublin by Paul Cullen who had been responsible for inviting Newman to become rector. There was no question of Cullen's high regard for Newman, nor of his unswerving support for the University; indeed, the Irish bishops recognized that Newman's reputation was a valuable asset, and he soon won their personal goodwill. Unfortunately there were, as in all Irish questions, many currents of feeling, political and national as well as religious, and Cullen had to take these into consideration. The Hierarchy was divided on methods of control and the distribution of responsibility, both matters that can cause indefinite delay and confusion in administration until established with precision, and, unfortunately, they were still unsettled when Newman took up his work.

The centre of the disturbance was Archbishop MacHale of Tuam; he had a high opinion of Newman and a low one of Cullen. MacHale wanted control of the University to be in the hands of the bishops, and the University to be staffed by Irishmen. The first list of professors drawn up by Newman contained the names of eight Irishmen, four Englishmen (one from Guernsey) and two Scots. This was a good proportion of Irish if the University was to appeal to people outside Ireland. An exclusively Irish staff (even assuming men of high enough qualifications were available) would have deterred English parents from sending their sons to the University; it is probable that the high proportion of Irish did in fact prove a deterrent.

The position was complicated by Cullen's habit of postponing decisions in matters of dispute, and his still more unfortunate habit of not answering letters; he preferred not to commit himself on paper with the consequence that he failed in common courtesy. In a letter to J. M. Capes (February 1857) Newman gave a half-humourous description of Cullen's behaviour:

> I will tell you his *rule* of acting, not once or twice, but his rule and principle, to let me ask a question in June, to let me call about it again and again, to let me write to him about it in July, to let me write to his intimate friend to get an answer for me in August, to give up all chance of one in September, and in January accidentally to find all along he has been telling others that he *has* decided it in the way I asked him not to decide it, though even now, in February, he has not directly or indirectly, answered me.

Cullen had some characteristics in common with Wiseman; neither liked making decisions especially if "No" had to be the answer. Both had lived in Rome for many years and it may be that the curial way of being slow to make decisions had become part of their own method of dealing with problems. In Rome this deliberation is usually justified, and, however long drawn-out proceedings may be, a decision is eventually reached; unfortunately, with Cullen and Wiseman, deliberation sometimes lapsed into procrastination.

Newman was not the man to force others to a decision; he could appreciate their problems however impatient he might be for a decision. Perhaps had Manning become vice-rector, the delays might have been shortened, but, equally well, his more trenchant methods might have caused even greater difficulties. Ireland was not England, and Cullen's problems were as much due to the conflict of opinions and prejudices amongst his countrymen as to anything else. The root of the trouble was not to be found in the constitution of the University nor in the division of opinion amongst the bishops; the fact was that there was no strong popular backing for the project in Ireland itself, nor could the essential finance come from such a poor people. Unless the University could achieve its original scope as the English-speaking Catholic University, it had small chance of survival. It soon became clear that parents in England, still less in North America, were not going to send their sons to a University in Ireland, a turbulent country of no reputation for learning or culture.

It is necessary to read the full story of Newman's Irish experiences to appreciate his patience and persistency. He groaned at times to his friends, but he steadily went forward. That story should also dispel the notion, sometimes held, that he was a donnish recluse with no experience of practical affairs. He was in fact a good business manager. His mother had discovered that after the failure of her husband; as Bursar of Oriel he had won approval; at St Clement's he had been a hard-working curate and had raised funds for a new church; St Mary's had meant more to him than a pulpit, and he had carried out his duties as vicar of the parish, building a new church at Littlemore and meeting the needs of that outlying district. As a Catholic he had founded and organized the Oratory at Birmingham. These tasks, however, were far from being as complicated or vexing as his work in Dublin proved to be. He had to create a University, draft its statutes and regulations, plan its studies, find a staff, watch the finance, prepare his own lectures, organize even the domestic arrangements, tour the country to win support, and carry on a voluminous correspondence with both friends and opponents. Even when he had gathered a staff, he had still to concern himself with the innumerable details of administration, or with furthering projects such as the foundation of the medical school, the launching of the periodical *The Atlantis,* or the building (and financing) of the University church.

The twofold nature of Newman's duties—as Superior of the Oratory and as Rector of the University—inevitably caused some difficulties, and a conflict of loyalties. The Fathers of the Oratory were determined not to lose their Superior, and he was equally sure that his first loyalty was to Birmingham and not to Dublin. The friction caused by the separation of the London Oratory and his consequent visit to Rome in 1856 pointed to the need for his more regular residence at his own Oratory. By the time he returned to Dublin in the autumn of that year, he had made up his mind that the time was coming for him to leave the University.

In November he wrote to Henry Wilberforce:

> Alas! you do not realize my work. My chattels stand about my room, the same confusion as on the night I came, from my inability to find leisure for removing them to their places. My letters are a daily burden; and did I not answer them by return of post, they would soon get my head under water and drown me. Every hour or half-hour I have people calling on me. I have to entertain strangers at dinner; I have to attend Inaugural Lectures—four last week; I have to stop Professors resigning and Houses revolting; I have to keep accounts, and find money when I have none. Besides the book I have just finished for Longman's [*The Office and Work of Universities*], I have three reprinting, which I am reading through and correcting; and I have to provide four Sermons in print for St Paul's Day, that for Sunday week not having the first word written yet. I have to lecture on Latin Composition and examine for Exhibitions. I then have to throw myself into quite a fresh world. And I have the continual pain of our Fathers sighing for me, if I am not there, and priests and Professors looking black, if I am not here.

It was not until March 1857 that he sent in his resignation. He wrote to each of the archbishops and bishops; the reasons he put forward were the increasing physical strain of the journeying between Birmingham and Dublin, and the prior claims of his own Congregation. "My age is now considerable; my contemporaries are dying or falling around me; I cannot at all tell what time is left to me for any work; and I should not like to be taken away without having given my last years to my Congregation at Birmingham." When he wrote those words he had passed his fifty-sixth birthday, but he had come to regard himself as an ageing man if not as an old man. There can be no doubt that he was feeling the physical and mental strain of his multiple duties.

Now that his withdrawal seemed likely, the bishops bestirred themselves to keep him. They appealed to the Fathers of the Oratory (20 July 1857).

> Sensible of the great services which Dr Newman has rendered to the cause of Catholic Education and Catholicity, not only by the prestige of his distinguished name, but also by the able and zealous manner in which he has discharged the duties of rector of our Catholic University, we are as anxious now to perpetuate his services to our rising University, as we were at first to secure them. . . . the connection of Dr Newman with the University is undeniably a very great gain, as his separation from it would be a loss, the magnitude of which it would not be easy to estimate.

Newman agreed to continue as rector for a time provided the bishops would be satisfied with shorter periods of residence and would appoint a vice-rector in whom he could place complete trust. The bishops, however, once more dilly-dallied. Newman therefore made his decision and sent in his resignation in a letter dated 12 November 1858 (exactly seven years after his appointment). He left Dublin after delivering the three lectures on "Literature", "Discipline of Mind", and "Christianity and Medicine" which are published in the second part of the volume *The Idea of a University*.

One episode in his Dublin years calls for special attention as it bears on his relations with Wiseman.

Newman had been informed on good authority that his name

was being considered in 1853 as successor to Bishop Hendren of Nottingham or as coadjutor to Bishop George Brown of Liverpool. He wrote in some alarm to Cullen.

> I feel most deeply and habitually, the office of bishop is not suited to me. Some things one is fitted for, others one is not. To say I am not a thorough theologian, and that I know nothing of Canon Law is obvious; I do not urge what is plain to anyone. But more than this, I have not the talent, the energy, the spirit, the *power of ruling* necessary for the high office of Bishop. This is neither humility nor modesty, but plain commonsense.

The next five years were to show that Newman underestimated his ability to rule and administer.

Nothing further was heard of this proposal, but, in the following year, another suggestion, emanating from Wiseman himself, as it would seem, came near to realization. Newman had felt the need for some more definite mark of his position as rector than the Irish bishops seem disposed to allow him; in his negotiations and appeals for a University his authority was not impressive. A Papal Brief naming him as rector was what he seems to have had in mind; he even thought of going to Rome himself. "I shall come back from Rome with a prestige as if I had a blunderbuss in my pocket." Cullen advised against such a visit but saw the necessity for the issue as soon as possible of a Papal Brief establishing the University under the patronage of the Pope.

The next news came from Wiseman in January 1854.

> At a third audience [with the Pope] I begged to make a suggestion long on my mind, and about which I consulted Archbishop Cullen at Amiens, and obtained his hearty concurrence. . . . It was that His Holiness would graciously please to create you bishop *in partibus,* which would at once give you a right to sit with the bishops in all consultations, would raise you above all other officers, professors, etc. of the University, and would give dignity to this itself, and to its head. The Holy

Father at once assented. . . . I must add that I have long wished
to do what I have done, even independently of the circumstances which appear to me to *require* it, for it appears to me to
end many difficulties, and place things on their right basis.
But ever since the Achilli judgment, I have felt that a mark of
honour and favour, and an expression of sympathy *from the
Church* was requisite, and this seemed to me the proper mode
of bestowing it.

I have only one thing to add, that I request the consolation
and honour of conferring on you the proposed dignity.

This definite statement left no room for doubt. Newman
thought that the bishopric "would be a real remedy against the
difficulties which lay in my way." He kept the information to
himself, but his own bishop, Ullathorne, was not so discreet; he
had heard of the Pope's intention and saw no reason for keeping it a
secret. Within a short time the news was widely known, and
Newman received many congratulations on his imminent elevation
as well as some gifts such as a pectoral cross and chain; some of
these came from hereditary Catholics.

Rome, however, had not yet spoken. The Brief establishing
the University was received in March 1854 but it contained no
reference to the proposed bishopric. Newman later recorded that,

Showing me the University Brief, he [Cullen] pointed out
to me the words "Newman, egregiis animi dotibus ornatus
etc.," and said in an awkward and hurried manner, "You see
how the Pope speaks of you—*here* is the distinction."

Ullathorne still assumed that the bishopric was a certainty. In
June he said to Newman, "Why are you not consecrated? It depends on you. You have only to name the time." At first it was
thought that the appointment had been postponed, but, as the
months passed without any sign from Rome, it became clear that
the proposal had been dropped. Neither Wiseman nor Cullen
made any later reference to the matter when they saw Newman
or wrote to him, and he was the last man to ask for explanations.

Had Wiseman, in his wonted enthusiasm, mistaken the Pope's intention? Or failed to pursue the matter? Was opposition voiced by Cullen or by some of the Irish bishops? Were Newman's denigrators at Rome—of whom Talbot was one—busily at work? These and other explanations have been put forward, but they are conjectures.

The last word may be left to Newman himself who wrote some years later:

For myself, I never asked anyone a single question, from first to last, on the subject, first of the delay, and then of the abandonment of the intention. It never occupied my thoughts. The prospect of it faded out of my mind, as the delay was more and more prolonged. I felt that to be a bishop *there* [Ireland] would have singularly helped me in my work; but I would never have been able to resign, if I had taken such wages. I might have been in Ireland till now. I am ever thankful to St Philip for having saved me from this.

CHAPTER XVI

DISSENSIONS

MRS BARBARA CHARLTON, under the year 1855, wrote in her recollections:[1]

> The Cardinal, responding to the influence of Manning, was cockering up the converts to such a puerile degree that these newly baptized misbelievers began to treat the old Catholics as the neophytes and themselves as ancient in the Faith, while in reality their peculiar antics and far-fetched ideas were making a caricature of Catholic religion.

She went on to complain that Wiseman had put Newman "on the shelf" by sending him to Ireland and then by keeping him at Birmingham.

It would be unjust to regard this outburst as typical of the majority of old Catholics, nevertheless it was a view held by a section of them, who, strangely enough, seemed to have resented their lost exclusiveness.

The contrariness of this opinion will be noted; on the one hand Wiseman was criticized for "cockering up the converts", and on the other for side-tracking the most eminent of them.

Wiseman's policy of welcoming the converts and of making the widest possible use of their talents was amongst his great services to the Church; this we can appreciate at our distance of time, but some contemporaries took a more short-sighted view and allowed their human feelings to cloud their judgment. "Think how many years I have lived as thy servant. . . ."

The regard that these same critics had for Newman is a curious factor in the situation. It is true that, with his strong sense of the past, he paid tribute to "that old school of Catholics which has

[1] *Recollections of a Northumbrian Lady, 1815–1866* (1949).

characteristics so great and so special"; it is also true that he disliked "extravagances" as he had said to Faber; but this alone would not account for the favour he gained in the eyes of the old Catholics. To them his own unobtrusive way of life and his ready consideration for the feelings of others would be more in keeping with their traditional reserve than the demonstrative style of Wiseman who some continued to regard as responsible for the public outcry of 1850. Few Catholics outside London knew Manning in 1855; to the casual observer he must have seemed entirely subservient to Wiseman; they had yet to learn that he brought to the Church his distinctive contribution.

Wiseman was well aware of the opposition to his policy, but he accepted it as part of his task. Manning undoubtedly came to regard some of the old Catholics as obstructive, and their preference for Newman may have contributed to the divergence that widened between the two former Anglicans. No doubt Manning's views were strengthened by Ward's strictures on the old Catholics. "When a Catholic," he once said in his sweeping manner, "meets a Protestant in controversy, it is like a barbarian meeting a civilized man." And Manning could write, "I look upon them [the old Catholics] as one of the greatest evils in England."

Wiseman did not allow these difficulties to deflect him from the path he had chosen; he was distressed by opposition but he would not take sides. His plea was that converts to Catholicism and those of long lineage in the Faith should combine for the good of the Church and not search out each other's imperfections and so lead to divisions. At times he did not hesitate to speak out. For instance, in *The Rambler*—the journal of a group of converts—for November 1856 there was an ungracious article reflecting on the intellectual shortcomings of "the little remnant of Catholic England." Wiseman replied in the *Dublin Review* in the following month; he gratefully recognized the value of the intellectual contribution of the converts but he warned them against pride.

But under the circumstances is there not something unkind, to say the least, in twitting these, in worldly estimation

less favoured brethren, with an intellectual inferiority, supposing it to exist? in reproaching them for not having possession of what had been taken from them, and asserting superio-
rity because one *has* had the advantage of it? Ought not such
honours to be meekly borne? Should the old family, so
touchingly described by our most eloquent writer as mys-
teriously dwelling in the quaint mansion among the trees, be
reprehended if it has grown up somewhat "living in the past",
while no present employment was allowed it? . . . It is not a
little to have "a past" on which to live, to have branches in
the family tree tipped with ruddy blossoms, and an occasional
lily brightly peeping through its gloomy foliage; to have in
one's pedigree the name of a man who was hanged, drawn and
quartered for the faith, or of a woman who was pressed to
death for conscience sake, of a learned writer or of a lady
abbess . . . a perpetual exile from home and country. . . . We
cannot but believe that an old plank torn and preserved from
the ancestral mansion will bear a youth more buoyantly and
more safely through the whirlpool to which he is hastening,
than scientific theories and philosophical refinements; and
while too many of these will be found shivered on the rocks,
or turned bottom upwards by stronger and ruder craft that
will follow, the solid old *robur* of simple faith enwrapped in
family recollections will gallantly outride the storm.

When Wiseman wrote those words he was not "cockering up
the converts"; he was paying tribute to those ancient families,
some of whom disparaged his work. Manning became a convenient scapegoat, but, in taking this line, Wiseman's critics were
being as unjust as some of the converts were in despising "the
little remnant."

Wiseman was a man of many projects and he eagerly encouraged others who wished to go forward; his was often the
inspiration and initial driving force. The achievements of his
thirteen years in London make a long and impressive list; churches,
new missions, schools, orphanages, reformatories, industrial
schools, prison chaplains, religious and teaching orders—all these

amongst others would be included. It is difficult now to appreciate the pressure of work upon him with only a small staff to assist him. At the same time he was preaching and lecturing in many parts of the country, work that not only brought encouragement to the faithful and to many a struggling priest, but made the Catholic Church better known to the public. Until their relations deteriorated he had the assistance of Mgr Francis Searle as his secretary— a man as large physically as himself. From their days at the English College in Rome they had formed a close friendship; Searle was a man of shrewd judgment and of sound business sense and it is true to say that without his control of the purse strings, Wiseman, impulsively generous as he was, would have been overwhelmed in debts. Searle was of an old Catholic family and his mind moved in a narrow groove. As a secretary he was a valuable servant, but, even had he had the time, he lacked the skill to get many of Wiseman's projects into practicable shape.

It was here that Manning proved so valuable. He had the ability to get things done and to follow them through in spite of criticism; a man of his type tends, perhaps inevitably, to regard those who hinder him as wilfully obstructive, if not as maliciously minded; he will push on one side the claims even of friendship if they in any way conflict with the purpose to which he has dedicated himself. The clash that came between Searle and Manning was distressing enough for Wiseman; it meant the loss of the confidant of many years on whom he had come to rely for all business affairs; it was the price that had to be paid for a more energetic realization of cherished plans. Tragedy—it does not seem too extreme a term—came, however, when Wiseman decided that he must have a coadjutor.

One element in the situation must be kept in mind. From about 1854 Wiseman's health began to fail. A number of illnesses afflicted him and brought not only much physical suffering but intermittent energy and impaired judgment. The conduct of the affairs of the Westminster diocese inevitably suffered, and there were complaints of day-to-day matters being neglected. He decided to ask for the appointment of a coadjutor with the right of succession (*cum jure successionis*). With the approval of the Chapter, he put forward the name of George Errington, then Bishop of Plymouth.

His name has already been mentioned in these pages—as Wiseman's schoolfellow and college companion, as his vice-rector at Rome, and as prefect of studies at Oscott. Two men, both over fifty years of age, could hardly have known each other more thoroughly. Their long association had been marked by a genuine personal affection, but, when they worked together, there had been clashes due largely to their contrasted temperaments. Errington was well aware of the likelihood of further difficulties if they both worked in Westminster and he tried to avoid the appointment, but Wiseman swept all his protestations on one side and, in April 1855, Errington became Archbishop of Trebizond with right of succession to the See of Westminster. It was understood, certainly in Rome and by Errington but not so clearly by Wiseman, that the new archbishop would carry out the normal duties of a diocesan bishop so that Wiseman could devote his time to those wider interests where his abilities could find full scope.

Difficulties arose when Wiseman allowed himself to become a kind of Court of Appeal and reversed some of the decisions of his coadjutor. An early example of this concerned W. G. Ward. Errington was a learned theologian and had long experience in the conduct of seminaries. When he visited St Edmund's College, which was at that period the seminary and school for the dioceses of Westminster and Southwark, he was disturbed to find that a layman, W. G. Ward, was in charge of the course in dogmatic theology. Errington did not approve of Ward's methods which were not on traditional lines. Errington himself was a traditionalist and had little sympathy with those who forsook the well-trodden paths. In view of this disagreement, Ward resigned, but was reinstated by Wiseman, not at the end of a discussion of the problem but almost casually, for he mentioned that Ward was to remain at St Edmund's just when Errington was in the train on his way to the college on a later occasion.

Errington regarded this action as proof that he and Wiseman could not work together, and he wrote to Rome suggesting that he should be removed "from my present position to any occupation, place or country the Holy Father may think fit." Talbot at once wrote a straightforward letter to Wiseman—a letter showing that Talbot's judgment had not yet been warped by self-conceit. He urged Wiseman to leave diocesan affairs to Errington according to the original understanding. The situation was eased when Errington went to Clifton to administer the diocese during an interregnum. Ward now decided definitely to resign, and with this difficulty out of the way, Wiseman urged Errington to return and carry out a visitation of the diocese. It was with well-grounded reluctance that Errington consented.

He did the visitation with the thoroughness that was part of his nature; it was true that he was severe where he found laxity, but many priests were grateful for the help and sympathy he gave them. Those who felt aggrieved at his censure were more vocal and some appealed, successfully, to Wiseman, who, however, paid a tribute to the "diligence, an exactitude, a labour, and a suavity which it would be difficult to surpass" with which Errington had carried out his difficult task—for it was the first visitation since the times of Cardinal Pole.

The right conduct of St Edmund's remained a problem; this was not only a question of teaching and discipline, but also of control. Wiseman had acted as if this concerned him alone, but students also came from the diocese of Southwark whose bishop, Thomas Grant, claimed a measure of authority and the right of consultation. Ullathorne wrote of Thomas Grant, "Of great simplicity and innocence of life, endowed with singular abilities and learning, quick and adroit in the management of affairs, he was untiring in the administration of his diocese, and in every good and charitable work." He had been one of Wiseman's students at Rome, and had later been rector during the years when the restoration of the Hierarchy was under discussion; his advice and assistance had been frequently sought by the bishops. Only a compelling sense of duty to his diocese could have led him to oppose Wiseman when the allocation of the property and funds of the old London District was in dispute on the setting up of the two dioceses of Westminster and Southwark. Eventually Grant felt obliged to appeal to Rome; this greatly distressed Wiseman, and he was even more vexed when Rome decided in favour of Grant.

Now they clashed again on this matter of the control of St Edmund's; the principle involved concerned also Ushaw and Oscott. Were the three colleges to be governed by the bishoprics in which the buildings were situated, or by all the bishops who sent students to them from other dioceses? Wiseman was strongly of the first opinion. The difficulties at St Edmund's were aggravated when, as we have seen, Herbert Vaughan, who had been appointed vice-president in 1855, and two other members of the staff joined the Oblates of St Charles when instituted by Manning in 1857. It is difficult to understand how such an imprudent step could have been taken. Vaughan and his colleagues could not live with the community at Bayswater; they could not be more than attached members, yet, and this was the serious implication, they placed themselves under the direction of their Superior, Manning, who, according to the statutes of the community, could overrule the wishes of the bishop and withdraw them at will. Did they themselves realize, did Wiseman himself realize, that this *imperium in imperio* was bound to cause friction? As we have seen, one of Wiseman's strongest desires was to have under his direction a body of priests who could supplement the work of the secular priests by undertaking any mission to which he directed them. He thought that he had at last achieved his purpose when Manning formed the Oblates of St Charles. It may be that Wiseman, who was no legalist, had not realized that Manning had the last word in the disposition of the Oblates; the original statutes framed by St Charles Borromeo had put the Oblates entirely at the service of the bishop, but Manning had secured his own control as Superior; by so doing he had defeated Wiseman's purpose and put his Oblates in the same position as the Oratorians and other congregations whose statutes had proved too restrictive. No doubt Manning had every intention of meeting all Wiseman's wishes, but he may have included this unusual rule to safeguard the position under Wiseman's successor. Errington and Manning had met in Rome when the rule had been under discussion. Errington had not shown any enthusiasm for the project.

Errington, with his knowledge of Canon Law and his insistance on its observance, was quick to see the dangers of this situation. In course of time, and Wiseman's ill health seemed likely to make the period short, he would be Archbishop of Westminster, and he had no wish to inherit a position to which, in his view, there were grave objections. Others too, though from varying motives, shared his misgivings. Was Manning, they wondered, trying to get control of St Edmund's? He certainly regarded the conduct of seminaries as part of the work of the Oblates as it was in Milan. Quite apart from the question of divided rule, he failed, at that time, to realize the strength of the St Edmund's traditions which went back to Douay and over the long years of exile to Oxford itself. Errington saw the need for improving the work of St Edmund's, but that, he considered, should be done under the supervision of the bishops and not by handing over the college to Oblates who were mostly converts and not themselves experienced in the well-established methods of seminary training.

The Chapter of the diocese took up the matter; they believed that under Canon Law, and in this Errington supported them, they had a right to call attention to the conduct of the seminary. Wiseman denied their authority to intervene. The situation was the more awkward as Manning was Provost of the Chapter. He, however, put no difficulties in the way when they asked to examine the rule of his Congregation, but he made it clear that this was an act of courtesy as the Chapter was acting beyond its powers. He refused to sign the petition to Rome which the Chapter drew up asking for a ruling on their authority to consider seminary affairs.

Errington took the side of the Chapter; this meant a complete breach between him and Wiseman, and it was indeed deplorable that the archbishop and his coadjutor should find themselves in opposing factions. In ruptures of this kind it is always difficult to know how far personal antipathies influence opinions. Errington certainly did not like Manning, nor did Searle, nor did some members of the Chapter. There is evidence that at this period Manning seemed cold and aloof and insensitive to the feelings of older men, the heirs of Catholic tradition in England. The opposition he roused was, however, not so much personal as due to resentment at the confidence Wiseman placed in him and at the haste with which he had been jumped up to the position of Provost. Wiseman had little skill in handling men and his failure to bring Manning forward without antagonizing others was part of the trouble.

It may also be noted that, according to a close observer, there was no strong personal sympathy between Wiseman and Manning. In some respects they were as different in temperament as Wiseman and Errington; indeed, it would not be an exaggeration to say that there was more in common between Errington and Manning than between either of them and Wiseman who was always ready to temper judgment with mercy; he held the reins loosely. Errington and Manning were both sticklers for the letter of the law; they insisted on obedience, and, provided that was unquestioned, they would do all that was possible to guide and support those under them. Wiseman's regard for Manning was a recognition of his administrative ability and of his singular devotion to the Church; he was the man to get things done.

During the summer of 1858 when the attack on the Oblates was maturing, Wiseman made a tour of Ireland. It was one of his great successes; everywhere he was acclaimed by Catholics with the warmest regard; immense congregations gathered to hear him preach and crowds flocked to see him wherever he went; he followed his custom of lecturing to mixed audiences on non-controversial subjects (such as "Ornamental Glass in the Catacombs"); he visited Trinity College and examined the treasures of its library; he attended civic receptions and banquets. Newman, who was not in Ireland at the time, reported the impressions he received from those who had shared in what was a triumphal tour.

We venture to affirm that there is no other public man in England who could have answered to the demand thus made upon his stores of mind with the spirit and intellectual power which the Cardinal displayed on the occasion.

It must have been with some sinking of the heart that Wiseman returned to London to face the discord in his diocese. As his

agent in Rome he sent J. L. Patterson, an Oxford friend of Newman and later president of St Edmund's, and Bishop of Emmaus.
He left at the end of 1858; his business was to put before the Pope
the case for the removal of Errington from Westminster, not on
canonical grounds, but because of the impossibility of the two
archbishops working together in harmony.

In a letter to Patterson soon after his departure, Wiseman
wrote:

> What I feel, of course, is the perfect solitude of my position.
> I literally have not a soul to speak to. . . . Searle is no longer *my*
> secretary, for he seems to be secretary of the Chapter; and
> instead of that confidence which has existed between us for
> twenty years, he has his own secrets and I mine, and we hardly
> speak. Is it not strange that almost all the plotting and the
> drawing up of documents against me should have taken place
> under my own roof, and that by my three *familiarissimi*—my
> Coadjutor, my Vicar-General [Canon Maguire] and my
> Secretary?

Manning followed Patterson to Rome to defend the Oblates.
Wiseman then wrote to Patterson:

> Dr Manning has started for Rome. He went yesterday, and
> may get there before this letter. He goes for his own affairs—
> the implied charges against him in the Chapter petition, and
> the necessity of meeting incidental questions. . . . I have told
> him distinctly that *you alone* are agent for my affairs.

The bishops met for the third Synod in July 1859. By this the
spirit of enthusiasm shown at the first Synod seven years earlier
had been weakened by dissensions among them, and it had to be
admitted that the majority of the bishops were at loggerheads with
their Metropolitan; the most disturbing fact was that Errington
himself led the opposition to Wiseman. On the control of the
seminaries, the Synod made decisions contrary to Wiseman's
wish. The majority approved a scheme by which the seminaries

would be placed under the supervision of a board of those bishops who sent students to them. Wiseman maintained that full control should be in the hands of the bishop in whose diocese a seminary was situated, and he hoped that he could get the Synod's decision reversed in Rome.

The next twelve months saw much going to and from Rome, and the account of the negotiations and of the manoeuvres between parties makes sad reading. Errington became obstinate when he found that Talbot had been accusing him of being anti-Roman and Gallican. These were terms of abuse and not of cool judgment, but as both, especially the second, were to become part of Manning's vocabulary, something must be said of their significance. By anti-Roman was meant the survival into the new age of the traditional reserve and insularity of the hereditary Catholics—characteristics that had been forced upon them by history. To be Gallican was to emphasize the authority of the bishops of a country against that of the Pope. Even in France this term had lost much of its seventeenth-century meaning; to apply it to the bishops and laity of England in 1860 was unintelligent. As in all questions, some were prepared to go faster and further than others; some had reservations on particular points of policy, but there was unquestioned loyalty to the Holy See, a fact that was made clear when the bishops withdrew all opposition once Rome had spoken.

It is best to regard these unhappy affairs as the growing pains of the restored Hierarchy. Only by actual experience could bishops and laity in a country that had been without a Hierarchy for three centuries discover what were their responsibilities and what was the extent of authority. Inevitably personal feelings entered into each dispute, and the difficulties became dramatized when such personalities as Wiseman, Errington and Manning were involved.

The outcome of the disputes must be summarized. On 22 July 1860, by the Pope's supreme authority, Errington was liberated from the office of coadjutor with right of succession in Westminster. The only reason given was that it had proved impossible for Wiseman and Errington to work in harmony and that their further association might be harmful to the Church in England. The fact that Errington was twice offered preferment in later years is evidence that there had been no canonical offence. He declined these offers and spent his remaining twenty-six years in quiet and faithful service to the Church, first in charge of missions in the Isle of Man and later teaching theology at Prior Park.

What part did Manning play in these disputes? He was directly concerned with the defence of the Oblates of St Charles, and he put the case with his usual clarity and cogency. He was not directly concerned with the problem of Errington's position, but he agreed that it would be better for Errington to be removed. He was, however, busily engaged in correspondence with George Talbot and on his visits to Rome he no doubt discussed the matter with those concerned. He kept Talbot informed of what was going on behind the scenes and gave his impressions of the persons who entered the dispute. The letters are open to the criticism that they displayed a spirit of uncharitableness towards those whose views were contrary to those of the writers. Manning was well aware that the information he gave to Talbot would be passed on to the Pope and to some of the Cardinals; he must also have known that Talbot would inevitably distort the facts in his own gossipy fashion. In his old age Manning described Talbot as "the most imprudent man that ever lived". That is a two-edged comment; in encouraging correspondence with such a tattler Manning himself was showing a lack of prudence and charity. Fortunately Pius IX seems to have taken Talbot's measure; he found his gossip amusing but he did not take it too seriously; thus the Pope's high regard for Thomas Grant was not affected by the animadversions of Manning and Talbot.

Against this defect of character must be placed Manning's achievements between 1854 and 1860. These were well described by Wiseman himself in a letter to Cardinal Barnabo (22 February 1860).[1] It is a fine tribute that deserves to be studied in detail; its length makes it impossible to reproduce here, but some indication must be given of its significance. Wiseman gave a list of what had been done under Manning's guidance; it included the completion

---

[1] Printed in full in Ward's *Wiseman*, II, 354–65. It is not printed in Purcell's biography of Manning. His chapter on "The Errington Case" is misleading and inaccurate.

of the church at Bayswater and the building of the community
house, a church and school in Pimlico and at Notting Hill, a
convent for the Collettines, and seven schools for the poor, besides the mission at Bayswater where, during the course of a few
years, the number of communicants had increased ten-fold.
Wiseman then referred to Manning's reputation as a preacher and
the constant demand on his services in the pulpit. "God has be-
stowed upon him in a special way the gift of converting others."
In his letter, Wiseman then turned to wider aspects of Manning's
work, especially to his skill in negotiating with government
officials in problems concerning Catholic Reformatories and
Orphanages and the safeguarding of Catholic children in workhouses.

Wiseman then dealt with the accusation "that he governs my
diocese, and that I see everything through his eyes."

When it was necessary to negotiate with the Government,
and with persons in high position, in matters that concerned
the interests of the whole of England; when it was a question
of founding or forming new works, which required largeness
of view and prudence—in such cases I have found no one
around me who has given me better counsel. Likewise when
I sought for light concerning the wants of the clergy in the
College or in the Mission, and upon the ecclesiastical spirit and
upon a thousand other matters of the highest importance, I
willingly grant I have often obtained from him advice and
sometimes comfort.

Perhaps it is in that last sentence that the root of the discord
may be found; men who had seen many years service in the
Church may have asked how a comparative newcomer like
Manning could give well-founded advice on the college (St
Edmund's) and "upon the ecclesiastical spirit."

The letter continues:

But in current and daily administration which forms the
government of a diocese, it is absolutely false that I have made

use of him as *e.g.* as though he were my vicar. Of the temporal concerns of the diocese I do not believe that I have ever spoken to him; nor do I believe that he has gained any information concerning them from me.

Wiseman asked a pertinent question. What bishop, having a man of such valuable qualities in his diocese, would have refrained from making full use of his services?

This outspoken defence of a priest who, in Wiseman's opinion, had been unjustly disparaged, may have played its part in later developments. Soon after this letter had been written Manning was made a Protonotary Apostolic, a position just short of a bishopric.

Errington was removed from Westminster soon afterwards, and it was thought that Wiseman's other difficulties would also be met in the way he desired. Rome, however, was in no hurry to make decisions; there was the hope that the bishops themselves would withdraw their opposition to their Metropolitan. All but two of them were in Rome for the canonization of the Japanese martyrs in May 1862. The Pope took the opportunity to call them together and, in Wiseman's presence, to exhort them to forget past differences and to work together for the good of the Church. Manning received jubilant accounts of this occasion from Wiseman and Talbot. The latter wrote, "There is no doubt that we enabled Cardinal Wiseman to gain a great triumph in Rome. I shall never forget the bishops' look after their last audience, in which the Pope gave them a severe lesson. Dr Ullathorne was very bitter after it, and so was Grant. They both received a solemn rebuke to meditate upon." The tone of that passage, with its cock-a-hoop references to two bishops of the quality of Ullathorne and Grant, is a sad commentary on the writer's own mentality, and, it must be admitted, on that of his correspondent in his least attractive aspect.

When, however, the official decisions were later received, they came as a shock to Wiseman and Manning. The government of the colleges was framed on the lines suggested by the majority of the bishops and not in accordance with Wiseman's opinion; the meetings of the bishops were also to be regulated as they had desired, that is, by previous notification of the subjects to be discussed and by majority decisions. One further matter was also determined as the bishops had desired—under the Roman Catholic Charities Act of 1860, all charitable and religious trusts had to be registered with the Charity Commissioners; Wiseman proposed that the Act should be ignored whatever the legal consequences, but the bishops thought otherwise, and Rome decided that each bishop should use his own discretion to protect the property and trusts of his diocese. Finally, it is said at the suggestion of Propaganda, the Oblates of St Charles were withdrawn from St Edmund's.

So, eventually, the causes for which Errington had fought were decided in favour of his opinions! It was a strange outcome yet it emphasizes that the deciding factor in the Pope's action in removing Errington was the personal incompatibility between Wiseman and his coadjutor as a threat to the smooth progress of the Church in England.

CHAPTER XVII

"UNDER A CLOUD"

NEWMAN was not caught up in the conflicts at Westminster. After his final visit to Ireland at the end of 1858 he spent more than thirty years at the Birmingham Oratory. It is difficult to think of a setting more suited to his genius or to the work that he alone could do. His vast correspondence, only a fraction of which has been published, brought help and guidance to a host of inquirers; the reprinting of his earlier sermons and writings and the new works that came from his pen extended his influence not only amongst Catholics but amongst thoughtful people of many shades of belief. Yet he felt that he was "under a cloud" and that the frustrations and misunderstandings he had to endure were preventing him from doing all that it was in him to do. It was not a matter of preferment, for which he had no wish; it was a deep sense of being hampered by the want of intellectual awareness of the dangers of the times and of any sense of the urgency of preparing men's minds for the problems he could see looming ahead —not political or social problems, for these were to him of subsidiary importance, but fundamental religious and spiritual problems affecting the salvation of men's souls.

In 1861 he wrote:[1]

I wish to do my part in destroying the feverishness and nervousness which is abroad, the vague apprehensions of some coming discoveries hostile to the faith, that spontaneous unwelcome rising of questionings and perplexities in the secret heart, which cut at the root of devotion, and dry up the founts of love, homage, loyalty, admiration, joy, peace, and all the

[1] *The Living Thoughts of Cardinal Newman,* by Henry Tristram (1948), p. 21. Newman was writing two years after the publication of Darwin's *Origin of Species.*

other best and noblest attributes of religion. It is perfectly true that obedience is acceptable to God, and may even be heroic, when performed amid darkness, dryness, and dejection; but few people except Saints can long endure so heavy a trial; and I shall think myself most highly favoured by the God of grace and truth if He shall enable me to suggest anything useful to any one soul who is under this special visitation. If I attain this object by lawful means, I shall not stand in need of any other consolation.

This same concern for the intellectual and spiritual preparation of the laity is more strongly expressed in a private memorandum written in 1863. The passage is long but it helps us to understand Newman's mind.

Rogers the other day asked Ward why it was that Catholics understood me so little, i.e. I suppose, why they thought so little of me. And the *Saturday Review* . . . said that I had disappointed friends and enemies, since I had been a Catholic, by doing nothing. The reason is conveyed in the remark of Marshall of Brighton to Fr Ambrose last week; "Why, he has made no converts, as Manning and Faber have done." Here is the real secret of my "doing nothing." The only thing of course which is worth producing, is *fruit*—but with the Cardinal, immediate show is fruit, and conversions the sole fruit. At Propaganda, conversions, and nothing else, are the proof of doing anything. Everywhere with Catholics, to make converts, is doing something; and not to make them is "doing nothing." And further still, in the estimate of Propaganda, or the Cardinal, and of Catholics generally, they must be splendid conversions of great men, noble men, learned men, not simply of the poor. It must be recollected that at Rome they have had visions of the whole of England coming over to the Church, and that their notion of instrumentality of this conversion *en masse* is the conversions of persons of rank. . . .

To me conversions were not the first thing, but the edification [building up] of Catholics. So much have I fixed upon the latter as my object, that up to this time the world persists in saying that I recommend Protestants not to become Catholics. And, when I have given as my true opinion, that I am afraid to make hasty converts of educated men, lest they should not have counted the cost, and should have difficulties after they have entered the Church, I do but imply the same thing, that the Church must be prepared for converts, as well as converts prepared for the Church. . . . Now from first to last, education, in this large sense of the word, has been my line, and, over and above the disappointment it has caused as putting conversions comparatively in the background, and the offence it has given by insisting that there was room for improvement among Catholics, it has seriously annoyed the governing body here and at Rome: at Rome on the side of the philosophy of polemic. I should wish to attempt to meet the great infidel &c. questions of the day, but both Propaganda and the Episcopate, doing nothing themselves, look with extreme jealousy on anyone who attempts it.

There is some exaggeration in that revealing passage, and a tinge of bitterness, but it does show the direction of Newman's thoughts and intentions. It has already been noted that the intellectual life of the Church was at a low ebb at that period; the political situation in Italy and France, with the threat to the temporal power of the Pope, preoccupied the minds of many leaders of the Church and hindered them from taking forward-looking views; but, while making every allowance for the exceptional pressure of material concerns, it must be admitted that Newman had reason in deploring the prevalent attitude towards the laity. In its crudest form this was expressed by Talbot in 1867 in a letter to Archbishop Manning.

What is the province of the laity? To hunt, to shoot, to entertain. These are matters they understand. . . . Dr Newman is the most dangerous man in England, and you will see that he will make use of the laity against your Grace. You must not be afraid of him.

During the ten years prior to that purblind statement, New-man's intentions had been checked several times.

In August 1857 he was invited by Wiseman to edit a new English translation of the Vulgate; the second Synod two years earlier had considered that a new version was desirable to replace the Rheims-Douay-Challoner text then in general use.

Newman wrote to Wiseman:

A greater honour, I feel, could not possibly have been done me than that which Your Eminence in that communication has conferred in selecting me for preparing an annotated English version of the Bible, and I beg Your Eminence, and, through you, the Episcopal body, to receive the heartful and most humble acknowledgement which so high and singular a mark of approbation and confidence demands at my hands.

He set to work enlisting the co-operation of Catholic scholars; the majority to whom he wrote were hereditary Catholics, the only two converts being Manning and Ward. He himself planned to write a long introduction which would "defend the Church and its position in the world in the nineteenth century as confronted with, and as against the penetrating knowledge, learning and ability of the scientific men and philosophers of the day."

For over a year he went on with his planning; he submitted his list of translators to Wiseman for approval, and they began their work. Then Wiseman passed on to him, without comment, a letter from the American bishops announcing that they were already engaged on a new translation and suggesting that they and the English bishops should combine to produce a new version. Newman seems to have been left to make what he could of the situation; he received no guidance from Wiseman nor from the bishops. Had he been of a more pushing nature, he could probably have got some kind of official decision. The prospect, however, of trying to reconcile the work of his own team with that of an American team daunted him. As he wrote in 1864:

I foresaw clearly that I should have endless troubles with publishers, American hierarchy, Propaganda, &c., &c., if I took this upon me. So I waited till I heard something more about it, but I have never heard till this day anything.

It is not surprising that he fought shy of such an Anglo-American enterprise, and it is difficult to see how it could have been successful. A translation done by a team of English scholars would have presented many problems of style, unless Newman proposed—though there is no hint of it—to use their work as the basis for a version completely rewritten by himself. American collaboration would have multiplied the problems. So the proposal was allowed to fade away, and Catholics in this country have had to wait nearly a century for a new English version of the Bible.[1]

The failure of Wiseman and the bishops to pursue the matter was in part due to the events recorded in the last chapter; until the disputes concerning Errington and the Oblates of St Charles had been settled, other business was put on one side. In later years Newman referred to Wiseman as "a man of large views and full of resource and suggestion, but he lived for the day, and every fresh event seemed to wipe out from his mind those which preceded it." The last sentence does not make full allowance for the troubles that beset Wiseman in his later years; Newman may not have been alive to the nature of those difficulties nor aware of the serious deterioration in Wiseman's health. Had they been able to meet more frequently, misunderstandings might have been avoided.

The fading-out of this scheme was a bitter disappointment to Newman for he had seen in this suggestion a substantial piece of work that he could do for the Church.

Against this disappointment could be balanced the successful foundation of the Oratory School in May 1859. It was founded in response to the need for a Catholic school conducted on the lines of the English Public Schools in which many of the converts had been educated; they wanted their sons to be brought up in a similar atmosphere and not in the somewhat monastic climate of the schools attached to the Catholic colleges. Some of the old

[1] It was in 1954 that the Hierarchy authorized for public use Mgr Ronald Knox's translation of the entire Bible.

Catholics were equally anxious for their boys to be trained on lines similar to those of the Protestant Public Schools.

The fate of the school was in the balance two years after its foundation when the staff resigned as a protest against the measure of authority given to the matron. Newman accepted their resignations and appointed a new staff under Father Ambrose St John as headmaster. From then the school flourished. The masters were laymen and they brought to the school the benefits of their Oxford or Cambridge days. It was charged against Newman that he was preparing the boys for the Universities, but this had no basis in fact. Newman himself took no regular part in the teaching, but he prepared the boys for performances of adaptations of the plays of Terence and Plautus, and he encouraged chamber music—thereby reviving his old love of the violin. The school, it has been said, was his "sole permanent contribution to English Catholic education, and in its continued existence the force and charm of his personality have achieved a kind of immortality. . . . The school's strength has been in character building and in the inculcation of public service rather than in pure scholarship, and the number of Old Boys who have attained prominence in public life is out of all proportion to its size."[1]

While the school was in its infancy, Newman became involved in the fate of *The Rambler*, the Catholic journal founded by a Balliol convert, J. M. Capes, in 1848. Its contributors were mostly lay converts and its contents were of a high standard of thought and learning; the writers were outspoken in their treatment of a wide variety of subjects and in their criticism of authority. A more pungent tone was given to its pages when Richard Simpson, an Oriel convert, became assistant editor in 1854; he took delight in startling his readers by expressing his opinions in extreme, even offensive, terms. We have already seen how Wiseman replied to one article which derided the old Catholics. This provocative spirit was bound sooner or later to cause trouble and to harm a journal that was doing good work. It may be noted, for instance, that the earlier part of Simpson's biography of Edmund Campion was published in *The Rambler*, but even then the author could not

[1] H. O. Evennett, *Catholic Schools of England and Wales* (1944), p. 70.

refrain from expressing his mischievous opinions on irrelevant topics.

The bishops became restive under this constant pin-pricking and they were seriously alarmed at some of the loose theology displayed by these clever laymen.

In 1856 Ullathorne wrote to Newman:

> I feel anxious about the latitudinarian spirit manifested in the writings of Simpson in *The Rambler*. Truths, and beautiful truths, are mixed with grave errors, and there is a restlessness of speculation, unguarded by the checks of the trained theologian, in Simpson.

Newman had much sympathy with the contributors to *The Rambler* who were, for the most part, friends of his; he knew how devoted they were to the Church and how desirous they were of using their abilities in its service, yet he could not but regret the tone of some of their writings and he thought they should avoid theological speculation. *The Rambler,* could, he felt, play an important part in preparing men's minds for facing the problems raised by the rapid advances then being made in knowledge, but this could be defeated by rashness of statement and by constant girding at authority. Liberty of discussion was, he knew, essential for progress in thought, but it must be liberty disciplined by the authority of the Church and within the limits rightly set by that authority. This conception was quite other than the growing liberalism in the world at large—the liberalism that Newman fought all his life—the view that "truth and falsehood in religion are but matter of opinion; that one doctrine is as good as another."

The tragedy of *The Rambler* as conducted by Simpson was that, by its irresponsible criticism, it must inevitably call down upon it the censure of authority and thus cease to be the means of educating lay opinion. That is what happened, and nothing took its place.

Sir John Acton became part proprietor of *The Rambler* in 1858. At the age of twenty-four he was an already portentously learned student of history. He had been at Oscott under Wiseman and in later years said, "We were proud of him; we were not afraid of him; he was approachable and generous, and no great friend of discipline." Acton had spent six years at Munich as the pupil of Dr Ignaz Döllinger whose work on Church history brought him wide fame. From him Acton learned that accurate research must be the basis of historical knowledge; every statement must be rigorously examined, and all questions should be fearlessly discussed. His influence on *The Rambler*, while raising its reputation for learning, did not restrain Simpson's reckless flouting of authority. Acton wrote to him, "You want things to be brought to bear, to have an effect. I think our studies ought to be all but purposeless. They must be pursued with chastity like mathematics." Simpson's integrity was not in doubt, but he could not attain Acton's detachment.

The time inevitably came when the bishops felt that some kind of check must be put on *The Rambler*. It was suggested that Ullathorne should ask Newman to use his influence with Simpson and Acton. Ullathorne wrote to Newman (16 February 1859):

> In London I met Cardinal Wiseman, Archbishop Errington, and Bishop Grant. After our business we talked about *The Rambler*. Our opinions were unanimous that something must be done. The point is to act with as much quietness and consideration as the case admits of. I mentioned my conversation with you, and your kind offer to write to the editor and Sir J. Acton. Cardinal Wiseman said it was like you, and that everything was safe with you. We agreed I should ask you, if you thought well, to write. It is our opinion that nothing short of Mr Simpson's retiring from the editorship will satisfy, as he plainly cannot judge what is and what is not sound language.

The immediate result of Newman's intervention was that Simpson resigned, and at the same time, urged Newman to become editor, a proposal that had the support of Acton.

The two men were never on easy terms; the more than thirty years that divided them was not a barrier, for Newman had a natural sympathy with younger men. The young cosmopolitan

scholar could not appreciate the cautiousness and sensitiveness of
the Oxford scholar who refused to be pushed further than he could
see his way. Acton wrote breathless letters to Newman; in one he
spoke of his difficulties "in the midst of a hostile and illiberal
episcopate, an ignorant clergy, a prejudiced and divided laity."
Eventually Newman called a halt to the correspondence. "To
talk to you," he wrote, "would be a recreation, but I am as sick
of penmanship as a pastrycook of tarts."

After some hesitation Newman accepted the fresh responsibility
of the editorship; his first number appeared in May 1859. It was
reviewed sympathetically, but with some reservations, by *The
Tablet*. The new editor's problem was appreciated.

> What we suspect to have been the actual ground of mis-
> giving about *The Rambler* is not so much any isolated views
> which were identified with it (displeasing as these may have
> been) as its general tone and temper. It was felt, in one word,
> that there was an absence, or deficiency, of "religiousness"
> about it. Things were habitually discussed in it in a cold, hard,
> worldly spirit. The grand mistake made in its administration
> seems to us to have been that of forgetting that Catholicism is
> an atmosphere, and not a mere creed; that it is a medium which
> colours almost everything which comes before us, except pure
> mathematics.

Newman needed time to effect the changes he had in mind,
but he was not given the time. He later wrote:

> I tried to make the old series of the magazine in keeping
> with the new; and, when faults were objected to in my first
> number I said to Mgr Manning, with a reference to the Great
> Eastern which was then attempting to get down the river, that
> I too was striving to steer an unmanageable vessel through
> shallows and narrows of the Thames, and that Catholic readers
> must be patient with me and give me time if I was to succeed
> eventually in my undertaking.

The parallel was apt; the "Great Eastern" was the wonder steam-
ship that failed.

The next step was a surprising one. Ullathorne called on Newman and suggested that, in view of the comments of *The Tablet*,
he should give up the editorship of *The Rambler*. It was sufficient
for his bishop to give a hint for Newman immediately to obey.
He believed that Ullathorne wanted him to resign, and he did so.
It is not known what was behind the bishop's abrupt action,
whether it was on his own initiative or whether it was proposed
by others; certainly it was unfair to judge the new *Rambler* by its
first issue only; no satisfactory explanation of this strange episode
has ever been given. Newman's comment in a letter to Henry
Wilberforce reveals his own feeling. "When I am gone it will be
seen perhaps that persons stopped me from doing a *work* which I
might have done. God overrules all things. Of course it is dis-
couraging to be out of joint with the time, and to be snubbed and
stopped as soon as I begin to act."

Unfortunately this was not the end of *The Rambler* matter. In
his last issue, July, Newman had contributed an article on "Consulting the Faithful in Matters of Doctrine." Part of his argument
was that in the period after the Council of Nicaea, many of the
bishops had been lax in their opposition to Arianism, and it was
left to the laity to champion Catholic truth. Some theologians
interpreted this as implying that the Church on that occasion had
failed in its teaching mission. The article was submitted to Propaganda by one of the bishops. When Ullathorne was in Rome
later that year he was asked to draw Newman's attention to the
matter and was told that the Pope was very displeased. In his
account of the episode Ullathorne wrote:

> Cardinal Wiseman was then at the English College at
> Rome. I told him all that had passed, and spoke to him
> gravely about the annoyances to which from time to time you
> had been subjected. . . . Also (I went) into the question about
> your treatment in the question of the Bible translation, etc.
> At last the Cardinal burst into tears, and said, "Tell Newman
> I will do anything I can for him."

Wiseman wrote at the time to Manning:

M

The late *Rambler* articles have given great pain, and Dr Ullathorne is charged with a mission of peace to Dr Newman. If he wished he could write an article explaining them rightly. I have spoken as well and soothingly as possible.

On his return to Birmingham, Ullathorne saw Newman who at once wrote to Wiseman asking for a list of the offending passages and the grounds for objection to them. When he had these (and he could obviously do nothing until he knew where he had offended) he promised to submit to the ruling of the Church if his subsequent explanations proved inadequate. Ullathorne approved this letter and himself wrote on Newman's behalf to Wiseman and to Propaganda.

Then came one of those silences that Newman found so mortifying.

Wiseman received the letter and both Manning and Talbot saw it, but it was not passed on to Propaganda, nor, of course, did the Pope see it. Wiseman did, however, receive from Propaganda a statement of the passages to which objection had been taken, but this was not passed on to Newman. It is true that Wiseman had a serious breakdown in health while in Rome and that Manning and Talbot were busy with the Errington affair, but this cannot excuse the failure to pass on documents of such vital importance to the reputation of any priest, let alone one of Newman's eminence. So the matter was allowed to drift. Those were anxious days in Rome with Victor Emmanuel and Garibaldi on the march, and Newman's trouble must have seemed a small item in the urgent affairs of the day. Even so, had Wiseman or one of his confidants passed on Newman's letter, or sent to him the list of offending passages, the matter could have been dealt with.

It was not until 1867 that the letter to Wiseman was at length brought to the notice of the authorities, and the whole matter was quickly resolved, but for seven years Newman had lain under the reproach of being suspected at Rome of unorthodoxy.

On Newman's withdrawal, Acton became editor of *The Rambler* with Simpson as his assistant; in April 1862 Acton changed *The Rambler* into a quarterly journal with the title *The Home and Foreign Review*, but this he gave up after eight issues. Newman did his utmost during *The Rambler* period to restrain Acton and Simpson; he urged them to avoid theological subjects and to adopt a less strident tone. At last he had to admit that the two men were beyond his influence and he withdrew from association with their publications.

The bishops were growing more and more irritated especially as Propaganda now voiced strong objections to *The Rambler* and insisted on restraint being imposed. Ullathorne at once wrote a letter to his clergy condemning *The Rambler* and its successor. As soon as Newman read this letter, he wrote to Ullathorne expressing his acceptance of his bishop's action. He particularly liked the bishop's clear statement of the grounds of his objections; Ullathorne's forthright dealings were in pleasing contrast, as Newman wrote to Ward, to Wiseman's manner "so vague as to leave no definite impression on my mind."

Ullathorne sent a copy of Newman's letter to Wiseman; this brought a letter from Manning.

> I believe *The Rambler* School to be small, but it is highly mischievous. The Cardinal has shown me the copy of Newman's letter, which I read with great thankfulness; not that I doubted what he would say, but I feared that he would not say it. He has a sort of sensitiveness about standing by his friends even when in the wrong, which is very honourable to his generosity.

Meanwhile the *Dublin Review* had lost much of the vigour it had in the days when Wiseman's mental powers were at full stretch. Wiseman had suggested that, when Newman took over *The Rambler*, the two papers should be amalgamated, but this proposal was dropped on Newman's withdrawal. Wiseman then decided to hand over control to Manning, who in 1863 persuaded W. G. Ward to become editor; the journal set out on a stormy passage of fifteen years. No one could any longer complain that the *Dublin Review* was dull; it became belligerent in tone and merciless to those who dared to disagree with Manning and Ward.

When Newman heard that Ward was the new editor, he commented, "Poor fellow, I wonder if he will burn his fingers as others, or have better luck." Ward proposed to visit Newman in the hope of enlisting his help, but, before his visitor came, he felt it wise to put on paper a statement of his attitude; in this he refers to his acceptance of his bishop's strictures on *The Rambler*.

> ... under no circumstances should I connect my name with the *Dublin Review*. I will add that I have suffered already so much from gossip about sayings of mine that I hope you will kindly allow me, when we meet, to keep clear of theological subjects.
>
> Nothing can prove what I have suffered in this way more clearly than the fact of the vague, deep suspicions which you have had of me now for eight years; and of the strange relief which you express in your last letter on finding me on the present occasion at once deferring to a definite judgment pronounced on definite grounds by the competent ecclesiastical authority. Why, if that authority in like manner pronounced certain writings of your own ... *de facto* to contain certain doctrines which had already been condemned at Rome as erroneous, I should not argue, but concur in the condemnation. I should do the like, of course, if the writings were my own. If I ever write on the subjects in question, I should say neither what Simpson has said, nor what you have said; but anyhow the true judgment about me lies, not with clubs or with coteries, but in my own acts, and with those who come after us.

From that time Catholic journalism lacked the distinction of thought and style that Newman could have contributed.

CHAPTER XVIII

APOLOGIA

THE year 1860 was fateful for Rome. Early in that year Piedmont, with the aid of Napoleon III, had established a kingdom north of the Papal States which stretched across the centre of Italy like a diagonal band with the Romagna in the north and the Patrimony of St Peter in the south. In May Garibaldi and his Thousand conquered Sicily and by summer were on the mainland heading for Naples. Cavour, the Prime Minister at Turin, pretending the need to protect Rome from the revolutionaries, sent the Piedmontese army through the Papal States; a small volunteer Papal force was swept aside and Victor Emmanuel marched south to intercept Garibaldi outside Naples. By the end of 1860 only the Patrimony of St Peter remained under Papal authority supported by the French troops in Rome who had remained after the fall of the Roman Republic in 1849.

The sending of these troops by President Louis Napoleon had been a true reflection of Catholic opinion in France where the Church had been steadily gaining ground under the influence through the years of Chateaubriand, De Maistre, Lamennais, Montalembert, Lacordaire and Dupanloup—men who varied in their intellectual and religious development but, in the earlier stages of their careers, united to revivify the Church in France. So strong was this Catholic opinion that, when the President became Emperor in 1851, he dared not withdraw the troops from Rome. His own tortuous and equivocal policy had resulted in the dominance of Piedmont whose Prime Minister was intent on uniting Italy under the House of Savoy. Austria was no longer able to safeguard the Papal States; other Catholic countries were anxious to come to the aid of the Pope, but the policy of non-intervention enforced by Palmerston prevented effective action. Only the

French troops, remaining at the whim of their designing Emperor, stood between Rome and the forces of Piedmont.

For ten years this precarious situation was maintained. Yet, as we have seen, the threatening political upheaval was not allowed to interfere with the mission of the Church. This point is well made by a recent writer.[1]

> It is odd that the Pope who is now, rightly, regarded by friend and foe alike as the founder of the "Modern Papacy", the Pope who recovered for the Holy See, throughout the Church Universal, an influence and prestige such as it had not enjoyed since the days of the Council of Trent, should also be regarded as having sacrificed the Church to the Papal State. The dramatic episode of Mazzini and Garibaldi in 1849 and the prolonged rearguard action by which Antonelli and Pio Nono tried to save their State from Piedmont, between 1859 and 1870, have helped to obscure the Pope's preoccupation with his unique spiritual office, to which, of course, his temporal sovereignty was wholly subordinate and ancillary. Much of this preoccupation cannot now be known. Thus he remained "the Pope of Prayer", but prayer is private; even so, his example in this may, for all we know, be his most important legacy. He granted an unprecedented number of audiences, he encouraged missionary activity in Africa, in Asia, and in America, which reached during his pontificate, proportions never previously attained; but great as was the personal and practical help which he gave to the missionary movement the story of that movement is the story of the pioneer priests who were faithful in the midst of dangers and suffering in distant places; it is not the Pope's story.

> But the important matter of the restoration of the Catholic hierarchies in England and in Holland is part of the Pope's story because he played a primary part in it, even though he played it at a distance; moreover the controversies aroused by those restorations had their bearing upon the central religious

---

[1] E. E. Y. Hales, *Pio Nono* (1954), p. 138. This book (by a non-Catholic) is the most balanced English account of the period.

and political storms of the century which flashed and rumbled round Rome.

The threat to the Papal States raised the question of the Temporal Power—that is, in the restrictive sense of the possession of sovereign territory. The Pope himself had no doubt that the States were essential for the secular independence of the Holy See, and that it was the duty of Catholic Princes to safeguard that possession; for this reason he did not maintain an effective standing army nor would he sanction conscription. In earlier years he had been willing to consider a federation of Italian States under the Pope as President, but the course of events and the excesses of the "liberators" and their anti-clerical and anti-religious tendencies had convinced him that a peaceful transition to a federation was impracticable without compromising the mission of the Church. So it was that, when at the end of 1859 Napoleon III suggested to the Pope that he should give up the Romagna, he replied:

> A project of such a kind presents insuperable difficulties; to convince oneself of that it is enough to consider my position, my sacred character, and the consideration I owe to the dignity and rights of the Holy See, which are not the rights of a dynasty, but rather the rights of all Catholics. The difficulties are insuperable because I cannot concede what is not mine.

Popular opinion in England was influenced by the uncritical account of the state of Italy which was spread about by many political refugees; thus the conduct of the Papal States was lumped with that of the Kingdom of the Two Sicilies, and the national "No Popery" tradition was a fertile soil for the growth of extravagant notions. Against such obsessions it was impossible for reasonable Catholics to make headway.

Wiseman accepted Rome's view that the States were a guarantee of the Pope's temporal independence; he busied himself in urging Catholics to contribute generously to Peter's Pence to make up for the loss of Papal revenue. A sum of over £6,000 was collected. Manning went further than Wiseman in three series of lectures he gave in 1860 and 1861; they were entitled *The Temporal Sovereignty of the Pope, Last Glories of the Holy See Greater than the First,* and *The Present Crisis of the Holy See.* The last was dedicated to Newman. "To you I owe a debt of gratitude for intellectual help and light, greater than to any man of our time; and it gives me a sincere gratification now publicly to acknowledge, though I can in no way repay it." The three booklets were collected in one volume published in 1862 under the title *Temporal Power of the Vicar of Christ.*

Manning set out to establish three propositions: "the temporal power of the Pope is ordained of God; the temporal power of the Pope has been the root, and the productive and sustaining principle of Christian Europe; the dissolution of the temporal power of the Pope would bring with it the dissolution of Europe." It must be admitted that Manning's exposition lacks substance; for instance it called for a far deeper knowledge of history than his to establish the second of these claims. Even Rome questioned his view that the loss of the Papal States would mean the reign of Antichrist in Rome, and he was constrained to modify this rash prediction.

The Rambler expressed somewhat liberal views on the question; Acton could not go the lengths of Rome, still less of Manning. This divergence was one of the reasons for ending *The Rambler,* and Manning was the emissary of official opinion to Acton, who wrote to Newman, "Manning's personal kindness was extreme. He gave me distinctly to understand that it was an official communication."

Newman's own view was more moderate than Manning's; the Temporal Power was one of those questions on which some latitude of opinion was legitimate. He disliked intensely the attempt being made to use the subject as a test of Catholic loyalty. It was at this time that Wiseman and Manning were forming an Academia of the Catholic Religion as an offshoot of the Roman Academy. Newman had agreed to become a member, but he threatened to withdraw if it was to be used to advocate extreme views on the Temporal Power.

It was not until 1866 that Newman made any public pronouncement on the subject. He then preached a sermon on "The Pope and the Revolution." He expressed the hope that Rome itself and some of the surrounding territory would remain under the Pope's authority, but should even this prove impossible, then "temporal power has been the means of the Church's independence for a very long period; but, as her Bishops have lost it a long while, and are not the less Bishops still, so would it be as regards her Head, if he also lost his. The Eternal God is her refuge, and as He has delivered her out of so many perils hitherto, so will He deliver her still. The glorious chapters of her past history are but anticipations of other glorious chapters still to come."

On the same day that Newman spoke those words, Manning preached on the same subject; it was Rosary Sunday on which the bishops had asked the faithful to pray for the Pope. Manning did not take the line of argument he had followed a few years earlier. He set out to establish, "1. that the Temporal Power of the Pontiff is a power ordained of God; 2. that it stands at least upon the same basis as all other rightful authority; 3. that it is sacred by every right common to other powers, and by rights and sanctions which transcend those of all other countries on earth; 4. that it therefore cannot be resisted, nor can any one excite resistance against it without sin against not only political justice, but against the ordinance of God."

Unhappily the problem of the Temporal Power led to excesses of statement that caused grave dissensions among Catholics. Fanatical advocates such as Veuillot in France regarded men of moderate views as traitors to the Church, and for a decade, this, and, as we shall see, the question of Papal Infallibility, embroiled the Catholic world in disputes that were conducted by some controversialists with distressing virulence, and made sport for Protestants and unbelievers.

Wiseman attended a Catholic Congress at Malines in August 1863. He himself spoke on the progress of the Church in England. The outstanding event of the Congress was Count Montalembert's two addresses, one on "A Free Church in a Free State", and the second on "Liberty of Conscience." Both were delicate subjects to handle in a Catholic assembly. He wanted governments to be neutral to religion, and he deplored the necessity of negotiating concordats to ensure protection for the Church. As to liberty of conscience, he argued that the Church should not rely on the civil power to enforce uniformity of belief; he referred to Spain and Naples which as "Paradises of religious absolutism have become the scandal and despair of all Catholic hearts." Strong objection was taken to some of Montalembert's statements, and representations were made to Rome. W. G. Ward privately published a pamphlet denouncing the first address on the ground that its argument would lead to religious indifferentism. The Pope did not publicly condemn Montalembert's views, but he thought that some needed qualifying; he made the comment that, though in practice, he would welcome liberty of conscience in Sweden and Russia, he could not accept it as a general principle. A letter to Montalembert from the Secretary of State expressed Rome's displeasure.

Montalembert had been told that Wiseman had been in part responsible for Rome's intervention. On hearing this, Wiseman wrote to a friend:

I have never written a word to Rome, nor given any authority to anyone to speak unfavourably of the Count's eloquent speech. Still less has it ever entered into my mind to denounce it to the Index, or ask to have it even reproved, still less condemned. Though I did not and do not agree in its political principles and tendencies, there was no error in it against faith or morals, which could have authorized anyone to denounce it, especially a stranger, in the presence of the Metropolitan. You may assure the Count of this, and of my undiminished respect and affection for him.

In explanation of this misunderstanding, Ward's son Wilfrid wrote, "it is probable that Mr Ward and Dr Manning had been understood as claiming the Cardinal's sympathy in their opposition to the speech."

There is no record of Newman's opinion of Montalembert's

address, but six months later in defining the liberalism to which he maintained a lifelong opposition, he was careful to distinguish it from the liberalism of Montalembert and Lacordaire. "I do not believe that it is possible for me to differ in any important matter from two men whom I so highly admire. In their general line of thought and conduct I enthusiastically concur, and consider them to be before their age." A tribute such as that was not calculated to please Ward and Manning.

The Malines Congress was followed a month later by one of Catholic scholars at Munich at which Döllinger was the chief speaker. In an address on "The past and future of theology" he pleaded for greater liberty for the theologian in discussing questions outside received dogmas. Errors should be fought with "scientific weapons" not by ecclesiastical censures, and by the power of informed opinion. Here he was arguing on lines congenial to Newman. But Döllinger went further; he deplored the low level of theological studies in Italy and argued that scholasticism was outdated. Finally he claimed that only in Germany were to be found "the two eyes of theology, knowledge of philosophy and history," and that Germany must become the preceptor of the nations!

Rome was naturally annoyed at the slur cast on Italian theologians and on scholasticism; there were, in fact, already indications of that revival of Thomism which was to be so encouraged by the successor of Pius IX. The Pope was more disturbed by the suggestion that discussion on theological and philosophical and even scientific questions should be conducted without full deference to ecclesiastical authority. He wrote to the Archbishop of Munich to express his displeasure.

This Papal Brief (21 December 1863) was a rebuff to those who wanted greater freedom of discussion. Döllinger's pupil, Acton, was so disheartened that he ceased publishing *The Home and Foreign Review*. Newman was full of sympathy with him and wrote (18 March 1864):

There is life and increasing life in the English Catholic body —clergy and laity—and, if there is life, there must be reaction.

I don't think that active and honest minds can remain content under a dull tyranny. It seems impossible to conceive that they can remain quiet under the supremacy of Manning and Ward.

Newman made a careful analysis of the Brief, and concluded:

If I understand this Brief, it is simply a providential intimation to every religious man, that, at this moment, we are simply to be silent while scientific investigation proceeds—and say not a word on questions of interpretation of Scripture, &c., &c., when perplexed persons ask us—and I am not sure that it will not prove to be the best course.

Shortly afterwards he again wrote, evidently with this Brief in mind, on the difficulty of discussing theories put forward by scientists, "hypotheses rise and fall; it is difficult to anticipate which of them will keep their ground, and what the state of knowledge in relation to them will be from year to year. In this condition of things, it has seemed to me to be very undignified for a Catholic to commit himself to the work of chasing what might turn out to be phantoms."

It is possible now, a century later, to appreciate Newman's prudence.

The letter to Acton, from which a quotation has just been made, was written while the preliminary passes were being made in the duel between Newman and Charles Kingsley, the outcome of which was the *Apologia pro vita sua*: a book that is among the classics of our language; that fact is of relative unimportance since the *Apologia* is far more than a masterpiece of English; it takes its place in the small group of self-revelations which the world classes with St Augustine's *Confessions*.

There is no need here to recount in any detail the circumstances that prompted Newman to write the history of his religious opinions. When Charles Kingsley rashly stated, "Truth, for its own sake, had never been a virtue with the Roman clergy. Father Newman informs us that it need not, and on the whole ought not to be", and when he failed to make a satisfactory apology, he opened the way to Newman's own public vindication. Superficially the contest was unequal. Kingsley was at the height of his popularity as a novelist, as a preacher and lecturer, and as an advocate of social amelioration; Newman had been all but forgotten by the public and, as we have seen, was subject to misrepresentation and even suspicion among his fellow Catholics.

It was providential that by this time he had renewed his associations with old Oxford friends; his diffidence, which did not grow less with the years, had been one of the reasons for the break in their intercourse, and they themselves felt cut off from the unknown society he had entered. There had been, in one sense, no loss of those Oxford friends who had remained Anglicans, for it was not by them that Newman was traduced; their affection had not grown less.

In June 1862 Newman and his former curate W. J. Copeland chanced to meet in London; from then onwards Copeland was a visitor at the Oratory and was there while Newman was writing the earlier parts of the *Apologia*. The news was perhaps spread by Copeland; soon a letter arrived from Keble; then Frederic Rogers, R. W. Church, Isaac Williams and others gladly renewed their friendship with one they still revered; there were visits and letters. So it was when Newman's devotion to the truth was questioned, old friends were at hand to strengthen him with their affection, and to supply information. Some extracts from letters to Copeland[1] must suffice to tell the story of those weeks of concentrated thought and composition.

31 March, 1864. I am writing my answer to Kingsley's pamphlet, and this is what I think. The whole strength of what he says, *as directed* rhetorically to the popular mind, lies in the antecedent prejudice that *I was a Papist while I was an Anglican.* Mr K. *implies* this. The only way in which I can destroy this, is to give my history, and the history of my mind, from 1822 or earlier, down to 1845. I wish I had my papers properly about me. It would be a great act of friendship, if you would let me

[1] *The Tablet,* 6 October 1945.

send you some pages in proof, in order to correct me, *if I have stated my facts incorrectly.*

19 April, 1864. I am very low—it is one of the most terrible trials that I have had. And I have to write against time, and to refresh my memory against time. Longman seemed to think an answer ought not to be delayed, if there was to be any—and people won't read a fat book—so the only way was to begin at once, and write as I printed. I do trust I shall be carried through it, but at my age it is a perilous toil. There will be at least five parts. The one on which I need your assistance is the fourth. It will be most kind if Keble looks at it too. The single point is, Have I made mistakes of fact, over-stated things, &c.? What I shall ask Keble (*as well as* you) to look at, is my sketch from (say) 1833 to 1840—but mind you, you will be disappointed— it is *not* a history of the movement but of *me*—it is an egotistical matter from beginning to end. It is to prove that I did not act *dishonestly*—I have doubts whether anyone could supply instead of me what I have to say—but, when you see it, you will see what a trial it is. In writing I kept bursting into tears—and as I read it to St John, I could not get on from beginning to end. I am talking of part 3. You can help me greatly between 1840 and 1845. But Church could help me quite as much. Yet from the day he saw me off at Johnson's, he has been so dead to me, that I could not get myself to ask him.

This led to a renewed association with R. W. Church to the great joy of both men.

17 June, 1864. The printers would not give me time to send you another slip or even a line to explain. I never have had such a time. It is the greatest effort I ever made; and for 10 to 12 weeks. One time I went on for 22 hours running. But it is over—and, I trust, has done my work—so I must be content and thankful and I am not much the worse for it, though very tired, and up to nothing at all.

16 May, 1865. I am this very day sending back to the Printer the *last* revise of my "Narrative of Religious Opinions" —i.e. my Apologia in its second edition.

The public did not take to the new title and the book has become known as Newman's *Apologia*. In its final form the book was pruned of the brilliant skirmishes with Kingsley.

By the time the final part had been published, Newman had the public on his side. He received many letters of appreciation but he was most heartened by the addresses that came to him from diocesan meetings of Catholic priests. One extract will serve as a specimen of others. The chairman of a meeting of the clergy of the diocese of Beverley wrote:

I was requested . . . to express to you as strongly and as earnestly as I could, how heartily the whole of the clergy of this diocese desire to thank you for services to religion as well-timed as they are in themselves above and beyond all commendation, services which the Catholics of England will never cease to hold in most grateful remembrance.

A quotation has already been given from Ullathorne's letter which was, in part, intended to disperse the idea that "you have been more occupied with your own thoughts than with the service of religion and the work of the Church."

There were a few discordant voices. Herbert Vaughan, for instance, wrote, "I have read it with a mixture of pain and pleasure. The egotism may be disgusting, but it is venial. There are views put forward which I abhor, and which fill me with pain and suspicion." It may be surmised that he was perturbed by the last chapter, "Position of my mind since 1845"; this must have been a difficult one to write for it touched on the measure of freedom of discussion that could legitimately be exercised by Catholics.

Manning said of the third part, "it is like listening to the voice of one from the dead", and after the publication of the *Apologia* as one volume in 1865 he wrote to Talbot that Canon Oakeley and

Dr Maguire "have been literally playing the fool about him [Newman] in this Kingsley affair." This presumably referred to their share in the address of appreciation sent to Newman by 110 of the Westminster clergy. Manning later wrote, "I know that Anglicans look on the *Apologia* as a plea for remaining as they are." What evidence Manning had for that statement is not known, but it may confidently be said that since its publication the reading of the *Apologia* has brought many to consider the claims of the Church, and, even if they have not submitted, they have gained a better understanding of its significance.

Talbot was in England in the summer of 1864 and he quickly sensed the changed position of Newman; he called at the Oratory but Newman was away. Talbot then wrote inviting Newman to preach a series of Lent sermons in Rome in 1865, "Where you would have a more educated audience of Protestants than could ever be the case in England." Newman replied:

> I have received your letter, inviting me to preach next Lent in your Church at Rome to "an audience of Protestants more educated than could ever be the case in England."
>
> However, Birmingham people have souls; and I have neither taste nor talent for the sort of work which you cut out for me. And I beg to decline your offer.

There is no record of Wiseman having read the *Apologia*; for the sake of his health he was living much out of London and was frequently prostrated by illness. He was obliged to leave the direction of affairs to his vicar-general and to Manning.

CHAPTER XIX

WISEMAN IN DECLINE

THE visit of Garibaldi to England in April 1864 was the occasion for enthusiastic demonstrations in his honour; the populace seized every opportunity to welcome him; he was received by the Prince of Wales, by the Prime Minister and foremost statesmen, by Anglican bishops and by the leaders of society. Men of strong religious faith such as Lord Shaftesbury and Gladstone were equally enthusiastic. In his biography of the latter, John Morley wrote, "Some were drawn by his daring as a fighter, and by the picturesque figure as of a hero of antique mould; many by sight of the sworn foe of Giant Pope."

Wiseman protested at this adulation of a man who had praised the Goddess of Reason set up by the French in 1793, and had written of "that hideous and immoral monstrosity the Papacy." The accuracy of Wiseman's quotation was questioned by *The Times*, but when Wiseman pointed out that he had used a translation published in that paper, the editor made an apology.

Manning issued a letter of protest in which he gave further extracts from Garibaldi's speeches to show his anti-religious attitude. Gladstone was certainly perturbed at this aspect of his hero. He wrote, "As to his Goddess Reason, I understand by it simply an adoption of what are called on the continent the principles of the French Revolution. These we neither want nor warmly relish in England, but they are different from its excesses, and the words will bear an innocent and even in some respects a beneficial meaning." An entry in Gladstone's diary implies that he attempted to get a more satisfactory declaration on religion from Garibaldi. "The utmost I could get from him was that it would be sad if the Italian people should lose its faith." Perhaps he would have felt more perturbed had he seen one of the portraits of Garibaldi circulated in Piedmont as early as 1850 showing him in the guise of Christ with his stigmatized hand raised in blessing. There has never been any satisfactory explanation for the cutting short of Garibaldi's visit; it may be that this revelation of his attitude towards religion was among the reasons for speeding his departure.

The year 1864 saw not only the composition of the *Apologia* and the visit of Garibaldi, but the issue from Rome of a document, *The Syllabus of Errors*, that was to cause an uproar. On 8 December the Pope published an encyclical *Quanta Cura* which condemned in emphatic terms such errors of the day as "naturalism" which ignores the primary place of religion, and those "liberties" which place Catholicism on the same level as other creeds. The encyclical was the Pope's indignant protest at the tendencies he saw operating in the world against the Church. Let it be recalled that he was not discussing paper theories; he could see these principles operating in Italy, principles with which he refused to compromise although their practical outcome might overwhelm him at any time. This encyclical would probably not have attracted much attention outside the Church; it was, however, sent out with a document that was not a formal papal pronouncement; this was "A Syllabus, containing the principal Errors of our times, which are noted in the Consistorial Allocations, in the Encyclicals, and in the Apostolic Letters of our most Holy Lord, Pope Pius IX." It was intended as a reminder to the bishops of what the Pope had said during his reign on a variety of matters; each error had a reference to the document in which it had been considered. The form of the Syllabus was maladroit, and to those unacquainted with Roman procedure, was misleading. The summary terms in which the condemned propositions were stated gave the impression of a universal application which was not always valid. Many of them, such as those on pantheism and rationalism, or on the Divinity of Christ, were only disturbing to extreme opponents of Christianity, but one in particular excited public controversy; this condemned the proposition that "the Roman Pontiff can, and ought to, reconcile himself and come to terms with progress, with liberalism, and with recent civilization." Discussion was befogged by the use of terms such as "liberalism" whose connotation varied from country to country. Newman, as we have seen, made a distinction between what was termed liberalism in France and what it meant elsewhere.

Rome was surprised at the storm aroused; what had been meant as an *aide-mémoire* for bishops was held up in the public press as a proof that the Papacy was opposed to the progress that most people regarded as the mark of the enlightened nineteenth century.

The French Government forbade the reading of the Syllabus in the churches. Bishop Dupanloup protested at this action, and he wrote a pamphlet in which he moderated the harshness of the Syllabus; for this he received the thanks of over six hundred bishops and the qualified approval of the Pope.

Newman's view was not publicly expressed at the time, for he would never be rushed into giving summary judgments. Two years later he pointed out that each abstract proposition had to be considered in the light of the particular circumstances in which it had originally been condemned. The Pope's experiences during the Roman Republic and in the later Piedmont aggression in themselves explained what he had in mind when writing of "progress" and "liberalism", words that had been used as battle cries against the Church. Moreover, the Syllabus was not in Newman's opinion an infallible pronouncement though it came with great weight and commanded every Catholic's serious attention. At the time he wrote to a friend that "the advisers of the Holy Father seem determined to make our position in England as difficult as ever they can."

Manning regarded the condemnations of those propositions affecting morals and faith as infallible utterances, and even those concerning political philosophy seemed to him to come within the same category as "politics are part of morals." W. G. Ward, writing in the *Dublin Review*, had no doubts that both the encyclical and the Syllabus were *ex cathedra* statements possessing "absolute infallibility", and wrote that those who withheld assent "act inconsistently with their Catholic profession, assume a non-Catholic position, and accordingly (while their indocility continues) excluded from the hope of Heaven."

Such extreme and, as he felt, unwarranted judgments distressed

Newman, and from that time may be noted the widening of the rift that was to divide him from Manning and Ward.

Two important matters called for decisions during Wiseman's last months; the first was whether Catholics could attend the Universities (particularly Oxford and Cambridge), and the second the movement for the "Unity of Christendom." Had Wiseman been in full health it may be that the University question would have been handled more sympathetically; as it was the lead fell to Manning, who, through Talbot, kept Propaganda informed of his opinions (and those of Ward) and urged decisive action. After Errington's removal, Wiseman had refused to have another coadjutor; in spite of strong pressure from Rome, where Ullathorne's name was under consideration, Wiseman begged to be allowed to pass his last years in peace, and at length his rather pathetic appeal was granted. One result was that Manning's influence increased and he was in constant correspondence with Rome and was there in the early months of 1863 and of each of the following years. When Manning formed an opinion he held it tenaciously and he pursued all legitimate means to win acceptance for it; it may be felt that at times his negotiations were in danger of becoming intrigues—and certainly his later correspondence with Talbot gives colour to this—but he used his considerable influence at Rome for causes which he regarded as of vital importance to the Church. He was occasionally at fault in his judgments and he was intolerant of opposition.

The University question was bound to call for a decision on policy sooner or later, but it came to the front when Newman had the opportunity, which he took after consulting his friends, of buying land at Oxford. He discussed the use of the site with Ullathorne who was anxious to have a more vigorous mission at Oxford. After their conversation Newman put his thoughts on paper for the bishop's approval.

1. I consider that there is considerable danger to the souls of Catholic youth who go to the Protestant colleges in Oxford.

2. I consider there is comparatively little danger in their going to a Catholic college there.

3. The former of these is the actual state of the case.

4. When I thought of our [Oratorians] going to Oxford, it was with a special view of meeting this actually existing danger.

5. If that danger ceased, I should not feel any special reason for going there.

Now you have told me that it is not unlikely that this danger *will* cease, i.e. that Catholic youth will be *prohibited* from going to Oxford, for your lordship said, to my surprise, that the idea of a Catholic university in England, which I thought not feasible, was still in contemplation. Before this great design, the notion of Catholic youth being on any footing at Oxford shrinks into nothing. . . . If then the present danger to young English Catholics is only temporary, Oxford has no stronger claims upon me than any other mission of a hundred souls.

A few days later the bishop made it clear that he could not sanction any move that might imply approval of Catholics attending the University. Newman then sent him the following statement:

1. That we have no intention at present to do more than accept your lordship's offer to put into our hands the Oxford mission.

2. That we do so with a view to the *future* foundation of an Oratory there; and for the same reason we buy the ground.

3. That we have no intention in any way to co-operate with the University, or with the colleges of Oxford, whether by taking lodgers, or private pupils, or in any other way.

4. That we propose to confine ourselves to the spiritual duties of the mission, taking the care of the present Catholics there, and doing our best to increase their numbers.

5. That neither now, nor in time to come, will we take part in any Catholic college there, or sell our ground for that purpose, without your Lordship's knowing our intention, so that you may write to Propaganda on the point if you so wish.

6. That we feel the kindness of your offer to write for us to Propaganda, but we will not avail ourselves of it—nor write ourselves—for this simple reason, that if we do, we shall give Propaganda the impression that we are contemplating something more than the performance of spiritual duties at Oxford.

7. That we contemplate, as our first step, to build a church on such a site as we can best provide for it.

Shortly afterwards Newman prepared a circular asking for contributions to the cost of building a church. Ullathorne asked him not to send this out but to allow him to read it at a meeting of bishops that was to be held at that time.

Wiseman had earlier been in favour of establishing Catholic Halls or Colleges at the Universities, but he now changed his opinion, probably under Manning's influence who had the strong support of Bishop Grant of Southwark, and, of course, of Ward. Newman went to see Wiseman in November to discuss the Oxford project; the Cardinal was too unwell for much conversation, and listened, as Newman said, "half querulously". It was their last meeting.

Manning's opinions were well known. He had stated them clearly in the first issue of the *Dublin Review* under Ward's editorship in July 1863. The article, entitled "The Work and Wants of the Catholic Church in England", will call for further attention; here we are concerned with his exposition of his views on the University question. He first set down the points in favour of Catholics going to the University, such as, the need for higher education of laymen who were now able to take a place in the public life of the country; the social advantages were also touched upon. Against these he placed his own strongly held opinion that the liberalizing tendencies of the University would be a grave danger to the faith of young Catholic students. Here, as we have seen, Newman fully agreed with him, though he thought there was equal danger to a youth entering business or taking a commission in the forces. Moreover he was realist to know that there were Catholic students at the Universities and that, in spite of prohibitions, some, at least, would continue to go there. Manning saw that simple prohibition would not solve the problem; this led him to consider the idea of a Catholic University in England.

Manning and Ward were alarmed at the possibility of Newman becoming once more associated with Oxford, though, as yet, there had been no specific suggestion that he himself would live there. They knew that his name would inevitably draw more Catholic students to the University, and in this they were undoubtedly right. Through Talbot they urged Barnabo, the Prefect of Propaganda, to give urgent attention to the matter. The bishops were therefore asked to meet in December 1864 to discuss the whole question. Before they met a series of questions[1]—"leading questions" would be a more correct description—was circulated by Wiseman's authority to a number of Oxford converts; a copy was not sent to Newman nor was he consulted. A son of Thomas Gaisford, the great Greek scholar, sent the questions and his answers to Newman. Some of his comments are worth noting as they indicate better than anything else the problem that was troubling many parents.

> I consider *myself* responsible that my son shall be brought up first as a Catholic Christian, secondly as an English gentleman, and tho' I hope that I am ready to take advice from wiser men, I decline to shift my responsibility on anyone.

> What is to become of my son at 18 if he does not go to Oxford? [The writer had already pointed out that he could not wait until a Catholic college could be established.] There must always be danger to him, and I think he runs less risk at Oxford than elsewhere; the bane of the old Catholics has been lying about idle at their parents' houses, or lounging on the Continent to pass the time between boyhood and manhood.

One implication of several questions was that the laity should not expect a better education than that available to the clergy. To

[1] See Ward's *Newman*, II, p. 540. It is difficult to believe these questions had more than Wiseman's formal approval.

this the reply came, "I don't see why the laity should be under-educated because the clergy can't have equal advantages."

When the bishops met they decided against the setting up of Catholic Colleges at the Universities, but they thought that parents should be dissuaded from sending their sons to Oxford or Cambridge. Ullathorne and Clifford were not in favour of a rigid prohibition. Propaganda approved the bishops' decisions. It should be noted that there was no absolute prohibition, nor did the bishops issue any general instruction on the matter. Rome had consistently opposed "mixed" (that is, Catholic with Protestant) education—indeed that had been the main reason for the encouragement given to the University of Ireland. The question of where parents were to send their sons was not faced.

When he heard of this decision, Newman gave up his proposal and sold the land. His comment was, "we are in a transition time and must wait patiently, though of course the tempest will last through our day." He added, "another Pontiff in another generation may reverse it."

The second important matter engaging Wiseman's attention at this time was the Association for Promoting the Unity of Christendom. The leading Catholic layman in this movement was Ambrose Phillipps de Lisle who was closely associated with Wiseman in the period before Newman's conversion. His expectations of wholesale conversions were pitched too high and undoubtedly affected Wiseman's earlier views. He hoped that the time would come when the Church of England as a body would submit to the Church of Rome. In 1857 he wrote to Barnabo claiming that there was a party (including ten bishops and two thousand clergy) in the Established Church working to this end, and he asked for the Pope's blessing on their endeavours. Barnabo was impressed and wrote an encouraging answer. The outcome was the formation in 1857 of the Association at a meeting of members of "the Roman Catholic, Greek, and Anglican Communities." Their immediate obligation was to pray for "a Corporate Reunion of those three great bodies which claim for themselves the inheritance of the priesthood and the name of Catholic." Their journal *Union* urged that individual conversions should not be the primary aim so much as the reconciliation of the whole body of any one Church. When de Lisle wrote to Newman he received a kindly reply, but he objected to the suggestion that individuals should not come over to the Church until all their fellows came in a body. "They have individual souls." "And then suppose, if these very dear and precious souls, say Dr Pusey, are taken away in this state, when grace has been offered them, and they have not followed it up."

Wiseman saw de Lisle and soon found that the talk of ten Anglican bishops was one of de Lisle's over-enthusiastic assumptions; he even thought that Samuel Wilberforce, Bishop of Oxford, was in that happy frame of mind! Wiseman put his finger on the fatal flaw in the Association's case—its contention that "Catholics, Greeks and Anglicans" were all equal, "three great churches", "the separated portions of the Church." It was the Branch theory in a new guise. Did he recall that just over twenty years earlier he had told Hurrell Froude and John Henry Newman that, to quote Froude, "not one step could be gained without swallowing the Council of Trent as a whole"?

Wiseman and the bishops asked Ullathorne to go to Rome to lay the matter before the Holy See; this was felt desirable as Rome, and indeed continental Europe, did not then understand the nature of the Anglican Church; this imperfect knowledge has been in evidence in later negotiations for Reunion. When the true facts were explained Propaganda issued a decree forbidding Catholics becoming members of the Association.

Wiseman was able to preside at the meeting of the bishops in December 1864, but from then he rapidly lost strength and energy, and by the end of January it was clear that all hope of recovery must be abandoned. Manning was then in Rome and, on 4 February, at Wiseman's wish, a telegram was sent to recall him; he arrived on the 12th; it is uncertain if Wiseman recognized him.

Nicholas, Cardinal Wiseman, first Archbishop of Westminster, died on the morning of 15 February 1865, at the age of sixty-three.

The scenes at his funeral astonished all who could recall the Cardinal's arrival from Rome in 1850. Vast crowds thronged the route and showed their respect for the great ecclesiastic whom, fifteen years earlier, they had burned in effigy.

CHAPTER XX

THE NEW ARCHBISHOP

WHILE Wiseman was on his deathbed, Newman composed *The Dream of Gerontius*. It was the expression of an intense consciousness, as he thought, of approaching death. The poem was written rapidly and was published in *The Month* in the spring of 1865. A generation later it was to inspire the music of the oratorio of the Catholic composer, Edward Elgar. This is not the place to consider Newman as a poet; his own modest opinion of "effusions which I have ever considered ephemeral" is not one that can be shared by those who give a high place among English Hymns to "The Pillar of the Cloud" ("Lead, Kindly Light"), and to "Praise to the Holiest in the Height" from *The Dream of Gerontius*. It is important, however, in any estimation of Newman's personality and genius to remember that he had the instincts of a poet; it found expression not so much in what he called his verse-making as in the imaginative insight it gave him of human nature, and in the quality of his prose.

By the time Newman's poem had been published, Manning had become Archbishop of Westminster. To many it must have seemed an astonishing appointment; fifteen years earlier the new archbishop had been an Anglican archdeacon.

After Wiseman's death, the Westminster Chapter had put forward three names for consideration—Errington, Clifford and Grant. The bishops gave their approval, but as Clifford and Grant withdrew their names, Rome was presented with that of Errington alone. This choice may have been prompted by the feeling that Errington had been ill-used in being removed from Westminster; at the same time his name would not have been put forward unless the Chapter and the Hierarchy had been convinced that he was the right man for this high office. The Pope who, by an act of supreme authority, had deprived Errington of the right of succession to Westminster, regarded this proposal as an affront, and he wrote to the bishops to express his surprise that they had supported this extraordinary recommendation.

Manning kept in close touch with Talbot throughout this period of anxiety and uncertainty. He himself favoured Ulla-thorne or Cornthwaite of Beverley. Other candidates he assumed would be put forward were Brown of Shrewsbury and Newman. The British Government discreetly supported Clifford. Manning's own name was not among the earliest to be considered. Ward, however, had written to Talbot soon after Wiseman's death to urge the claims of Manning. The two met shortly afterwards and Ward wrote to his wife, "I have given up about all hopes of Manning's appointment. He says himself there is not the remotest chance of it," and he added that he would not go to Rome as "it is most important that there should be no idea about his intriguing in Rome." Manning certainly did not lift a finger to promote the consideration of his own name. Talbot, however, did all he could with the Pope and the Cardinals to urge Manning's suitability. There was another advocate at Rome, R. A. Coffin,[1] who had just become Provincial of the Redemptorists in England. He dis-cussed the question of Wiseman's successor with the General of his congregation who took him to see Cardinal Reisarch; Coffin urged that Manning should be considered; the Cardinal reported the conversation to the Pope. At one stage the Pope was so non-plussed that he suggested that Talbot should become Archbishop. Talbot at once wrote to Manning who replied, "I trust you will be sent to us." Was this one of Pio Nono's jests? It was easy to get a rise out of the humourless Talbot. So the discussions went on until the Pope decided to reserve the question to himself. At one stage he seems to have favoured Ullathorne, and it would have been a good choice, but eventually, after much thought and prayer, he decided on Manning.

Though the choice may have been unexpected, it had a sound basis. As early as 1859, according to Bishop Patterson, Wiseman had hoped that Manning would be his successor, but the Erring-ton dispute and the opposition to Manning's growing influence

[1] An Oxford convert who had accompanied Newman to Rome in 1846, and had, for a few years, been an Oratorian.

may have deterred Wiseman from pressing his idea. Manning's own explanation is reasonable. In recalling that he had gone to Rome as Wiseman's procurator in 1862, he added, "All these years had brought me into the closest relations with Pius IX. He had charged me with commissions of a very delicate kind. All this gave me an experience of Rome and a knowledge of the people there, which led on to my being where Pius IX placed me in 1865." It will be recalled that during his years at the Accademia Ecclesiastica, Manning had frequent audiences with the Pope who had kept him in Rome longer than Wiseman desired. Indeed, it is probably true to say that the Pope knew Manning personally better than he knew any member of the English Hierarchy. To this should be added the striking tribute to Manning that Wiseman sent to Propaganda in 1860; in this, it will be recalled, emphasis was laid on the access Manning had to government circles and his success in carrying out negotiations. At a period when relations with other governments were of pressing importance to the Papacy, this fact may have had its part in the Pope's decision.

Manning's appointment as archbishop was loyally accepted by the Hierarchy, by the Chapter of Westminster, and by the generality of priests and laity. Whatever may have been their former sentiments towards him, they set these aside in obedience to Rome.

There was a pleasant exchange of letters between the new archbishop and Newman. In reply to an invitation to the consecration on 8 June, Newman readily accepted, but begged to be excused the dinner that would follow; he went on to refer to rumours that Manning had recently proposed that he should be made a bishop *in partibus*; Newman begged that nothing more should be heard of the matter. In reply Manning recalled the earlier proposal when Newman was rector of the University of Ireland, and added, "I think that such an intention ought not to have been suspended. And I have for more than two years done my part to accomplish it. . . . But your wish must be final with me."[1]

Newman stayed with his friend Frederic Rogers (Lord

[1] On the day of his consecration, Manning received a letter from Ward accusing Newman of "(1) Disloyalty to the Vicar of Christ, and (2) Worldliness."

Blachford) for the consecration. R. W. Church has left an interesting glimpse of this resumption of friendship.

> I was in London for a couple of days last week at Rogers', and met Newman, who was staying there. He had come for Manning's consecration. It was the first time I had seen him for twenty years nearly. He was very little changed in look or general manner or way of talking, except that he seemed almost stronger in body. He was in good spirits, very hearty, and talked very freely about all sorts of things; reminding us every now and then that he was across the border, but without embarrassment, and without any attempt to flaunt anything in our faces. It was a much more easy meeting than I could have supposed possible. We seemed to fall into the old ways of talking. He talked about Manning, and about his own position, and his differences of views about education. He thought that Manning had certainly plans, but no one knew what they were; it was clear, however, that Newman did not much expect them to be what he would lay most stress upon. He spoke of the difficulty of getting interest or money for anything but immediate objects; the poor, or the training of priests; while literature, and higher education, and the education of the laity, no one cared much about or thought worth efforts. He spoke of his own school at Birmingham, and of the effect of its example in making the other schools, even the Jesuit schools, less Continental in their ways and more English, as in trusting boys and giving up *espionage*. The effect was as if he was working his own way, and giving up the general course of affairs to Manning and those who went with the current.

Shortly after this meeting Rogers and Church made a present of a violin to Newman. He was delighted and wrote, "On Saturday I had a good bout at Beethoven's Quartets, and thought them more exquisite than ever."[1]

[1] A letter of Edward Fitzgerald, dated February 1883, shows that the violin was still in use; "... pathetic as the notes of the violin which some one says are from time to time to be heard from within his room at the Birmingham Oratory."

In September came another reunion; the three great personalities of the Oxford Movement—Newman, Keble and Pusey—met for the last time. Newman had arranged to go down to Hursley to see Keble, and, by chance, Pusey was there. Newman wrote to Ambrose St John:

> As we three sat together at one table, I had a painful thought, not acute pain, but heavy. There were three old men who had worked together vigorously in their prime. This is what they have come to—poor human nature! After twenty years they meet together round a table, but without a common cause or free outspoken thought; kind indeed, but subdued and antagonistic in their language to each other, and all of them with broken prospects, yet each viewing in his own way the world in which those prospects lay.

It was the last time that Newman saw Keble who died six months later. Newman then wrote:

> Keble seems to have received all doctrine except the necessity of being in communion with the Holy See. . . . Till he saw that, (or that he was not in the Church), he was bound to remain as he was, and it was in this way that he always put it.

Reference was made in the last chapter to Manning's article on "The Work and Wants of the Catholic Church in England." This may be regarded as setting out some of the objectives he had in mind when he became archbishop. They are here summarized.

1. Establishment of diocesan seminaries for the education of the priesthood.
2. Provision of adequate education for the poor and middle classes.
3. Higher literary and scientific education for laymen.
4. Practical efficiency and more public usefulness in our laymen.
5. Provision for foreign missions.

The greatest danger he considered was "tame, diluted, timid or worldly Catholicism." This could only be combated by "downright, manly and decided Catholics, more Roman than Rome, and more ultramontane than the Pope himself." He was of the opinion that English society despised the first form of Catholicism, but would respect the second form.

For more than a decade he had watched Catholic affairs from the centre; judging from his later policy and conduct, he seems to have drawn some definite conclusions from what he had seen of the trials and difficulties to which Wiseman had been subjected. First there was the need for strict discipline among the clergy. The Pope had written to him after his appointment urging him "to maintain the discipline of the clergy against the world and against our own relaxations." Secondly, the archbishop must have greater control over the regular clergy; there must be no suggestion that the regulars were in some way superior to the secular clergy. In other words, the archbishop must be complete master in his own house.

Outward signs of the direction in which he was moving may be noted. He insisted on Roman vestments being used and on the altars being ornamented in Roman fashion; the Italian pronunciation of Latin was introduced. The Roman collar was to be worn, and a secular priest was to be known as "Father", a title previously limited to the regular clergy.[1]

Among the earlier questions with which Manning had to deal was the continued effort of the Association for Promoting the Unity of Christendom to gain a hearing. The decree of September 1864 forbidding Catholics to become members had been a setback, and the leaders felt that their position had been misunderstood. They had therefore asked Wiseman to forward to the Holy Office an address of explanation. This he agreed to do, but died before he could do so. The address, signed by nearly two hundred Anglican clergymen, was sent to Talbot who agreed to lay it before the Holy Office. Meanwhile Manning had published at the end of 1864 a letter to Dr Pusey entitled "The Workings of the

[1] It may be noted that the collar and the title have been widely adopted in the Anglican Church.

Holy Spirit in the Church of England." In a friendly tone the author maintained that there could be no question of corporate reunion as the Anglican Church was not a branch of the Catholic Church; it was not a question of reunion but of submission to the Holy See. This provoked Pusey to write his *Eirenicon*, of which more must be said in the next chapter.

Talbot consulted Manning on the kind of answer the Holy Office should give to the Anglican address. Manning was most emphatic on the need for a clear and definite statement on "(1) the exclusive unity of the Catholic and Roman Church, and (2) its exclusive infallibility, and (3) the universal duty and necessity of submission to it." He was in Rome that September to receive the Pallium, and took the opportunity to discuss the question with the Holy Office. The answer was ready by the end of the year. It followed the line of thought suggested by Manning, who then issued a Pastoral Letter on "The Reunion of Christendom." He sent the draft to Ullathorne who thought that some sentences were too sharp in tone, and Manning modified these though Grant and others thought they were justified.

Consultation with Ullathorne became part of Manning's procedure and proved beneficial, for Ullathorne united the old Catholic tradition with loyalty to the Holy See and an understanding sympathy with converts. At times Manning allowed himself to write harsh comments on Ullathorne, who, on his part, was bluntly critical of the archbishop, but they worked together to do valuable service to the Church.

This first Pastoral Letter is one of Manning's most agreeable productions. He welcomed the fact that so many Anglican clergymen could have joined in the address on reunion. "A change has visibly passed over England. Thirty years ago its attitude towards the Catholic Church was either intense hostility or stagnant ignorance. It is not so now. There is still much hostility and ignorance. But the hostility is more civilized and the ignorance is breached on all sides." The most interesting part of the Pastoral, however, is the passage in which he refers to the Nonconformist Churches which were then on the threshold of their period of great influence in public affairs.

They are souls for whom Christ died, robbed of their inheritance by the Anglican separation, from which they by legitimate process have separated in turn. Their state of privation is all the less culpable, as they have been born into a diminished inheritance of truth, with a greater difficulty of rising to it again. They are, moreover, marked by a multitude of high qualities of zeal, devotion to duty, conscientious fidelity to what they believe. If they are rougher in their language against the Catholic Church, they are more generous and candid adversaries; more vehement but less bitter, and altogether free from the littleness of personality and petty faults which sometimes stain the controversy of those who are intellectually nearer the truth. For such men it is our duty to cherish a warm charity and a true respect, and not disproportionately to waste upon those who stand nearer to us the time and sympathy which is their due. The time is come that the Catholic Church should speak, face to face, calmly and uncontroversially to the millions of the English people who lie on the other side of the Establishment.

Manning's suggestion that more thought should be given to those outside the Anglican Church was a timely reminder that the field of the Catholic Apostolate was not limited to one section of the people. As we shall see, he himself was to make a number of close contacts with leaders "on the other side of the Establishment."

One of his main purposes was revealed at a meeting called to consider a suitable memorial to Cardinal Wiseman. Manning presided and it was decided that a Cathedral should be built. He promised to support the scheme, but, significantly, he added that for him the urgent needs of the thousands of children of poor Catholic parents must come first. Funds were generously subscribed, but, beyond buying a site, Manning refused "to pile up stones and bricks."

It may have been this preoccupation with work of urgent importance that prevented Manning from giving energetic support to Talbot's scheme for rebuilding the Church of St Thomas of Canterbury in Rome. Talbot was deeply hurt at the failure of the English laity to provide the necessary funds. He received consoling messages from Manning, but little active support, and, for a time, there was a coldness between them.

One more episode involving Talbot calls for notice.

The English College at Rome under its rector Dr Neve, an Oxford convert and a warm admirer of Newman, had not maintained the standard it had achieved under Wiseman; its difficulties could have been remedied had the situation been put before the bishops, but another method was used. Talbot had been made Delegate-Protector of the college in 1867, and shortly afterwards it was announced that Dr Neve had resigned. He certainly regarded himself as dismissed; he wrote, "Talbot never said a word of his reasons for dismissing me, so I asked him. He replied that I was so fresh from Eton and Oxford that I did not understand Catholic young men. I remarked that he was fresher from both places." With Manning's approval, Talbot appointed an Irish priest, Henry O'Callaghan, as rector; he had been in charge of a small house of studies in Rome for the Oblates of St Charles which had been set up after they had been removed from St Edmund's. This change was made without any reference to the bishops who were all directly concerned as they sent students to the college. They had to accept what had been done, but the high-handed way in which the change had been made did not make for good relations with their archbishop. The college was now, in effect, under his control with one of his Oblates as rector.

Manning's intention of setting up a diocesan seminary apart from St Edmund's was carried out in 1869. He took over Cupola House, Hammersmith, which had been a convent since the days of Catharine of Braganza. Dr Weathers became president but control remained in the hands of Manning. He kept the seminary going at considerable expense during his lifetime, but it did not survive him.

CHAPTER XXI

NEWMAN'S TRIBULATIONS

PUSEY'S *Eirenicon*, published at the end of 1865, had as sub-title, "The Church of England a Portion of Christ's Holy Catholic Church, and a Means of Restoring Visible Unity." It took the form of a letter to Keble; in it Pusey argued that the great obstacle to union was not the teaching of the Roman Church as formulated by the Council of Trent, but the extravagant devotions to the Virgin Mary which were permitted, and the extreme interpretations allowed on such subjects as purgatory and indulgences. At the same time Pusey issued a reprint of Newman's Tract 90.

Newman corresponded with Pusey on the *Eirenicon*, and at length decided to publish an answer, but he had no wish to hurt his old friend. "If I shall say anything which is in the way of remonstrance, it will be because, unless I were perfectly honest, I should not only do no good, but carry no one with me—but I am taking the greatest possible pains not to say a word which I shall be sorry for afterwards." *A Letter addressed to the Rev. E. B. Pusey, D.D.*, was published early in 1866.

Newman limited himself to two points. As extravagances in devotions are, *ipso facto,* not the norm, it is unjust to use them as a criterion; the accepted doctrine of, and devotion to, Our Lady is, in the order of things, a legitimate development of the teaching of the Fathers of the Church.

In one passage Newman objected to Pusey taking Faber and Ward as authoritative exponents of Catholicism. Of Ward he wrote:

Do not his energy, acuteness, and theological reading, displayed on the vantage ground of the historic *Dublin Review* fully account for the sensation he has produced, without supposing that any great number of our body go his lengths in their

view of the Pope's infallibility? Our silence as regards their
writings is very intelligible: it is not agreeable to protest, in the
sight of the world, against the writings of men in our own
Communion whom we love and respect. But the plain fact
is this—they came to the Church, and have thereby saved their
souls; but they are in no sense spokesmen for English Catholics,
and they must not stand in the place of those who have a real
title to such an office.

This was to put elaborately what he had said in a private letter
to Pusey. "As to Ward's notions, they are preposterous."
The position Newman had come to occupy in the educated
world may be judged by the fact that *The Times* reviewed his
Letter to the length of seven columns of small print.[1] This was
written by R. W. Church. One passage deserves quotation.

> There is only one person on the Roman Catholic side
> whose reflections on the subject English readers in general
> would much care to know. Anybody could tell beforehand
> what Archbishop Manning would say; but people could not
> feel so certain what Dr Newman might say. Dr Newman has
> given his answer; and his answer is, of course, in effect the
> same as that of the rest of his co-religionists. He offers not the
> faintest encouragement to Dr Pusey's sanguine hopes. . . .
> What Dr Pusey asks is, in fact, to pull the foundation out from
> under the whole structure of Roman Catholic pretensions.
> Dr Newman does not waste words to show that the plan of
> the *Eirenicon* is impossible. He evidently assumes that it is so,
> and we agree with him. . . . A stand made for independence
> and good sense against the pressure of an exacting and over-
> bearing dogmatism is a good thing for everybody, though
> made in a camp with which we have nothing to do. He goes
> far enough, indeed, as it is. Still, it is something that a great
> writer, of whose genius and religious feeling Englishmen will
> one day be even prouder than they are now, should disconnect
> himself from the extreme follies of his party.

[1] 12,000 words! Unthinkable today either for subject or space.

Ward prepared an article on Newman's *Letter* for publication in the *Dublin Review*; in this he criticized some of Newman's arguments. Ward submitted his draft to Ullathorne who, as Newman's diocesan, felt it would be improper for him to give an extra-judicial opinion; he suggested that Clifford of Clifton might be consulted. This was done, and, later, Clifford wrote to Ullathorne, "I wrote back to say that I was not a fit person to be censor of the article in question, inasmuch as I greatly admired Dr Newman's *Letter*, and had failed to discover in it either Protestantism or anti-Catholic sentiments, or any attempt to cast a slur on foreign Catholics." Manning persuaded Ward not to print the article, and he himself did not go further with a book he had planned on Our Lady. It was to this Newman referred in his *Letter*. "We are to have a Treatise on the subject of Our Lady soon from the pen of the Most Reverend Prelate; but that cannot interfere with such a mere argument from the Fathers as that to which I shall confine myself here."

Manning wrote to Newman to thank him for the *Letter*. "All this cannot fail to do much good, and I trust your treatment of it will have a wide effect." He thought that Newman's reply was "the driest possible." Yet at the same time letters were being exchanged between Manning and Talbot in a very different tone. Talbot thought there was nothing new in Newman's argument from the Fathers, and went on to express his fears that "*The Home and Foreign Review* and the old school of Catholics will rally round Newman in opposition to you and Rome. Stand firm!" Then he added, "Dr Newman is more English than the English. His spirit must be crushed." To this Manning replied (25 February 1866):

What you write about Dr Newman is true. Whether he knows it or not, he has become the centre of those who hold low views about the Holy See, are anti-Roman, cold and silent, to say no more, about the Temporal Power, national, English, critical of Catholic devotions, and always on the lower side. . . . In one word it is Worldly Catholicism, and it will have the worldly on its side, and will deceive many.

It may seem that the views of such a man as Talbot are not of much importance; as estimates of Newman they are, of course, valueless; their significance lies in the fact that Talbot had considerable influence in some Roman circles and encouraged those attacks on Newman that distressed all who appreciated his true quality. It is doubtful if Talbot's chatter really affected the Pope's judgment; Newman himself expressed his gratitude for the kind way in which the Holy Father always spoke of him.

Manning's attitude is more puzzling. No wonder that, a few years later, Newman wrote to him, "I do not know whether I am on my head or on my heels when I have active relations with you."

Newman's *Letter* was attacked in *The Tablet* and *The Weekly Register*; but he had his defenders, notably Ullathorne and Clifford. As Newman's bishop, Ullathorne spoke with special authority. He wrote:

> Little can they know of him on whom they pronounce their hasty and unauthorized judgments, who presume to tell the world that Dr Newman has derogated from the devotion which good Catholics pay to the Virgin Mother of our Lord. . . . Is petty cavilling from Catholics without authority to be the present reward for a masterly exposition of the subject the most difficult for a Protestant to comprehend, and which has made that subject classical in the English tongue? In vain have I striven to find what Dr Newman has written derogatory to devotion to the Blessed Virgin, or beyond the limits of theological prudence. I cannot fail to observe the earnestness with which he puts forth his whole soul in exalting each glorious privilege of the Immaculate Mother of our Lord.

Newman wrote to Ullathorne, "I was not prepared for such extreme kindness and tender considerations for me as it displays."

Pusey wrote to commiserate with him on the attacks he suffered from his fellow Catholics. Newman replied, "Thank you for your sympathy about the attacks on me, but you have enough upon yourself to be able to understand that they have no tendency to annoy me—and on the other hand are proof that one is doing a work."

Both as Anglican and Catholic he had become inured to misrepresentation as well as to direct attacks; he had become content to state his views as carefully and as clearly as he could and to leave the question at that. He did not engage in prolonged controversies in the public journals, but left his printed word to do its own work, confident that time would do its own winnowing. "We must have patience", was his advice to those who called for loud protestations and a fighting policy.

He was, however, to be called upon to suffer yet another disappointment in 1866. It will be recalled that he had sold the land at Oxford which he bought in 1864; another opportunity came a year later and he bought a plot in St Aldate's Street; it was as if he could not drive Oxford out of his thoughts. Ullathorne asked him if he still wanted the Oxford mission, but Newman said that the land was "for the chances of the future, not as connected with myself." The bishop replied that he would not say anything more for twelve months; he then again asked if Newman would undertake the mission and build a church at Oxford. It seems strange that Ullathorne did not realize that his proposal was bound to lead to trouble; he was, however, deeply concerned at the poor state of the mission at Oxford with its wretched buildings and its ineffective work. There was need for a priest of high quality who could raise the prestige of the Catholic Church. The bishop had the right, and, indeed, the duty of opening missions anywhere in his diocese; had he acted promptly, there would have been an outcry, but little could have been done about it, and the mission would soon have become firmly established. Unfortunately Ullathorne hesitated, or was it Newman who suggested a more cautious policy? The bishop decided to write to Propaganda to secure its approbation; he thought this would be given as he had received a letter from Cardinal Barnabo early in 1865 in which he had encouraged the bishop to develop the mission. "But if," he wrote, "Father Newman be not disposed to undertake it, the bishop should provide that some learned and worthy priest be placed there to meet the needs of the Catholics of the town. . . . As for Father Newman I know he has often suffered disappointment at finding that his undertakings cannot be carried through; so I wish you to take care to encourage him, for his piety and zeal for souls are not called in question."

Manning was alarmed when he heard of this fresh petition to Propaganda. He at once wrote to Talbot urging the need for "a stronger declaration against the Protestant Universities. I think Propaganda can hardly know the effects of Dr Newman going to Oxford." Manning saw that, with Newman in charge of the Oxford mission, with the prospect of an Oratory, there would be an additional inducement to Catholic parents to send their sons to that University.

On 10 June Newman wrote to a friend, "It is all but certain we are going to Oxford. Our bishop proposed it to me in three successive years, and I could not refuse, but look on the prospect of being there with extreme dismay." Apart from personal reluctance at "opening wounds which are quite healed", he welcomed the opportunity of opening an Oratory at Oxford at some future date.

Barnabo asked Ullathorne for further information. In reply the bishop wrote, "Father Newman does not intend to change his residence from Birmingham, but to place at Oxford some Fathers of the Oratory, and to make visits there from time to time." Newman, however, felt that his own position should be made quite clear, and he told Ullathorne that "Cardinal Barnabo should clearly apprehend that I feel no calling whatever to go to Oxford, except it be in order to take care of Catholic undergraduates, or to convert graduates."

Both Newman and Ullathorne knew that there were young Catholics at Oxford, and, unless a rigid prohibition were imposed, some would still go there just as others would go to Cambridge. It seemed better in their eyes to accept the situation and make proper provision for their care—the existing mission at Oxford was so poor and so inadequately staffed that it could make no impact. Manning wanted a definite prohibition imposed and was not prepared to condone the presence of any Catholics at the Universities.

Meanwhile Cardinal Reisach had arrived in England to study the problem. With Manning he spent some days with Ward at St

Edmund's, and also visited Oscott, and was taken to Oxford to see the ground Newman had purchased. He did not, however, see Newman. This extraordinary failure to discuss the question with the person most closely concerned can only be ascribed to Manning's decision as he was responsible for the Cardinal's movements. It is an action like this that makes it difficult to believe that his conduct was free from animus; it seemed as if he were determined to force his opinion at all costs. He had, in fact, a reasonable case, and the majority of the bishops supported him, and his belief that, with Newman at Oxford, more Catholics would go there, was a fair presumption. Yet he chose to treat Newman as a person of no importance. When the Cardinal left, Manning wrote to Talbot, "he has seen and understands all that is going on in England."

In December 1866, Propaganda replied to Ullathorne's petition; an Oratory could be opened at Oxford under Newman's direction provided it did not prove to attract more young Catholics to the University. The condition was attached that Newman himself must not take up residence there. Ullathorne told Newman of the first part of this decision, but shirked telling him at the same time of the condition attached. Newman at once made plans for taking up this new work; then his bishop informed him that Propaganda would not allow him to live at Oxford. At once all Newman's hopes fell to the ground; it was a hard blow, but his friends persuaded him to wait before making a decision.

Manning wrote soothingly to Ullathorne who had suggested that Newman should be at hand when the bishops met in Low Week to discuss—among other business—the University question. "A few words from you or from him, distinguishing the Oxford Oratory from the other question, will, I hope, suffice to satisfy a large number of those who are full of respect and regard to Dr Newman, and enable them to feel glad of anything which gives him a work at Oxford." On reading this Newman commented, "Do I go to Oxford with an intention of bringing young Catholics there? The answer is plain. I have no such intention there, nor ever had. But the answer will be as fallacious as the question is ensnaring, unless I add my going there will in fact attract Catholics there." That kind of subtle distinction bewildered plodding minds and made them wonder what Newman was up to.

Meanwhile the Catholic press had printed gossip from Rome to the effect that the proposed Oxford mission had been inhibited, and one paper hinted that this was because there were doubts of Newman's orthodoxy. At once his friends came to his defence. An address, dated 6 April 1887, signed by some two hundred laymen headed by Lord Edward Fitzalan Howard,[1] assured him of their loyalty. "Every blow that touches you inflicts a wound on the Catholic Church in this country." Manning described the Address as "a revelation of the absence of Catholic instinct, and the presence of a spirit dangerous to many." It was on this occasion that Talbot described "the province of the laity" as "to hunt, to shoot, to entertain," and added, "Dr Newman is the most dangerous man in England."

It was clearly time for Newman's relations with Rome to be put on a sounder basis. He himself would not go there; for a man sensitive to fine shades of meaning in words, the conduct of a conversation in a language he knew imperfectly, was a sufficient deterrent, so in May 1867 he sent two of the Oratorians, Ambrose St John and Henry Bittlestone, to Rome on his behalf. The Pope gave instructions that every courtesy and attention should be shown to them. Ambrose St John proved a resolute defender of his Superior, and was determined to get all doubts and suspicions swept away. He found that Newman's article "On Consulting the Faithful on matters of Doctrine" was still held against him. Newman sent him a copy of his letter to Wiseman which had never reached Propaganda. When he saw the letter Barnabo was "thunderstruck" and declared that it put matters right. It then appeared that while one eminent theologian had questioned some of Newman's statements, another, equally eminent, could see nothing to criticize, and Father Perrone, the most noted of Roman theologians, warmly defended Newman.

It had also been said that Newman advocated sending young Catholics to the old Universities and that boys were prepared for

[1] Uncle of the 15th Duke of Norfolk, who was educated at the Oratory School.

them at his school. St John soon showed how thin was the evidence for both these criticisms. Another complaint was that Newman had not remained to the dinner after Manning's consecration; that such a trifle should have been a cause for criticism indicates the lengths to which some of his detractors were prepared to go.

Barnabo, once the facts had been put to him, showed great friendliness; he said there would be no objection to Newman visiting the Oxford Oratory, if established, provided he did not reside there. St John also saw Cardinal Reisach—"very bland and courteous—apologized for not calling on you . . . he spoke highly of you." A long talk with Talbot, in which St John spoke plainly, seems to have shaken his complacency; he suggested that Newman might be made a Protonotary Apostolic!

The Oratorians' audience with the Pope was gratifying. As always he expressed his confidence in Newman and said he must not mind reports that got into the papers, but, on one point, he was adamant; he could not encourage anything that would lead Catholics to go to Protestant Universities. He was not content with expressing his regard for Newman; he asked Cardinal Cullen for his opinion on the orthodoxy of Newman's writings. The choice was sound as there would be no language problems, and Cullen had known Newman and his publications for many years. The Cardinal was able to assure the Pope that there could be no question of Newman's orthodoxy. This opinion was, at the Pope's request, made known to Newman to whom it came as a great consolation in a period of anxiety.

Undoubtedly this visit did much to clear the air and to combat the activities of those who seized every chance to disparage Newman in Rome. Ward was, of course, not responsible for any of the town-talk or small-minded fault finding; his opposition was in the open and not a back-stairs business. He did however regard the permission to open an Oratory at Oxford as a disaster, "because of his [Newman's] surpassing power of influencing young men, united with what I consider the unsoundness and disloyalty of various of his views . . . I wrote to everyone I could think of in Rome." That Newman was not allowed to reside in Oxford was at least something gained. With characteristic overstatement,

Ward added, "There is no act of my life on which I look back with so much gratitude to God as the having been able to take part in so sacred a cause."

At their meeting in Low Week 1867 the bishops asked Propaganda to approve of each of them publishing a Pastoral in his diocese pointing out the grave dangers of young Catholics going to the Universities. A rescript dated 6 August instructed the bishops to carry out their proposal. There was still no absolute prohibition, as Manning would have liked, but the rescript contained the sentence, "it is next to impossible to discover circumstances in which Catholics could without sin attend non-Catholic Universities."

When he learned of this decision, Newman wrote to his bishop to withdraw from the Oxford mission. Ullathorne replied, "I receive the announcement of your decision with a sense of pain both acute and deep. I have no hesitation in saying it, as my complete conviction, that you have been shamefully misrepresented at Rome, and that by countrymen of our own. . . . I still trust the time will come when the facts of the case will be better understood in Rome, and when justice will be done to you".

Propaganda urged that a Catholic University should be founded in England. The outcome of this suggestion may be briefly given here. After some years of hesitation and under further pressure from Rome, action was taken. The result was the Catholic University College at Kensington established in 1874 and abandoned in 1882. Manning had taken the whole matter into his own hands. He did not consult Newman, nor the Jesuits with their long tradition of educational work. A well qualified staff was collected and they did good work, but the rector was incompetent and mismanaged the finances. Eventually Manning had to wind up this ill-conceived experiment. Yet, with better organization, less rigidity of control and a wider use of lay interest, it might have succeeded. The college was established in a part of Kensington that was to become before the end of the century a cultural centre, with its museums, the Royal College of Music, colleges of art, science and engineering, as well as the offices of the University of London. The Catholic University could have taken its place with its distinctive contribution to scholarship and learning.

In 1895 Leo XIII gave permission, under some safeguards, for Catholics to attend the Universities.

CHAPTER XXII

THE VATICAN COUNCIL

WHEN the University question had been settled and there was no longer any danger of Newman going to Oxford, Manning felt that the time had come to improve their personal relations. Canon F. Oakeley, their Oxford contemporary, offered to act as mediator. The triangular correspondence should be read in full as it brings out so well the feelings of the protagonists.[1] Newman stated at once that the root cause was "the difficulty I have in implicitly confiding in him", and that he felt that York Place[2] was a centre of opposition, not so much as coming from the archbishop himself as from his *entourage*; there was, too, the undoubted muttering that persisted at Rome. He could not rid himself of the suspicion that the source of the innuendoes was the archbishop, who, had he so wished, could have checked the gossip.

Manning on his part had believed that certain printed attacks on his views had been inspired by Newman, and he had been hurt by references to himself in *A Letter to Dr Pusey*. Newman was able to prove that he had known nothing of the article and pamphlet specified by Manning before they were published; at the same time he could see nothing reprehensible in the fact that some writers had criticized Manning's opinions. "I have felt much of late years, though I have said little about it, the great injustice of those who put out strongly their views, and then accuse others as wanting in peace and charity, who, on this provocation, feel bound to show that there is another opinion on the point, and that there are good Catholics who hold it."

The correspondence was carried on over a period of four months; it ended with a brief note from Newman containing the

[1] Purcell's *Manning*, II, pp. 327–46.

[2] Wiseman had moved from 35 Golden Square in 1855 to 8 York Place (now 108 Baker St., W. 1.). The block retains its external appearance above shop level except for the intrusion of a cinema façade.

sentence already quoted, "I do not know whether I am on my head or my heels when I have active relations with you"; he added, "In spite of my friendly feelings, this is the judgment of my intellect."

Reviewing the correspondence twenty years later, Manning commented, "His last was in terms which made a reply hardly fitting on my part. For years we never wrote nor met."

What was the root cause of this estrangement? We can dismiss implications of jealousy or rivalry; each, in moments of irritation, spoke or wrote words that could be interpreted as expressions of personal feelings, but these were not typical of either of them.

The explanation lies in a statement made by Manning in 1887 that, on three questions, "Newman was not in accordance with the Holy See. I am nobody, but I spoke as the Holy See spoke." The subjects were "(1) The Temporal Power; (2) the Oxford Question; and (3) the Infallibility." Manning and Ward (and it may be added, Vaughan) were firmly convinced that they knew, *before Rome had spoken*, the mind of the Holy See, and that opposition to their views was an act of disloyalty. Newman held that, *until Rome had spoken*, it was legitimate to discuss questions on which the Church had not yet pronounced judgment; "I prefer much wherever it is possible," he wrote in *A Letter*, "to be first generous and then just; to grant full liberty of thought, and to call it to account when abused." When the Church had spoken, Newman accepted the decision and controversy was closed.

Manning's habit of mind was such that, having reached an opinion, he could not believe that other Catholics could differ from him without betraying the Church; he could not sympathize with their intellectual difficulties. Moreover, he held each opinion in its absolute form. This intense assurance of the absolute truth of his own opinions determined his attitude towards persons; they were in, or out of, his favour according to their acceptance or refusal of his views. This is seen in his varying opinions of Bishop Grant and of Bishop Ullathorne. He was prepared to renounce friends and even relatives in his devotion to what he believed to be the mind of the Church. This surrender of human ties was part of his asceticism; he was ready to pay that price. The strange thing is that he should have persisted in regarding such friendships as unaffected.

Newman accepted *ex animo* "the whole revealed dogma . . . as it is infallibly interpreted by the authority to whom it is thus committed", and he regarded any Catholic who did otherwise as unfaithful. Manning and Ward wanted to extend the scope of dogma far beyond the declared utterances of the Church, and it was here that Newman was bound to clash with them. It may be noted that the decisions eventually given by Rome were rarely couched in the stringent terms advocated by Manning and Ward.

Accounts have already been given of the conflict of views on the Temporal Power and on the Oxford question; we must now turn to the even more contentious subject of Papal Infallibility. It must be emphasized that previous to the Vatican Council of 1870, the Infallibility of the Pope was not an article of faith. There were two aspects of the matter that were under discussion. First, was it wise to seek for any such definition at that time; was it opportune? Secondly, was it possible so to define Papal Infallibility and to limit its application as to prevent it from becoming too great a burden on conscience? No Catholic denied the doctrine of the infallibility of the Church—that the Church was divinely protected from error; the point at issue was whether the doctrine of Papal Infallibility should be defined as an article of faith, and if so, in what terms.

Newman's opinion was expressed in a letter to Ward in February 1866:

As to writing a volume on the Pope's infallibility, it never so much as entered into my thought. I am a controversialist, not a theologian, and I should have nothing to say about it. I have ever thought it likely to be true, never thought it certain. I think, too, its definition inexpedient and unlikely; but I should have no difficulty in accepting it were it made.

Ward sent this letter to Manning to prove that Newman minimized Catholic doctrine; what Ward meant was that Newman did not accept the extreme view of Papal Infallibility that Ward and Manning regarded as the mark of the loyal Catholic.

Newman also felt that a definition of Papal Infallibility of the unlimited kind that would satisfy Manning and Ward would be an additional obstacle to non-Catholics considering the claims of the Church. He and those who agreed with him were labelled "inopportunists" as opposed to the ultramontanists who were also eager to see an increased centralization of the authority of the Church.

Through the pages of the *Dublin Review*, Ward carried on an unrelenting warfare against those who dared to question his opinions. We have seen how he regarded *The Syllabus* as an infallible pronouncement; indeed, he took the view that all the Pope's utterances were infallible and must be accepted as such by all Catholics, otherwise they were "unsound", "disloyal", "enemies of the Church," and "low-type insular Catholics." Manning, while agreeing with Ward's opinions, was to some extent a restraining influence, particularly in preventing direct attacks on Newman; Ullathorne did all he could to encourage this restraint. He took a moderate view; he was prepared to welcome a pronouncement on infallibility, but, like Newman, he wanted its exercise to be carefully safeguarded. Clifford of Clifton and Archbishop Errington were firmly of the opinion that any definition would be inopportune; they had the sympathy of three other English bishops. Manning had the support of Cornthwaite of Beverley, and Grant of Southwark. The other bishops approximated to the position taken up by Ullathorne.

This question divided Catholics not only in England but in continental Europe and across the Atlantic. In France, Bishop Dupanloup was the powerful leader of the inopportunists; his fiercest opponent was the layman journalist Louis Veuillot, whose vituperative extravagances made even Ward's comminations seem mild.

In Germany the leading inopportunist was Döllinger; most of the bishops of that country were also inopportunist but they repudiated Döllinger's extreme opinions. Both the Austrian Cardinals, Schwarzenberg and Rauscher, were also inopportunists.

P

Newman was not therefore taking up a peculiar position; he was but one of many responsible Catholics in this and other countries who thought that the time was not ripe for the definition of Papal Infallibility. Ward's sweeping condemnation of such a strong body of opinion was indefensible.

It was in December 1864 that the Pope first suggested the summoning of an oecumenical Council; over three hundred years had passed since the Council of Trent had met to combat the Reformation. Pius IX felt that the renewed attacks on the Church and its freedom could best be met by calling together the bishops for consultation. The controversy caused by the encyclical *Quanta Cura* and the accompanying *Syllabus of Errors* shortly afterwards, underlined the need for decisions on many questions. After consulting the Cardinals and a number of bishops, the Pope announced on 29 June 1867 that he would call such a Council. It was in keeping with his own serene and cheerful spirit that he should have taken such a decision at a time when the very existence of the Papal States was in the balance.

It should be stressed that the Council was not primarily called for the purpose of discussing Papal Infallibility; the five preparatory Commissions indicate the true scope of the deliberations: (1) faith and dogma, (2) discipline and canon law, (3) religious Orders, (4) Oriental Churches and missions, and (5) Church and State. Those bishops, however, who held ultramontanist views were intent on the discussion of the Infallibility and on its definition as stringently as possible; thus, when the Pope announced the summoning of the Council, Manning and Senestréy (Bishop of Ratisbon) made a vow to do all they could to obtain the definition.

No attempt will be made in these pages to describe the course of the Vatican Council of some seven hundred bishops, which opened on 8 December 1869.[1] We are concerned with the part

---

[1] The most satisfactory account is given in Abbot Cuthbert Butler's *The Vatican Council* (1930). Contemporaneous reports need to be read with caution; the writers, for the most part, were hostile observers who had to rely on rumours and chance remarks; the oath of secrecy was well observed. The debates were of a high standard of responsibility. Reporters tended then, as now, to over dramatize differences of opinion. It may be noted that, after a mental breakdown, George Talbot had been removed from Rome before the Council met.

taken by Manning, with the attitude of Newman, and, to a less degree, that of his bishop, Ullathorne.

One result of Cardinal Cullen's entirely favourable report on Newman's writings was that the Pope intimated that he would like Newman to come to Rome to take part in the preparatory work of the Council. The invitation brought Newman a sense of rehabilitation, but after some hesitation he declined it; he felt that as he was not a trained theologian he could not render the service suggested; moreover, there was the bothersome obstacle of language, and his own conviction that he was too old for the strain involved. He considered, however, that the invitation gave him freedom to express his views to his bishop, and Ullathorne, on his part, kept Newman aware of what was happening as far as the oath of secrecy allowed.

The Council had been at work for three months before a move was made to get the question of Papal Infallibility brought on at an earlier date than seemed probable, but it was not until the middle of May 1870 that at length the subject was opened in a general debate. During the previous months the exponents of various views had been hard at work enlisting support, writing pamphlets, drawing up petitions and counter-petitions and discussing tactics. Manning was the unresting leader of those who wanted the definition; Dupanloup was the leader of the inopportunists. The accounts of the preliminary manoeuvres make fascinating reading; inevitably opponents were accused of intrigue, but there was nothing reprehensible in the way in which contending sides marshalled their supporters and sought to win over those who were uncommitted.

The one questionable move was Manning's success in keeping opponents off the deputation (or commission) *de Fide*, which was concerned with preparing the presentation of the Infallibility question to the Council. Deputations dealing with other subjects had represented varying opinions, and this was in accordance with the Pope's wishes. Not only opponents but those holding moderate views resented Manning's action, and the controversy was sharpened. His relentless advocacy had already alienated some bishops. "Heretics," he said prejudging the issue, "come to a

Council to be heard and condemned, not to take part in formulating doctrine."

In February 1870 Ullathorne wrote to Newman:

> Be assured, my dear friend, that whatever mischief is doing outside by our own newspapers, to which so many of us are alive, moderation will be the upshot in the Council. If you could see, as I see, schemata [proposals] brought in, only to be pulled to pieces and sent out again, bleeding in every limb, to be reconstructed by the special deputations by the light given in the Council, you would realize how the general sense of the Fathers prevails over party views and idiosyncrasies. . . . The Pope spoke very kindly of you the other day.

This letter had been a reply to one from Newman which was to cause extreme annoyance to the supporters of Manning, but gave much satisfaction to those of moderate views. Newman had been provoked and disgusted at the continued attacks in the English Catholic press on those who doubted the wisdom of a definition of Papal Infallibility. Ward was, of course, as intemperate and intolerant as ever, but he had now been joined by Herbert Vaughan who had bought *The Tablet* in 1868.

Looking back on what happened, Newman wrote, "One thing I could do without impropriety—*liberare animum meam*—to my Bishop, and that I did. I did so with great deliberation in one of the most passionate and confidential letters I ever wrote in my life." It was one sentence in that letter that caused the uproar.

"Why should an aggressive insolent faction be allowed to 'make the heart of the just to mourn, whom the Lord hath not made sorrowful'?"

The letter was not marked "Private".[1]

Ullathorne showed it, as he later explained, "to some four of the English bishops, all your friends," amongst whom was Clifford, who borrowed it, and, naughtily, made a copy. It was

---

[1] It is so marked in Ward, II, p. 287, but not in the original at the Birmingham Oratory.

not long before its contents were widely known. Archbishop
Errington, for instance, wanted to have it translated into Italian.
Soon quotations—sometimes garbled—appeared in the English
and German papers. Ullathorne wrote in great distress to Newman, who, at first, did not recognize the words "aggressive
insolent faction" as his own, but a more careful reading of his
draft showed that they were indeed his. On the whole he was
rather pleased at Clifford's indiscretion. "I am glad I have done it,
and, moreover, I am not sorry that, without any responsibility of
my own . . . the general drift of what I wrote has been published."

Clifford was a leading inopportunist and he was supported by
Amherst of Northampton; when they showed signs of suffering
from the heat of a Roman summer, Manning suggested they
should both go home.

Nearly two months were spent on the Infallibility debates.
The final vote was taken on 18 July when 533 approved and two
dissented; many refrained from voting or had returned to their
dioceses. Of the bishops who had felt that the definition was inopportune, not one withheld his assent when the decision had
been reached; they accepted it, in Clifford's words, "as the voice
of the Church, and as such undoubtedly true."

The definition by itself closed a long, and sometimes acrimonious, controversy, but it opened a new question: how would
it be interpreted? As Newman wrote to a friend:

> The dogma has been *acted on* by the Holy See for centuries
> —the only difference is that now it is actually *recognized*. I
> know this is a difference—for at first sight it would seem to
> invite the Pope to *use* his now recognized power. But we must
> have a little faith. Abstract propositions avail little—theology
> surrounds them with a variety of limitations, explanations, etc.
> No truth stands by itself—each is kept in order and harmonized
> by other truths. . . . Future Popes will explain and in one sense
> limit their own power. This would be unlikely, if they merely
> acted as men, but God will overrule them. Pius has been over-
> ruled—I believe he wished a much more stringent dogma than
> he has got. Let us have faith and patience.

Manning at once issued a Pastoral which extended the meaning and application of the new dogma to the utmost limits; the
kind of definition he and Ward had desired had not been accepted;
it was nearer the moderate view of Ullathorne who, in his
Pastoral, explained that:

> The definition does not extend infallibility to the private
> teaching of the Pope, still less to his conversation, or to his
> ordinary actions, or to his judgment of causes as between man
> and man. To nothing of this kind does it reach; they are ex-
> cluded by the very terms. It is only when he exercises a certain
> office in a certain way that he is declared to speak without
> error.

It looked as though these varying interpretations would open
a new controversy, but, in 1871, Bishop Fessler of Austria, who
had been General Secretary of the Council, published a pamphlet
The True and False Infallibility of the Pope;[1] he had submitted his
manuscript to Pius IX who had it examined by the theologians;
he then wrote a letter to Fessler thanking him for "having brought
out the true meaning of the dogma of Papal Infallibility." Here
then was an opinion that could be taken as authoritative; in substance it followed the same lines as Ullathorne's explanation in
his Pastoral. Fessler showed that the dogma was strictly limited to
questions of faith and morals, and, "the Pope must express his
intention, by virtue of his supreme teaching power, to declare this
particular doctrine on faith and morals to be an integral part of the
truth necessary to salvation revealed by God, and as such to be
held by the whole Catholic Church; he must publish it, and so
give a formal definition in the matter."

This interpretation, having the Pope's approval, closed the
discussion. It may be noted that Fessler had also stated that the
Syllabus of Errors was not issued *ex cathedra* and was not therefore
an infallible utterance. Ward tried to find a loophole, and came
dangerously near implying that the Pope had made a mistake.

[1] The title of the translation made, at Newman's suggestion, by Ambrose
St John.

Newman welcomed Fessler's pamphlet as he hoped it would see the end of "tyrannous *ipse-dixits*"; it "clearly proves to us that a moderation of doctrine, dictated by charity, is not inconsistent with soundness of faith."

The years since 1870 have proved that the carefully worded definition of the dogma of Papal Infallibility was a true expression of the mind of the Church. Manning's extreme views have not been accepted; Newman's fears have proved unfounded.

Three days before the Pope gave his assent to the dogma Napoleon III declared war on Prussia; on 4 August the French troops began to leave the Papal States. A month later came the battle of Sedan and the end of the second Napoleonic Empire. On 20 September the Piedmontese troops arrived at the gates of Rome; after a token resistance, the Papal forces surrendered. Pius IX became "the prisoner of the Vatican", and the Council was suspended *sine die*.

CHAPTER XXIII

MANNING, NEWMAN AND GLADSTONE

WHILE the Vatican Council was discussing Papal infallibility Newman published his *Essay in Aid of a Grammar of Assent*, in which he discussed the relation between knowledge and belief, a problem that had exercised his mind for many years. The book is not easy reading, but it repays every minute spent upon it. Even the reader who has small aptitude for a carefully reasoned argument on abstract ideas, will find here much to interest him in the illustrative material drawn from the author's wide-ranging knowledge. It was not a book to make a popular appeal, but its importance was quickly recognized amongst those most fitted to judge. W. G. Ward wrote in its praise in the *Dublin Review*, and Newman was pleased that, in the midst of their controversies, they could find "a point of agreement between us on an important subject."

During the previous two years he had reached a wide public by republishing his Anglican sermons in eight volumes, *Parochial and Plain Sermons*. W. J. Copeland had offered to supervise the publication. Newman hesitated; would it not be necessary to revise them in accordance with his changed position? At last he wrote to Copeland:

I took an early opportunity of asking a great authority at Rome, and he told me that provided I did not give scandal to unreasoning Catholics by bringing my own name in close connexion with the republication, I need not under the circumstances alter the text. It is on that friendly advice I am now acting in accepting your friendly Editorship. Did I think the volumes likely to do harm to religion, (e.g. suppose they had been the sermons of a Unitarian) I could not consent to republish them—and my feeling is, that on the whole they are good as far as they go—and therefore I have no difficulty.

The first volume appeared in 1868, and within six months 3,500 copies had been sold. This encouraged Newman to republish more of his earlier writings. In 1873 he recalled this work in a letter to Copeland:

You have been of the greatest use to me in the matter of the sermons, and I only regret you have had so much trouble; but you have not had it for nothing. Unless you had broken the ice, I could have republished nothing which I wrote before 1845-6. The English public would not have borne any alterations—and my own people would have been much scandalized had I made none. They murmured a good deal at the new edition of the Sermons, as it was—but, since you, not I, published them, nothing could be said about it. After this beginning, I took courage to publish my Essay on Miracles and the *British Critic* Essays, uncorrected, but with notes corrective of the text. This too made some disturbance but very little—and then I published at Rivingtons my University sermons—and then I went on to mix Anglican and Catholic Essays together—and now I hear no criticisms on these measures at all. . . . My view has ever been to answer, not to suppress, what is erroneous—merely as a matter of expedience for the cause of truth, at least at this day. It seems to me a bad policy to suppress, Truth has a power of its own, which makes its way, it is stronger than error.[1]

Newman regarded his *Grammar of Assent* as "my last work. I say work because 'work' implies effort—and there are many things I can do without an effort. This is the fifth constructive work which I have done—two as a Protestant, three as a Catholic."[2]

[1] *The Tablet,* 6 Oct. 1945.
[2] As a Protestant: *Prophetical Office, Lectures on Justification.*
  As a Catholic: *Development of Christian Doctrine, Idea of a University, Grammar of Assent.*

He gave a friend a glimpse of some of the "many things I can do."

> As to my engagements here, a Superior must have them. We are very few Fathers, and each has his work—one has the jail—another the orphanage—two have the school—another has the parish—another the Poor Schools. The great *domestic* works, the care of the Library, the Sacristy, the Accounts, necessarily in great measure fall to me, at least at intervals. Now I am at the Library. The Oxford matter, correspondence & accounts, took up an untold mass of time—and tired me, so that they wasted more. And now that I am getting so old, I wanted to go through all my correspondence &c., &c. which will be close employment for some years.

The first copy of the *Grammar of Assent* was put into his hands on his sixty-ninth birthday, so he had some excuse for feeling that his main writing work was done, but one further contribution to controversy was required of him.

It might have been thought that by 1874, public controversy about Papal infallibility would have died down; amongst Catholics it had, of course, ceased. But Gladstone had other ideas. His first ministry had been defeated in 1873 on his Irish University Bill. This had roused the opposition of Cardinal Cullen on the grounds that it would strengthen the policy of mixed (Catholic with Protestant) education, and that no provision was made to grant funds for the Catholic University. Manning had urged Cullen to accept the Bill, and he had told Gladstone that he thought the Irish hierarchy would accept it. He soon found that he was mistaken, and warned Gladstone that the Bill would be opposed. It seems strange that, in view of his own strong opposition to mixed university education, Manning should have assumed that the Irish bishops would support a measure endowing "non-catholic and godless colleges, without giving one farthing to Catholics." Gladstone had tried to get round the religious difficulty by a clause prohibiting the appointment of university professors and lecturers in theology, modern history, and moral and mental philosophy. Did Manning

think that this curious limitation of the scope of a university was a
sufficient safeguard for young Catholics? Cullen was certainly not
prepared to condone a scheme which divorced religion from
education.

This was the second time that Manning had burnt his fingers
over the Irish University problem. Disraeli, when he became
Prime Minister in 1868, had proposed to grant a charter to a
Catholic University in Dublin. Manning supported the scheme
and gave Disraeli the impression that the Irish bishops would also
approve. When, however, they insisted that control must be
entirely in the hands of the bishops, the proposal had to be dropped.
Disraeli felt that Manning had misled him. Did the memory of
this add piquancy to the portrait of Cardinal Grandison in *Lothair*?
—a portrait that combines some characteristics of Wiseman and of
Manning.

In September 1874 Gladstone spent a fortnight at Munich with
Dr Döllinger, who had rejected the dogma of Papal infallibility
and was in association with the Old Catholics. On his return,
Gladstone got into touch with Acton. The first result of his reflections was an article on "Ritualism and Ritual", which contained a passage that heralded the outburst to come. He scorned
the fear that the Church and people of England could be Roman-
ized:

> when Rome has substituted for the proud boast of *semper
> eadem* a policy of violence and change of faith; when she has
> refurbished, and paraded anew, every rusty tool she was
> fondly thought to have disused; when no one can become her
> convert without renouncing his moral and mental freedom,
> and placing his civil loyalty and duty at the mercy of another;
> and when she has equally repudiated modern thought and
> ancient history.

Gladstone followed up this by publishing in November 1874
his pamphlet *The Vatican Decrees in their bearing on Civil Allegiance:
a Political Expostulation*; by the end of the year 145,000 copies were
in circulation, of which 120,000 were in a sixpenny edition.

The passage just quoted was the text of the pamphlet; the Syllabus and the Vatican Decrees provided the material for an argument that was developed with considerable verve. The author made use of quotations from Manning's lectures of 1860 on the Temporal Power in which it had been claimed that on its destruction "the laws of nations would at once fall in ruins." Reference was also made to an address given before the Academia in 1873 on "Caesarism and Ultramontanism"; in this Manning had maintained that it was for the Church and not for the State to determine the limits of their jurisdictions. It must be remembered that Gladstone was not raising an academic issue; he was writing at a time when the Pope had withdrawn to the Vatican after the occupation of Rome. There was the possibility that the Catholic Powers might intervene in order to restore the Temporal Power. There was, moreover, another immediate situation that raised specific problems. Bismark's *Kulturkampf* to subject Church to State in Germany had already led to the imprisonment of two Catholic archbishops and nine bishops. Gladstone argued that what was happening in Germany was the adverse reaction of its government to the Vatican Decrees; other governments were similarly affected. He therefore demanded that an authoritative pronouncement should be made that the Vatican Decrees in no way impaired the civil allegiance of Roman Catholics.

The concluding pages weakened the force of the pamphlet; in these Gladstone complained that his Irish University Bill had been defeated by the "direct influence" of the bishops; nor could he refrain from the gibe that more converts came from the upper classes than from the poorest people for whom "the original gospel was supposed to be meant. . . . If the Pope does not control more souls among us, he certainly controls more acres."

Manning at once sent a letter to the press in which he stated "that the Vatican Decrees have in no jot or tittle changed either the obligations or the conditions of civil allegiance." A second letter described Gladstone's pamphlet "as the first event that has overcast a friendship of forty-five years." Gladstone objected to this statement which seemed to him astonishing considering that for some years they had neither met nor corresponded. "I

wondered, too, at your forgetting that during the forty-five years
I had been charged by you with doing the work of Antichrist in
regard to the Temporal Power of the Pope." In his reply Manning
tried to distinguish friendship and its expression, as if friendship
could be put into cold-storage during periods of angry discord and
then brought out again unimpaired. In a later memorandum
Manning averred that his disagreement with Gladstone was due to
the influence of Acton who "inspired him with his own
animosity."

Within a few months Gladstone had more than twenty printed
replies on his desk. Amongst the earliest was Ullathorne's *Mr
Gladstone's Expostulation Unravelled*, a hard-hitting reply which
made good use of Gladstone's *Church Principles*. Then in January
1875 came Newman's *Letter Addressed to His Grace The Duke of
Norfolk*. This was followed by Manning's reply which bore the
same title as Gladstone's pamphlet. His argument was in the main
limited to the question of civil allegiance, but he had much to say
on the *Kulturkampf* in Germany and on the seizure of the Papal
States. In his introduction he referred to pamphlets written by
Ullathorne, Clifford and Vaughan. He had refrained from reading
Newman's pamphlet before writing his own "so that I may be
clear of seeming in any way to refer to what he has said, if in anything, which I hope is not likely, there were a divergence."

At the opening of his *Letter* Newman pointed out that the true
significance of the Vatican Decrees could not yet be assessed.

> None but the *Schola Theologorum* is competent to determine
> the force of Papal and Synodal utterances, and the exact inter-
> pretation of them is a work of time.

He went on to lay the blame for misunderstandings, such as
Gladstone's, on the intemperate advocates of extreme views.

> I own to a deep feeling, that Catholics may in good measure
> thank themselves, and no one else, for having alienated from
> them so religious a mind [i.e. Gladstone's]. There are those
> among us, as it must be confessed, who for years past have

conducted themselves as if no responsibility attached to wild words and overbearing deeds; who have stated truths in the most paradoxical form, and stretched principles till they were close on snapping; and who at length, having done their best to set the house on fire, leave to others the task of putting out the flame. The English people are sufficiently sensitive of the claims of the Pope, without having them, as if in defiance, flourished in their faces. Those claims most certainly I am not going to deny; I have never denied them. I have no intention, now that I have to write upon them, to conceal any part of them. And I uphold them as heartily as I recognize my duty of loyalty to the constitution, the laws and the government of England. I see no inconsistency in my being at once a good Catholic and a good Englishman.

Newman's approach was different from that of Ullathorne or of Manning. They had dealt with the misunderstandings revealed in Gladstone's pamphlet and with his shortcomings in the interpretation of facts; as immediate answers their replies were effective, but Newman's pamphlet is still read because he was concerned not so much with making legitimate debating points, important as these were, as in examining fundamental principles. Thus his section on "Conscience" is as pertinent and as illuminating today as when it was written.

When Gladstone came to write his second pamphlet *Vaticanism: an Answer to Replies and Reproofs*, he gave most of his attention to Manning. He made a distinction between the moderate views expressed by Newman and Clifford on the one hand, and on the other the more extreme opinions of Manning and Vaughan. Gladstone paid a fine tribute to Newman. "In my opinion his secession from the Church of England has never yet been estimated among us at anything like the full amount of its calamitous importance," and he described Newman's work as that "of an intellect sharp enough to cut the diamond, and bright as the diamond which it cuts." He implied that Newman had not done anything as a Catholic comparable with his work as an Anglican; this, he regarded, as a serious loss to the religious life of the day.

This implication disturbed Newman; it seemed to him to suggest that he had wasted his talents since his conversion. He therefore added the following note to the second edition of his *Letter*.

It is indeed a stern question which his words suggest, whether, now that I have come to the end of my days, I have used aright whatever talents God has given me, and as He would have had me use them, in building up religious truth, and not in pulling down, breaking up, and scattering abroad. All I can say in answer to it, is, that from the day I became a Catholic to this day, now close upon thirty years, I have never had a moment's misgiving that the communion of Rome is that Church which the Apostles set up at Pentecost, which alone has the adoption of sons, and the glory, and the covenants, and the revealed law, and the service of God, and the promises, and in which the Anglican communion, whatever its merits and demerits, whatever the great excellence of individuals in it, has, as such, no part. Nor have I ever, since 1845, for a moment hesitated in my conviction that it was my clear duty to join, as I did then join, that Catholic Church, which in my own conscience I felt to be divine. Persons and places, incidents and circumstances of life, which belong to my first forty-five years, are deeply lodged in my memory and my affections; moreover, I have had more to try and afflict me in various ways as a Catholic than as an Anglican; but never for a moment have I wished myself back; never have I ceased to thank my Maker for His mercy in enabling me to make the great change, and never has He let me feel forsaken by Him, or in distress, or any kind of religious trouble. I do not know how to avoid thus meeting Mr Gladstone's language about me: but I can say no more. The judgment must be left to a day to come.

There were still those at Rome who searched Newman's publications for anything that seemed censurable. Cardinal Franchi of Propaganda wrote to Manning to express concern for some remarks made in the *Letter*. His reply was emphatic. "Earnestly do I beseech your Eminence that no *public* action be taken in reference to the pamphlet of Father Newman." He admitted that it contained "slight blemishes" but he set down twelve reasons for not taking action. His own pamphlet had in fact been criticized for seeming to suggest the possibility of smoothing out the difficulties between the Holy See and the Italian Government. Manning's agent in Rome, Father H. O'Callaghan, wrote to him shortly afterwards.

The Holy Father said to me this morning that he understood you were afraid that he was going to condemn Fr Newman, but that he had no such intention, though he would have wished some friend might let Newman know that there were some objectionable passages in his pamphlet. He had heard, he said, that good had been effected by it, and that the notion of Newman's opposition to the Pope was completely dispelled.

Ullathorne was also asked for his opinion. His answer was as emphatic as Manning's, but expressed in warmer terms though written in his own brand of Latin. He wrote that Newman "has a tender and compassionate heart, and exercises a great influence in conciliating to the faith minds in trouble; and especially has he reconciled many to accepting the Vatican Decree on infallibility. And the recent pamphlet has been welcomed by the whole Catholic press in England with one accord; and especially did Cardinal Cullen in a pastoral letter praise it highly."

Some months later Cardinal Franchi again wrote to Ullathorne giving him a list of "censurable propositions"; these included what we should now regard as mild criticisms of the Renaissance Popes; one sentence was thought to be disrespectful: it read, "Now, the rock of St Peter on its summit enjoys a pure and serene atmosphere, but there is a great deal of Roman *malaria* at the foot of it."

Ullathorne replied: "Fr Newman has often complained that the authorities at Rome do not deal with him directly and openly, but by intermediaries and secretly. I strongly urge that if anything is to be done, he be written to directly and openly."

No more seems to have been heard of the matter, and New-man was apparently unaware of this fresh attempt to disparage him.

He had at this time to suffer a great personal loss. Ambrose St John had been busy translating Bishop Fessler's *True and False Infallibility*; his health had been precarious and he broke down under the strain of his many labours. He died on 24 May 1875 at the age of sixty. For thirty-three years he had been Newman's affectionate disciple and friend, and the loss was hard to bear.

A former pupil of the Oratory School came to see Newman shortly after the death of St John.

"Dr Newman said, 'You must have something to remember him by.' He went to the bookcase to find one of Fr Ambrose's books for me, and then, suddenly, holding on to the bookcase, began sobbing."[1]

---

[1] Viscount Fitzalan, *The Tablet*, 6 Oct. 1945.

Q

CHAPTER XXIV

CARDINAL MANNING

IT is with a sense of relief that one turns from the controversies of the period to consider the work achieved by Manning as archbishop. Not that the arguments backwards and forwards were of less consequence; they were essential to the development of the Church, but their very importance tends to overshadow the devoted work of what may be termed day-to-day Catholicism. Manning's genius was not for the discussion of fundamental ideas; he could write a cut-and-thrust article or pamphlet that served its immediate purpose, but the limitations of his mind rarely permitted him to go far below the surface. His great work for the Church was done in the field and not in the study.

It has already been noted that Manning had refused to do more than collect subscriptions towards the Cathedral to be built as a memorial to Wiseman. He had stated plainly that the care of the children had prior claims on him.

In his Anglican days he had given much of his thought and time to problems of the education of the children from poor homes. From the beginning he had fought against the secularization of the schools; education, he held, must not be divorced from religion; that principle guided him throughout life. Wiseman had made the care of the children one of his main concerns, and by appointing Manning as his Inspector of Schools in 1856 he gained a powerful ally in this work. In the tribute he paid to Manning in 1860, Wiseman bore witness to the value of this co-operation not only in the building of new schools but in securing equitable treatment for Catholic children in reformatories and workhouses; in addition a Catholic reformatory and an orphanage were built.

No charitable work was dearer to Manning's heart than this crusade for the rescue and care of the children. It was not therefore surprising that, on the foundation laid by Wiseman, he, in his turn, gave much of his energy and organizing ability to extending that work. Wherever Catholic children were in danger of being lost to the Church, he carried on a ceaseless warfare on their behalf.

During 1866 he issued three Pastorals on the needs of the children of the poor. His programme included the provision of new schools and the rescue of children from workhouses and Poor Law schools, and from such voluntary institutions as Dr Barnardo's Homes, where they would be brought up in a Protestant atmosphere. The strength of his appeal was recognized by *The Times*. "Nobody here wishes to make public charity the means of religious 'seduction', or to induce the hungry to sell the soul's birthright". This was a kindly thought, but it was not in keeping with hard facts. The commentator went on to say that the Catholics must "organize a system of protection for the poor, to see either that they are kept out of the workhouses, or that once in they are not compelled to change their faith." It was an unnecessary adjuration. The small Catholic community with its limited resources had not been backward in accepting its responsibilities, but there were obstructionists in Government offices and on Boards of Guardians who did not share the scruples of *The Times* on "religious seduction." The difficulty was that the transfer of Catholic children was not obligatory on the Guardians. Each Board had to be approached separately and persuaded to act. It proved a long task but Manning persisted until, in 1886, the last of the Metropolitan Boards gave way; this distinction was reserved for the Board of St George's, Hanover Square. They capitulated after Manning in a Pastoral had written, "The Guardians of St George's continue their stubborn refusal to transfer our poor children to schools of their own religion. This Board is the richest and represents the highest and most educated parish in London. It now stands alone in the metropolitan district for this unjust and ignoble oppression of the poor."

The increasing influence of Manning may be seen in the notice taken in the newspapers of his Pastorals; comment was often critical but his views were regarded as of interest to their readers; to us their numbers may seem insignificant compared with modern circulations, but it was an influential section of the community.

At a meeting in St James's Hall on 14 June 1866, Manning founded the Westminster Diocesan Education Fund; the scope of the work included not only the building of schools, but also the general protection of poor children. Nearly £8,000 were subscribed within twelve months and twenty new schools were opened. This supplemented the work of the Poor School Committee set up in 1847 to which Privy Council grants were paid.

The Education Bill introduced by W. E. Forster in the House of Commons in February 1870 roused considerable controversy. Its purpose was not to establish a system of state schools with compulsory attendance, but, as Forster explained, "to complete the voluntary system and to fill up gaps." Elected School Boards were to be responsible for providing schools where they were needed; the necessary funds were to come from an education rate, and, according to the original draft of the Bill, voluntary (denominational) schools were to receive grants from this source. This is not the place for an account of the storm that arose over the proposal to aid denominational schools out of the rates. The outcome was that the Act as it was passed in August put all voluntary schools outside the rates, but continued the Privy Council grants. The Cowper-Temple clause forbade the teaching in the Board Schools of any "religious catachism or religious formulary distinctive of any particular denomination." This conclusion to a heated debate gave small satisfaction to anyone. Gladstone himself could not see how it was possible "to include religion, and to exclude dogma." The Board Schools were at least not to be completely secularized, but time was to prove that neutral-tinted Bible-teaching formed little more than a thin crust over the abyss of rationalism.

Catholics had therefore to face the task of providing their own schools out of their own funds. During the critical months the Poor School Committee did all it could to put the Catholic case before Members of Parliament, but they were fighting a hopeless battle. Unfortunately just at that period the bishops were in Rome for the Vatican Council. It has been suggested that, had they been in England, more favourable consideration would have been given to the Catholic problem. This is, however, doubtful. Stronger advocacy might well have led to less acceptable decisions. While it is true that, under Wiseman's guidance and influence, public opinion had become more tolerant of the Church, the anti-Rome feeling had been strengthened by the popular belief that the Pope alone prevented the complete unification of Italy. Moreover there were vague suspicions of what was going on in the Vatican Council.

Manning did what he could to influence the Prime Minister, but Gladstone was at that time absorbed in his projected Irish land legislation and could give but occasional attention to the school problem. Both of them feared secularized schools. Manning wanted the Catholic schools to retain their distinctive character within a national system; if that was not possible, then all voluntary schools should be equitably treated and given the same financial support as the proposed Board Schools. As an alternative, he suggested that grants from the rates should be made in proportion to the funds raised by the schools themselves. "In the last three years," he wrote, "we have opened in London thirty new schools and have gathered out of the streets three thousand children. Give me time, and just proportionate help, and there will not be one of our children without a school."

When the Bill became law, Manning persuaded the Hierarchy to accept the limited aid that was offered, and to work with the new Boards in the hope that more favourable treatment could be gained. Ullathorne would have preferred Catholics to refuse the grants. Manning wrote to him:

> It seems to me that our best course is to co-operate to the utmost of our power, and thereby to obtain a share in the treatment of questions which may affect us. If they should offer to include our clergy in any Boards, I think we ought to accept it. We can but retire, if in conscience bound.

And later:

> The Boards may destroy our lesser schools by reporting them to be insufficient or inefficient. The effect of this in Lon-

don would be to destroy one half of our schools. By opening negotiations with the Board, as I have with the Privy Council, I hope to save them. By standing aloof from the Boards we should be exposed to the danger of their hostility.

Manning found it possible to work with the London School Board and he expressed his thanks on several occasions; he saw to it that the Catholic schools received all that the law allowed, but this left a great financial burden to be shouldered by the Catholics —a burden they still have to carry. An Education Crisis Fund established in 1870 eventually raised nearly £400,000 and provided for over 70,000 new school places. The small group of wealthier Catholics gave generously, but the money also came from those whose shillings had as much value as the rich man's pounds.

The school problem was linked with the great increase in the number of Irish Catholics who flocked to England in the middle years of the century. Most were miserably poor; some were destitute. There was considerable justification for Manning's remark that he had "given up working for the people of England to work for the Irish occupation in England." It was therefore inevitable that he gave much thought to Irish problems, and in some respects, he was ahead of his time in the conclusions he reached. One of his outstanding publications was his *Letter to Lord Grey* (1868). He set out the elements of the problem in these words:

> So long as there exists upon the statute-book any penal enactment against the Catholic religion; so long as the Catholic people of Ireland are deprived of a *bona fide* Catholic education; so long as a Protestant Church Establishment is maintained by law over the face of Catholic Ireland; and so long as the people of Ireland fail to derive from the land such subsistence as the labourers and farmers of England and Scotland derive from the soil: there must be a just discontent, which will be the misery of Ireland and the danger of England.

The Disestablishment of the Irish Church in 1869 removed one cause of grievance. On the schools question Manning pointed out that there were some 5,000 schools containing nearly 700,000 Catholic children and only 25,000 Protestants. "It is not permitted to teach publicly the Catholic religion, to use Catholic books, or to put up a crucifix." He stressed the need for solving the land problem: "it is the chief and paramount condition on which the peace of Ireland depends. In comparison with this question, all others are light." Security of tenure and freedom from arbitrary power were essentials of prosperity. In one passage he wrote feelingly of his personal association with the Irish in London:

> I am day by day in contact with an impoverished race driven from home by the land question. I see it daily in the destitution of my flock. The religious inequality does indeed keenly wound and excite the Irish people. Peace and goodwill can never reign in Ireland until every stigma is effaced from the Catholic Church and faith, and the galling injustice of religious inequality shall have been redressed. This, indeed, is true. But the "Land Question", as we call it, by a somewhat heartless euphemism, means hunger, thirst, nakedness, notice to quit, labour spent in vain, the toil of years seized upon, the breaking up of homes, the miseries, sicknesses, deaths of parents, children, wives.

Even when violence broke out, he kept his sense of proportion. He condemned the Fenians, as Rome did, but he could write: "No greater self-deception could be practised on ourselves than to imagine that Fenianism is the folly of a few apprentices and shop-boys. Fenianism could not have survived a year if it were not sustained by the traditional and just discontent of almost a whole people." For a time Manning was out of favour with the Irish because he would not condone Fenianism, and so strong was the feeling against him that it was thought prudent to cancel a visit he was to have made to Dublin at Cardinal Cullen's invitation.

Manning corresponded with Gladstone on Irish questions, but it is impossible to say with what degree of influence. The value to the statesman lay in knowing the opinions of the leading Catholic in this country who was himself in touch with the Irish Hierarchy; we have seen how Manning went further than the Irish bishops were prepared to go in the University question, but on other matters he was a more reliable guide.

Closely linked with the problems of the Irish Catholics in England was the total abstinence movement to which Manning gave powerful support. He had seen for himself the terrible results of intemperance amongst the Irish in the slums of London. It is difficult, almost impossible, for people of today to picture the degradation caused by excessive beer and spirit drinking at the period of which we are writing. We may be tempted to smile at some of the extreme methods used to combat what was a dreadful evil; thousands and thousands of men and women were rescued from shame and despair by those crusaders who, scorning ridicule and obloquy, dared to go down to the slums and dark places of our cities and urge drunkards to renounce the cause of their degradation. To talk of temperance was ineffective; it was either the pledge, or a life of debasement. Amongst those crusaders Manning must be given a leading place. He himself took the pledge. The League of the Cross was largely his creation; its leaders regularly reported to him, and he spoke at innumerable meetings. He was particularly effective on an outdoor platform; no interruption or abuse could ruffle him; he was tireless in his advocacy, and his efforts were wonderfully rewarded. The Annual Whit Monday rally of the League at the Crystal Palace was an important engagement in his busy life. His zealous work for the League was criticized by some priests and laymen, but, as in other matters, once Manning had made up his mind in which direction lay his duty, nothing could make him swerve from his course.

Wiseman had done much to give the Catholic Church a place in the national life; his popular lectures to audiences of the general public helped to familiarize people with the sight of a Catholic prelate on the platform. He spoke on cultural subjects and avoided controversial issues. In this he prepared the way for Manning's bolder policy. When a good cause claimed his support, he did not hesitate to stand side by side with men of other Churches.[1]

Writing in 1892, A. W. Hutton could say:

[1] On one occasion he shared the platform with Francis Newman; they had probably not met since their Balliol days.

Five-and-twenty years ago no dignitary of the Establishment and no conspicuous Nonconformist minister would have been willing to appear on the same platform with a Catholic ecclesiastic, nor could any such ecclesiastic have taken a useful or an influential part at meetings summoned to promote some social reform. He would have been reckoned out of place and superfluous.

Manning changed all that. The first notable occasion was the opening of the Mansion House Fund for the relief of the poor of Paris after the Prussian siege was raised at the end of January 1871. He at once got into touch with Archbishop Darboy, the President of the Paris Committee, but the archbishop was later taken as a hostage by the Commune. Manning did all he could to save him; he wrote to Bismark and to Gladstone to beg their intervention, but it was to no purpose, and on 24 May Archbishop Darboy was shot.

As a member of this Mansion House Committee, Manning had shown himself so energetic and effective that from that time his help was frequently sought, and gladly given, in many good causes.

In July 1872 he was president of the International Prison Congress, and he then expressed his attitude towards problems of social welfare.

When I was called upon to preside over this meeting, I felt it my duty to do so as neutrally as possible. That is to say, holding a profound conviction that, on all those occasions which lay on my conscience a public duty, I am bound to be as outspoken, I may say as explicit and determined, in expressing what I believe, as my office requires; so, on all other occasions, when I am not bound to make these declarations or to bear these testimonies, I desire to identify myself with the majority of those whom I love and respect. . . . It is the constant desire of my heart to work with my countrymen in everything that can promote the welfare of our people, or that

will, like this Congress, world-wide in its character, promote
those sympathies which bind Christian nations together.

Later in that year he was one of the founders of Hospital Sunday, and in the December he was invited to preside at an
Exeter Hall meeting of the Agricultural Labourers' Union, which
had been recently formed by Joseph Arch who had been a
Methodist local preacher. Manning declined to preside as he felt
that it might prejudice the cause of the Union for a Roman
Catholic archbishop to be in the chair; he offered to move the
main resolution on the condition that Charles Bradlaugh, the free-
thinker, took no part in the proceedings as had been suggested.
At the meeting Manning spoke feelingly on the lot of the farm
workers; he recalled his Lavington days and the intimate knowledge he had then gained of their lives. Later in the meeting, when
Charles Bradlaugh came on to the platform, Manning left the
Hall.

This meeting has its importance as the prelude to his later
interest in the problems of labour.

Up to 1873 Manning had occupied the house in York Place
that had been Wiseman's last residence; an opportunity came for
moving to a larger building in Westminster. The land bought for
the cathedral of the future was the site of the old Bridewell in
Tothill Fields. Nearby was a building intended as an Institute for
the Guards whose married quarters were across the way. The
Institute had failed and the building was for sale. Father John
Morris, S.J., who had been Manning's secretary for some years,
described the new Archbishop's House.

It was substantially built and very spacious, but when that
had been said the praise it deserves is almost exhausted. But the
Cardinal liked the austerity of its bareness and openness. There
was not a bedroom in it, when he bought it, and the upper
floor was undivided. He put up three little rooms or cells in
each of its corners, in one of which he slept and died. During
the day he encamped in one of the large rooms of the floor
below, dwelling behind a screen, with his books and papers

on the floor and tables, all round his chair. The other great
rooms on that first floor were admirably adapted for the reception of the crowds who thronged them on certain occasions.

Father Morris, who had previously served Cardinal Wiseman,
added some notes on Manning's personal characteristics.

It was the Cardinal's habit to sit close to a blazing fire, and
Newman's[1] orders were to keep it at white heat. To my fancy
he was like St Thomas of Canterbury, who was extremely
thin and chilly. He was also like the Saint in the keenness of
his senses, which, with the exception of his hearing, remained
to the very end. Not long ago he sent for me to talk over
something that had happened when I was his Secretary, and
his memory proved better than mine. His mental clearness
and vigour in extreme old age were very remarkable. This
also was characteristic, that in money matters he was one of
the most generous of men. If a difficulty could be solved by
his opening his purse-strings he was sure not to hesitate. Then
again, he was an excellent man to have to transact business
with. I remember the change when he succeeded Cardinal
Wiseman. Long before his death, Cardinal Wiseman was
under the influence of the disease that killed him. It became
very difficult at last to get one's business done. I used to hide
away my papers as I entered his room, and then produce them
when the propitious moment had come; but Archbishop
Manning was ready for work at any time, and indeed he had a
faculty, that his nephew Father Anderdon shared, of being able
to turn to severe literary labour immediately after dinner. His
dinner was simplicity itself, and practically he had but one
meal a day. That spare, emaciated frame needed singularly
little nourishment.

In March 1875 Manning was promoted to the dignity of Cardinal with the title of the Church of SS. Andrew and Gregory on

[1] Newman was his butler; he had also been Wiseman's butler. The name
inevitably caused some amusement.

the Caelian, from which St Augustine of Canterbury had set out
on his mission to England in 597. The news was received with
wide satisfaction in England. The Catholic laity subscribed a large
sum towards the necessary expenses of the position; Manning
added this to the endowments of the diocese. He received numerous letters of congratulation. Amongst others was the following:

> My dear Lord Cardinal,
>
> I beg you to accept the congratulations of myself and this
> house on your recent promotion. It must be a great satisfaction
> to you to receive this mark of the confidence placed in you by
> the Sovereign Pontiff. And it must be a source of true pleasure
> to your brother and his family and to your other relations and
> friends.
>
> And as regards the Protestant world, it is striking to ob-
> serve the contrast between the circumstances under which you
> return invested with this special dignity, and the feelings which
> were excited in England twenty-five years ago on occasion of
> the like elevation of your predecessor, Cardinal Wiseman.
>
> That the temporal honours, to which you have attained,
> may be the token and earnest of those which come from God
> alone, is the sincere prayer of yours affectionately,
>
> John H. Newman.

Manning went to Rome at the end of 1877 to receive the Red
Hat from the Pope. It proved to be the last act of a friendship of
over twenty years. The aged Pope's strength was gradually failing;
he saw Manning several times but prolonged conversation was
impossible. He died on the evening of 7 February 1878; his last
words to Manning a few hours previously had been, "Addio,
carissimo!"

Before the Conclave to appoint a successor, there was some
discussion whether, in the state of Italian affairs, a foreigner or an
Italian would be preferable as Pope. A few of the Cardinals
favoured a foreigner, and the name of Manning was suggested.
He himself considered that an Italian Pope was essential—"one
who knows and loves Italy, and is known and loved by Italians"—

and this was the general opinion. Gioachino Pecci was elected and took the name of Leo XIII. He was only two years younger than Manning but he was to reign for a quarter of a century and to add to the prestige of the papacy.

CHAPTER XXV

CARDINAL NEWMAN

NEWMAN republished in 1877 some of his Anglican writings in two volumes with the title *The Via Media or The Anglican Church*. The first volume contained his lectures on "The Prophetical Office of the Church" delivered in St Mary's forty years earlier; the second volume was a miscellany of papers including Tract 90. The Preface to the new edition was the last considerable piece of writing from his pen. It is important as revealing his mind towards the end of his long life.

He discussed the three offices or functions of the Church:

Christianity, then, is at once a philosophy, a political power, and a religious rite: as a religion, it is Holy; as a philosophy, it is Apostolic; as a political power, it is imperial, that is, One and Catholic. As a religion, its special seat is pastor and flock; as a philosophy, the Schools; as a rule, the Papacy and its Curia. . . .

Truth is the guiding principle of theology and theological inquiries; devotion and edification, of worship; and expedience of government. The instrument of theology is reasoning; of worship, our emotional nature; of rule, command and coercion. Further, reasoning tends to rationalism, devotion to superstition and enthusiasm, and power to ambition and tyranny.

Newman developed this theme with the wisdom and insight of a man who, for half a century, had reflected on the great issues involved. It is a pity that this clear exposition of his conclusions is hidden away in a volume that is not likely to attract the attention of the general reader.

At the end of the year, Trinity College made him an honorary Fellow, "a mark of extreme kindness to me from men I have never seen." He at once wrote to Ullathorne to make sure that acceptance would not be misconstrued, and spoke of his longing "to see once more, before I am taken away, what I thought I should never see again, the place where I began the battle of life." He visited the college in February 1878, and, to his delight, he met his former tutor, Thomas Short, then in his 89th year. At the dinner given in his honour, Newman, as one who was present recorded, "made a speech of perhaps ten minutes in length or a little more, in a delightfully simple, natural and genial vein. . . . I remember the exquisite finish of his expressions and the beautiful clearness of his articulation and the sweetness of his voice."

His other college, Oriel, also wished to pay tribute to one of its most famous members; W. W. Ouless was engaged to paint Newman's portrait for the college, and, at the same time, a second one for the Oratory at the wish of his Birmingham friends.

With the accession of Leo XIII, it was thought by prominent Catholic laymen that the time had come for Rome to signify its approval of Newman's work. The Duke of Norfolk, Lord Petre, and the Marquis of Ripon (a convert of 1874) took up the matter, and they asked Manning to lay before the Pope the strong desire of the laity that Newman should be raised to the cardinalate. The suggestion could not have been a welcome one to Manning. He genuinely feared Newman's influence and doubted his orthodoxy. As late as 1890 he still had those doubts. A young friend recorded the following conversation in that year.[1]

"From an observation you made," he said, "I gather that you are under the impression that Doctor Newman is a good Catholic." I replied that such was my vague belief. He retorted, "Either you are ignorant of the Catholic doctrine, or of the works of Doctor Newman." . . . After asking which of Newman's books I had read, he proceeded to tick off on his tapering fingers, in his usual way, ten distinct heresies to be found in the most widely-read works of Dr Newman.

[1] J. E. C. Bodley, *Cardinal Manning*, p. 16.

Whatever Manning's personal feelings may have been, he agreed to forward the petition to Rome, nor did he do so in grudging terms: such was not his style once his mind was made up. He wrote of Newman:

> The veneration for his powers, his learning, and his life of singular piety and integrity is almost as deeply felt by the non-Catholic population of this country as by the members of the Catholic Church. In the rise and revival of Catholic Faith in England there is no one whose name will stand out in history with so great a prominence.

The Duke of Norfolk later explained the motives behind this desire to see Newman honoured.

> I do not think that any Catholic has been listened to by those who are not Catholics with so much attention, respect and, to a great extent, sympathy as Newman. But while numbers were brought by him to see and to accept the truth, I felt very strongly that the full outcome of his labours was most unhappily limited by the impression which was made to prevail by a certain school of well intentioned people that he did not really speak the mind of the Church or represent the beliefs which the Church called upon her children to accept.

The Duke himself mentioned the request to the Pope. Manning's letter, which he had given to Cardinal Howard who was returning to Rome from England, did not arrive until after the Duke had seen the Pope. When he did get the letter, the Pope at once gave his approval. In January 1879, the Cardinal Secretary of State informed Manning of the Pope's decision. This letter was sent to Ullathorne who was delighted to pass the news on to Newman. He wrote, "I also take the liberty to express my own personal hope that you may decide on accepting, moved by that great affection I have always felt towards you, and not unconscious of the honour it would confer on the Church in England and on this diocese especially."

Newman was overcome at this unexpected recognition; for him it meant "the cloud is lifted from me for ever." He had one doubt; would he be expected to live in Rome? His age and increasing infirmities made him shrink from such a prospect. He talked the problem over with Ullathorne and then put his difficulty in writing.

For I am, indeed, old and distrustful of myself. I have now lived thirty years *in nidulo meo*, in my much-loved Oratory, sheltered and happy, and would therefore entreat His Holiness not to take me from St Philip, my Father and Patron.

Ullathorne sent this with a covering letter to Manning. He explained that "nothing stands in the way of his most grateful acceptance except what he tells me greatly distresses him, namely, the having to leave the Oratory." Next day he wrote again (did he suspect Manning?), "If the Holy Father thinks well to confer on him the dignity, leaving him where he is, I know how immensely he would be gratified."

Newman, too, wrote to Manning.

I could not be so ungracious, whether to the Holy Father or to the friends at home who have interested themselves in this matter, as to decline what was so kindly proposed, provided that it did not involve unfaithfulness to St Philip.

Manning sent Newman's first letter to Rome but did not send Ullathorne's covering letter. As there were rumours already circulating that Newman had refused the honour, Ullathorne wrote direct to Rome to explain the situation. Meanwhile Manning had left for Rome; a few days later there appeared in *The Times*, in prominent type, a notice saying that "Dr Newman has excused himself from accepting the purple." Newman was horrified at this breach of confidence. The matter was, as yet, private between Rome, Manning, Ullathorne and himself; nor had he, in fact, declined the cardinalate.

Manning must have taken Newman's letter at its surface value,

R

and have jumped to the conclusion that the dignity had been re-fused. Had he read Ullathorne's letter carefully, he would have understood the true significance of Newman's difficulty—one that the Pope could remove at a word. It is hard to avoid the con-clusion that *The Times* announcement came from Manning or from one of his secretaries.

Ullathorne certainly believed that Manning had deliberately put a wrong construction on Newman's letter. Some years later Ullathorne (who had, on retirement, been made a titular arch-bishop), expressed his views on this unhappy affair.

> What do you think? He lectured me as though I had been a boy for suggesting Newman's promotion to the cardinalate, and urging it so strongly. Manning said to me: "You do not know Newman as I do. He simply twists you round his little finger; he bamboozles you with his carefully selected words, and plays so subtly with his logic that your simplicity is taken in. *You are no match for him!*" . . . [Ullathorne] plainly told the Cardinal that he himself [Manning] was no match for New-man. He distrusted Newman, whilst the Archbishop [Ulla-thorne] told him that there was no honester man on earth; that his only aim in this world was to advance the cause of religion.

When Newman saw the announcement in *The Times* he at once wrote to the Duke of Norfolk to say that there could be no truth in the report as the matter was still under consideration. The Duke acted promptly. He called together his friends and they sent a note to *The Times* in which they expressed their pleasure at the honour offered to Newman. He then sent Newman's letter, a copy of the resolution passed by his friends, and a strongly expressed letter to Manning. This time Manning did not falter. The Pope at once granted permission for Newman to remain at his Oratory. Ullathorne received the news on 1 March and hastened to con-gratulate his friend. Manning wrote to Newman to explain that he had misunderstood his wishes, "an error which I have repaired the instant I knew it."

This strange episode suggests several questions. Was Manning directly or indirectly responsible for that notice in *The Times*? Was he too eager to see a refusal in Newman's hesitations? Why did he not send Ullathorne's explanatory letter to Rome with Newman's?

Such questions cannot now be answered, but it is of interest to note the words used by the Pope some years later when he received a verbal message from Newman. "My Cardinal! it was not easy, it was not easy. They said he was too liberal; but I had determined to honour the Church in honouring Newman. I always had a cult for him. I am proud that I was allowed to honour such a man."

Letters and addresses of congratulation poured into the Birmingham Oratory. Not the least significant was one from Archbishop Errington in which he wrote of "the long, laborious, and wise course you have followed in the service of God's Church."

Newman arrived in Rome on 24 April 1879. He had a long audience with the Pope, and on the day, 12 May, when the official act of conferring the cardinalate was carried out, he spoke of the resistance he had always offered to Liberalism in religion—"the doctrine that there is no positive truth in religion, but that one creed is as good as another." This notable address was a fitting summary of his life's work.

It was typical of Newman that, on his return to England, he broke his journey to visit his former curate, J. R. Bloxam, Rector of Upper Beeding. The inhabitants of that Sussex village must have been highly excited at the arrival of a real Cardinal!

The two English Cardinals met twice; once when Newman was in London, and again when Manning was in Birmingham. Newman appreciated the work Manning was doing, and, in 1881, during a sermon at the London Oratory, he quoted a passage from a recent Pastoral in which the need for Catholic education for Catholic children was once more emphasized. Newman went on to express his admiration for the great work Manning had done in putting this principle into practice.

CHAPTER XXVI

LAST LABOURS

MANNING's efforts on behalf of the children of poor Catholics were ceaseless, but in his last period he devoted much of his thought to the problems of labour. In 1874 he gave a lecture at Leeds on "The Dignity and Rights of Labour." A few extracts will indicate his attitude.

> I claim for labour the rights of property . . . the working man carries his property with him as ready money. He can buy with it, and he can sell it. He can exchange it. He may set a price on it.
>
> Labour has a right not only to its own freedom, but it has a right to protect itself.
>
> Whatever rights, then, capital possesses, labour possesses.
>
> I am one of those who are of opinion that the hours of labour must be further regulated by law. I know the difficulty of the subject; but I say the application of unchecked political economy to the hours of labour must be met and checked by a moral condition.
>
> Is it possible for a child to be educated who becomes a half-timer at 10 or even 11 years of age? Is it possible for a child in the agricultural districts to be educated who may be sent out into the fields at 9? I will ask, can a woman be the mother and head of a family who works sixty hours a week?
>
> The homes of the poor in London are often very miserable. The state of the houses—families living in single rooms, sometimes many families in one room, a corner a-piece. These things cannot go on; these things ought not to go on. The accumulation of wealth like mountains, in the possession of classes or of individuals, cannot go on, if these moral conditions

of our people are not healed. No Commonwealth can rest on such foundations.

In a digression he objected to the growing use of the term "proletariat", which he described as pedantic.

It was inevitable that the bugaboo word "socialist" was hurled at him, but he made no claim to advance a carefully thought-out economic plan, though he was at one time attracted by the theories of Henry George. His function, as he conceived it, was to urge at all times the need for justice and charity between man and man. As particular problems came to the front, so he applied his mind to ameliorative measures.

He may have been aware of the important work on social problems done by Catholics on the Continent—such as Bishop Ketteler of Mainz, Charles von Vogelsang, Albert de Mun, La Tour du Pin and Charles Périn. There is, however, no evidence that Manning had studied the writings and proposals of these and of other Catholic thinkers. He had more in common with John Ruskin, whose *Unto This Last* was published in 1862. The two men were friends; Ruskin frequently visited Archbishop's House. Of *Fors Clavigera*, Manning wrote to the author, "It is like the beating of one's heart in a nightmare", a peculiarly apt description of that strange collection of letters on social and other subjects. They were both members of the Metaphysical Society founded in 1869 by James Knowles to bring together men of very varied ways of thought—Tennyson, Huxley, Mark Pattison, Tyndall, Dean Stanley, R. H. Hutton, W. G. Ward, J. D. Dalgairns, and others. At one meeting Ruskin read a paper on "Social Policy", and at another Manning gave one on "The Soul before and after Death." He had hoped that Ruskin would be converted to Catholicism, and there are passages in that author's works that show how near he drew to the Church. On problems of social justice the two men had much in common, but neither attempted to draw up a policy for long-term action.

Manning was appointed in March 1884 to the Royal Commission on the Housing of the Working Classes; his name on the warrant followed that of the Prince of Wales; the problem of pre-

cedence must have caused a headache to officials, but as he was
called "Cardinal" and not "Archbishop of Westminster" the
decision was, presumably, in recognition of his princely rank; it
was, more significantly, a recognition of the place he had come to
take in the life of the country. He attended the meetings of the
Commission regularly and advised the secretary on the drafting
of the Report. A few months after its publication he spoke at the
Mansion House on the subject and he pointed out two obstacles to
reform: the reluctance of Vestries to carry out their duties, and,
the heartlessness of the owners of slum property. He suggested
that a central authority should have power to compel Vestries to
act, and he wanted all property to be registered so that the owners
would be known.

> If only those in London who have heads and hearts to care
> for the condition of the poor, and who have been aroused
> within the last six months to the consciousness of an intolerable
> evil, would continue and sustain this movement by their own
> self-denying efforts, I believe there would be found the dyna-
> mic force that would put the law into operation; and then
> gradually and with patience, with those kindly and generous
> modes of treatment with which alone human affairs can be
> governed, we shall find a full and complete remedy for these
> sufferings of the population.

It would take too much space to detail all the causes for social
betterment that had Manning's support, either from the platform,
in conferences, or in the pages of the monthly Reviews and in
The Times. He urged that the government should organize the
emigration of poor people, not by ones and twos, but in groups
so that they could establish communities in the colonies. The
Anti-Slavery Society had his strong approval, and at one of its
meetings he spoke eloquently on the responsibilities of Empire.

> I know no people on the face of the earth so bound by strict
> obligations to give freedom to men as we. We are bound by
> the liberty which is an heirloom from our ancestors, the liberty
> of our own land in which slavery became extinct and serfdom

could not survive; on the coast of England if a slave set a foot he was free. We are bound by the great federation of our Christianity, which binds us in sympathy, not only with Christians but with the whole human race. We are bound by the wrongs we have done in the past, by the deep and indelible memories of the wrong which England has inflicted on the African race in centuries gone by; we are bound by the memory of the reparation which England has nobly made; and lastly, by the responsibility of the great Empire which has been entrusted to us—for imperial power is a stewardship— laying on us the obligation to serve all peoples and nations with whom we come in contact.

He supported the Shop Hours League in its campaign for the closing of shops one hour earlier on one day a week. The Co- operative Clothing Company sought and gained his patronage. He turned his mind to the problem of unemployment and de- clared that "every man has a right to work or to bread." At the same time he pointed out the inadequacy of the Poor Law and the inequalities in its administration.

W. T. Stead and Bramwell Booth had his sympathy in their campaign for the protection of young girls, and when their method of collecting evidence brought the two men into court, he sub- scribed to the Stead Defence Fund.

Nor did he limit his influence to his own country. When in 1887 the Knights of Labour (a kind of federation of Trade Unions) in the United States seemed in danger of being proscribed by Rome as a secret society, he joined forces with Cardinal Gibbons to pre- vent such a catastrophe, and he urged the importance of the views of local bishops being given full consideration in Rome in prefer- ence to those of "officious persons" who saw things from a distance.

It is hardly necessary here to narrate again the story of the Dockers' Strike of 1889. Certainly it was the most dramatic of Manning's interventions in the world of labour, but it should be seen as one incident in a long series of efforts to gain justice for working people. The dockers were claiming an extra sixpence a day—the "dockers' tanner." They won public sympathy and funds were contributed generously to maintain the women and children. At length the directors gave way; then deadlock was reached on the date when the new wage should begin. The directors wanted 1 January 1890; the dockers, 1 October 1889. A Mansion House Committee failed to effect an understanding. Manning was not prepared to give up. One of the Committee recorded that "day after day from ten in the morning till 7 or 8 at night he spent interviewing, discussing, negotiating"—he was then in his eighty-second year! At last, he went down to Dockland and appealed to the Strike Committee. He begged them not to prolong for one hour the privations of their wives and children, and he persuaded them to compromise on the date when the new terms would begin. Some days had to pass before the directors would agree, but at last, "the Cardinal's peace", as it was called, was achieved.

Newman, now eighty-eight, dictated a note of congratulation to Manning on his work as a peace-maker and on the proof that he gave of the Church's close concern with the welfare of the poor.

His work for so many public causes did not lessen Manning's concern for education, nor did it draw his mind away from his pastoral care of the priests of his diocese—they remained his primary charge, and, although some found him strong-handed, they had in him a bishop to whom they could turn at all times for help and encouragement.

He gave his approval to the Voluntary Schools Association founded by Herbert Vaughan in 1884; by this Catholics, Anglicans and Wesleyans made common cause in their endeavours to get more favourable consideration from the government. Manning was also a member of the Royal Commission (usually called the Cross Commission) set up in 1887 to review the working of the 1870 Act. This Commission recommended that rate aid should be given to all voluntary schools. This had long been Manning's claim, but he went further; he proposed that a national education tax should be levied and that all schools should have grants from this fund. No political party at that time would have dared face the outcry of "Rome on the rates", so the Commission's proposal fell to the ground.

Of all Manning's publications *The Eternal Priesthood* published in 1883 has had the longest life. Its twenty brief chapters set before the priest a high ideal of pastoral work and conduct. Much of it is a commentary on the decisions of the Fourth Provincial Council of 1873, the only one held while he was archbishop. At that Council there had been signs of disunion; this was partly due to friction between the religious orders (the regulars) and the secular clergy. Manning would have preferred the term "pastoral clergy", but there were technical objections to this. The trouble was a legacy of the privileges the orders, especially the Jesuits and Benedictines, had been allowed in penal times; with the coming of the Hierarchy there was need to establish more normal relations between the bishops and the regulars. It was a long fought struggle in which Manning had the support of the bishops. The difficulties were resolved by the Papal Bull of 1881, *Romanos Pontifices*.

Manning permitted himself little relaxation, and, indeed, when the activities mentioned in the last few pages are considered, it is a wonder that he could find time for periods of ease. He liked to have people at lunch and to enjoy their conversation. Thus Ruskin noted one such occasion in 1880 when the Cardinal "told me delicious stories all through lunch." And John Richard Green, the historian, in a letter to his wife in 1877, recorded a meeting with Manning at The Athenaeum.

I have just been having an hour's talk with my Cardinal, and I must have an hour's talk with you to save my Protestantism! Manning is certainly a charming controversialist, courteous, full of information, with exquisite felicity of expression, and lending himself with perfect ease to every turn of topic—which I always take to be the essential difference between conversation and dissertation. We talked of Bryce, and Colonies, and Irish character, and Italian scenery, and English education and a hundred other matters till "his Eminence" had to rise to go.

Meanwhile Newman was passing his last years quietly at the Oratory. Age with its physical infirmities did not impair his

mental vigour. He had hoped to pay another visit to Rome in
order to put to the Pope his views on the need for preparing
educated Catholic opinion for the coming attack that was inevitable from the rapid extension of scientific inquiry not only in
the natural world but in criticism of Biblical texts and in historical
research. His health, however, prevented him from making such
an arduous journey. He was able to get to Oxford in 1880 and
again in 1884; two years later he spent three days with Dean
Church at the Deanery, St Paul's. The Dean wrote to a friend,
"He was so bright, so kind, so affectionate; very old and soon
tired, but also soon refreshed with a pause for rest, and making
fun of his old age."

In July 1888 Newman went to St Dominic's Priory, Stone, to
see Archbishop Ullathorne who was staying there. He received
the nuns, and then "he rose and blessed the community and returned to the guest room, still leaning on Archbishop Ullathorne's
arm. There he consented to rest for a short space, and take some
refreshment, the Archbishop pouring out tea for him and holding
it to his lips. To see these two venerable men thus together, one
waiting on the other, and supporting his feebleness was a sight
never to be forgotten."

It was their last meeting. Ullathorne died on 21 March 1889 at
the age of eighty-three.

We get another glimpse of Newman in that year from a letter
by Aubrey de Vere to Hallam Tennyson.

I paid my annual visit to Cardinal Newman, sleeping one
night at the Oratory. I found him considerably weaker than
last year in his body but strong and clear in his mind. He is now
89. He looks forward to his end with a very bright and peaceful though humble Hope, equally unlike the coldness of the
Sceptic or Stoic and the presumption of the Puritan enthusiast.
On no face, that of man, woman, or child, have I seen a smile
like his, so rich in charity, sweetness and pathos, and yet often
with a gleam of humour fleeting across it. It is a strong contrast to that strange look of *intensity* into which his features
more often fix themselves.

The end was drawing near. John Henry Newman died on 11 August 1890 in his ninetieth year.

On 20 August, the day after the funeral at Rednal, a Requiem Mass was celebrated at the London Oratory. Cardinal Manning gave the discourse. It is a fine tribute, gracefully worded and generous. To read it in the light of their known relations, is to make one wonder why they should ever have clashed or why they so rarely corresponded or met. He spoke of "my love and veneration for my brother and friend of more than sixty years." Such an expression must raise once again the problem of Manning's view of friendship. One can only shake one's head and pass on.

Manning himself was beginning to feel his age. He liked to talk about earlier days, and, as Newman had done, to turn over old records and put his papers in order.

It must have been with peculiar pleasure that he received Leo XIII's Encyclical of 15 May 1891, *Rerum Novarum*, which summed up and approved the movement for social justice which had been much in the minds of a number of far-seeing Catholic leaders in western Europe for some years. Not least among them was Manning; his own work of this kind had not met with wholehearted approval from some of his clergy nor from some of the laity, but now the Pope had put his seal upon it.

Manning could look back on a well-ordered diocese, and on the disappearance of some of the problems that had been inherited from the penal days of the Church. He could now see the Church in England, no longer ostracized, but taking its place in the religious, political and social life of the country. He had striven to the utmost for that Church, and, although there were policies and actions open to question, he had done a good work.

He died on 14 January 1892 in his eighty-fourth year. The vast crowds who paid tribute to him were witnesses to the high place he held in the thoughts of his countrymen.

CHAPTER XXVII

THE THREE CARDINALS

IN the opening chapter a picture was sketched of the state of the Catholic Church in England in the early years of the nineteenth century. The two Relief Acts of 1778 and 1791 had removed the most onerous of the penal laws; freedom of worship was granted to Catholics. It was but slowly that they accustomed themselves to this liberty of which they had been deprived for more than two centuries; it was like coming out of a dark passage into bright sunshine; eyes had to be focused and thoughts and emotions adjusted to the new conditions. A large work was awaiting them. Churches had to be built and schools established; there was a lack of priests.

It was providential that just at that time the English seminaries and schools and religious communities that had preserved the traditions, were forced to leave France and the Low Countries and return to their mother land after their long exile. French emigré priests, for a period, gave great service to the newly freed Church in England. To guide all this were four vicars-apostolic, and as one studies the records of their lives and labours, and those of their devoted priests, one cannot but marvel at what was achieved within a generation. Friction and discord were inevitable while duties and functions were being harmonized, but, the Church steadily gained confidence in a country where Papists and Popery were regarded with suspicion and even with repugnance.

The Emancipation Act of 1829 restored citizenship to the Catholics, and, as in the period after the Relief Acts, an apprenticeship, as it may be termed, had to be served before the notion of taking part in the national life could become familiar.

The forties of the century saw the great influx of poor Irish Catholics, and the accession of a group of converts from the Anglican Church, many of whom had come under the influence of Newman. The Church was called upon to bring these new elements into one with the existing Catholic community.

A mere listing such as this in a few paragraphs of the problems of the first half of the century, serves to bring out the complex nature of the task that had to be faced. The doubling of the number of vicars-general in 1840 relieved the pressure on those responsible for guidance, but this could not meet the full need. It was desirable that the normal governance by bishops should be reinstituted as soon as possible. This came at mid-century, but, in view of the special problems of the English situation, Rome decided to retain a certain measure of supervision through the Congregation of the Propaganda to whom the bishops had to make their reports.

The task of unifying the various elements into one body, and, at the same time, of promoting the life of the Catholic community and of bringing it again into full association with the Universal Church, could probably not have been accomplished by one of the older generation of vicars-apostolic. They were the right men for their day and generation; devout and self-denying, they were, by the force of the circumstances in which they laboured, rather limited in their outlook, and lacked, for the most part, close contacts with the Catholic Church outside their own country.

Wiseman brought to his work in England advantages of personal ability and experience that were of outstanding value. His long residence in Rome and the European range of his mind made it natural for him to see the Church in England in terms of the Universal Church. It is probable that he never fully appreciated the historical reasons for the comparative isolation of the Church in this country, nor the inevitable persistence of habits of restraint in forms of devotion; not that he failed to pay tribute to the sacrifices made by the old Catholic families, but to enter their minds and see things as they saw them was an all but impossible task for one who had not grown up in their society. Many of them regarded his more demonstrative methods with suspicion, and his first Pastoral as Cardinal-Archbishop gave them cause to doubt the wisdom of his appointment. It was an unfair judgment as the unexpected result of that Pastoral was largely accidental, and his brilliant riposte gained more sympathy for Catholics than had been lost during the fit of national hysteria. His friendly relations

with converts, and the speed with which he gave them opportunities of serving the Church shocked some of the older generation, but time has vindicated his bold policy. He had been quick
to see the value to the Church of the accession of men of their
intellectual quality, and there is no doubt that his own eminence
as scholar and theologian carried weight with them. There had, in
fact, been no Catholic apologists in England who could meet such
men on their own ground. It is only necessary to read Wiseman's
contributions to the early *Dublin Review* (such as those reprinted
in *High Church Claims*) to realize that here was a writer who
spoke not only out of his great learning but with the voice of
authority.

He was undoubtedly too optimistic in his hopes for large-scale
conversions, but this was in part due to the misleading impressions
he had received from earlier converts such as Phillipps de Lisle;
this optimism was, however, part of that buoyancy of spirit that
characterized him; a set-back could quickly prostrate him, but he
as quickly recovered and went forward with renewed enthusiasm.

Wiseman's confidence in the future was an inspiration to
others. Priests could be sure of his encouragement in any plans for
extending their work. It is true that he was impatient of details of
administration, and his lack of method, and his open-handed
generosity, and his faith that any money needed would come,
were the despair of his secretaries and of those who had to worry
about finance. Yet this boldness of conception was needed at that
time to compel the Church in England to break out of the bonds
of old restrictions. A more cautious or business-like leader would
have been less effective.

A long list could be made of the good works initiated by
Wiseman and developed by Manning. The record given in
earlier chapters is a testimony to his great energy and resourceful-
ness. As he surveyed the existing state of the Church, his vivid
imagination recognized the needs and possibilities, and his mind
was fertile in ideas for building up the greater Catholic Church in
this country.

Nor was he content with reanimating the Church from within,
or with the needs of his own diocese. He wanted Catholics to take

their proper place in the national life. By his visits up and down the
country and by his popular lectures, he did much to break down
the barricades of prejudice. He knew that the first step towards
sympathy is acquaintanceship and knowledge. Many Englishmen
had not knowingly spoken to a Roman Catholic, let alone seen,
or spoken to, a Cardinal. He therefore used every possible opportunity to bring the Church to public notice, expounding its tenets
and explaining its policy. He delighted in public functions and
great occasions, and this too was of service to the Church, for most
Englishmen, however undemonstrative they may seem, share this
delight. For the first time for three centuries a Cardinal became an
accepted leader in public life. This is not to say, of course, that all
the animosity and misrepresentation piled up during the past
centuries could be swept away by one man within a few years.
Wiseman's achievement was to take the first, and most difficult,
steps towards the rehabilitation of the Church. His successors
found the way easier for his pioneering.

Good men of narrower vision complained that Wiseman
could initiate a project but had not the patience to see it through;
he could not bend his mind to details of organization. It was perhaps as well that he could not do so. Had he cumbered his time
with the consideration of the minutiae of rules and regulations, he
would have achieved far less. This refusal to bother with the letter
of the law led to trouble later on; the discord between the bishops
and the regulars was partly due to Wiseman's failure to study the
rules by which they were bound.

Such defects as these count little if we take the larger view of
his achievement. It was his function to lead the Catholic Church
in England out of the twilight that followed the long years of
proscription into the light of day and to take its place not only
in the national life but in the wider life of the Church in the
world.

It was a tragedy that during the last years of his life Wiseman
was afflicted with sickness that impaired his physical and mental
vigour. More and more he became reluctant to make decisions,
and his hope that a coadjutor would take much of the burden off
his shoulders was frustrated by his inability to share responsibility.

The spectacle of two good men at variance did harm within the Church. It was the same inability that caused friction with the bishops, and the fact that Rome felt obliged to decide issues against his wishes added sorrow to his last years.

While it is impossible to discount Wiseman's period of decline, it is right that we should base our estimate of his services to the Church on the years when he was in full vigour. When the complex problems he had to face are considered, and a comparison is made between the position of the Church before he came to England and at the time of his death, the greatness of his work can be appreciated. It was far from being the work of one man; the devoted labours of bishops and priests and laity were essential for any advance, but Wiseman was their leader and in him they found an example of courage and of never failing inspiration at a period when Roman Catholics were looked at askance and Roman Catholicism regarded as an alien creed.

His successor was a man of very different temperament. Manning's outstanding characteristic was his will power. He lacked the intellectual distinction of Wiseman and Newman, nor had he their imaginative genius. Few men have been so utterly devoted to the Church; he was ambitious but it was for power to strengthen the Church and not for self-aggrandizement. When he left the Church of England, he threw away the certainty of high preferment for a future in which there seemed small prospect of advance for a convert clergyman. Nor did he intrigue for personal benefits. A careful study of the facts of his life must absolve him from self-seeking. It would not be necessary to make such a statement were it not that some critics have attributed unworthy motives for which there is not a scrap of evidence.

During the first period of his Catholic life, he became Wiseman's trusted lieutenant. This was not a matter of compatibility of temperaments, but Wiseman found in him one who shared his plans for the Church, and, at the same time, had the necessary driving power and administrative ability. Once Manning had taken up a position, nothing, save his own will, could move him. The qualification is necessary for Manning did, on occasion, change his attitude without any apparent compelling need. In his

Anglican days, for instance, his views on the Dr Hampden appointment were suddenly altered, and, as a Catholic, his later opinions
on the Temporal Power were not in keeping with the extreme
position he had taken up some years earlier. Such instances, and
others, prove on examination to be expressions of Manning's
strong political instinct. The term is not used in a derogatory
sense. The power to govern, to rule, and to order is essential for
the well-being of the Church community just as much as it is for
the political community. Manning had this power to a marked
degree; it will be recalled that his early inclination had been for a
Parliamentary career. Now, as Newman pointed out in a passage
previously quoted, expedience is the guiding principle of government but carrying with it a tendency towards ambition or tyranny.
Manning was prepared to accept the logic of facts just as any
leader must do if he is to accomplish even part of his plans. Thus
the occupation of Rome was a fact, and any fresh consideration of
the Temporal Power had to take that fact into account with all
other relevant facts.

The intransigence of Manning, during the period when he
clung to any one opinion, was lamentable and it led him into conduct
that must be regretted. He was unable to believe that those who
differed from him were honest or truthful. Soon after Newman's
conversion, Manning had surprised Gladstone by affirming that
the bond between those who had gone over to Rome was "their
want of truth." This uncharitable attitude towards those of different views was unfortunately strengthened by the influence of
W. G. Ward whose intellectual powers easily overrode Manning's
lesser mental ability. Ward himself recognized Manning's limitations. He once said to his son Wilfrid, "Be careful what you say
about scholastic philosophy to Manning when you see him. He is
sensitive to generalities, but densely ignorant of all particulars.
Say to him, 'Scholastic principles are true ones, but need adapting
to the times, etc.,' That will quite satisfy him." The significance of
this remark can be seen in Manning's books; once he departs from
generalities, he becomes less convincing.

Can we here find one of the causes of his misunderstanding
with Newman? Manning seriously feared Newman's influence;

s

he could not appreciate the purpose of much of Newman's writing—his desire to strengthen the intellectual forces of Catholicism in a world that was rapidly moving towards rationalism. Manning recognized the same danger, but his remedy was reiterated pronouncements, and he was suspicious of careful argument designed to meet intellectual difficulties; he feared that in doing so the fullness of Catholic teaching might be weakened. That was at least a tenable opinion; what was regrettable was that Manning allowed himself unworthy means for checking Newman's influence.

On his own ground, the practical affairs of the Church, Manning could move forward with complete confidence. He ruled his own diocese in a way impossible to one of Wiseman's temperament; discipline was imposed, but, the priest who accepted that rule was sure of every help and sympathy in his work. So, too, when he handled such problems as the provision of schools and institutions for poor children, his hand never faltered. His final phase, his crusade for social justice, again called out his political instinct which was the more effective because of his warm-hearted and generous charity to all in distress. It is not without significance that W. G. Ward was not interested in such matters; in these Manning was his own mentor.

When we consider the contribution made by Newman to the life of the Church we find ourselves in a different atmosphere from that in which Wiseman and Manning lived for they were essentially leaders and rulers. Although Wiseman in his early years seemed destined to be a great scholar, his true work was to be done in guiding the Church in England through a difficult period of its history. The imagination refuses to see Newman as a diocesan bishop; he found his right place in the Oratory; there he could exercise his great intellectual gifts and, in spite of the hindrances he had to suffer, he accomplished his unique work.

When they were both nearing the end of life, Newman said to Ullathorne, "I have been indoors all my life, whilst you have battled for the Church in the world."

Manning had the same thought in saying, "Newman from the beginning to the end was a recluse—at Oriel, Littlemore and

Edgbaston; but I from the beginning was pitched head over heels into public life."

Neither statement should be taken absolutely; Littlemore and the Oratory were Newman's work, nor could one remote from practical life have carried on the struggle for the Catholic University in Ireland. The measure of truth in these statements is that Newman was a profound thinker with the susceptibilities of a poet, and such a man must have periods of solitude if his true work is to be done. Newman's powers needed the sun of human affection to bring them to fruition. Few men have had, or have treaured so highly, such a great company of friends. Even the break with Anglicanism did but interrupt the friendships of youth and maturity. His contemporary E. B. Pusey wrote in 1879 when they were both old men, "You may assure your friends that nothing either has or can come between my deep love of John Henry Newman." It was this sensitive affection that made it possible for him to understand the intellectual and spiritual problems of those who sought his guidance. A few sentences from a statement made by the Duke of Norfolk have been quoted in an earlier chapter; he went on to say, "no one was able to bring Catholic truth to the intelligence of his countrymen as Newman could, because, among other reasons, he could show them that he understood, in a way no other Catholic writer did, the difficulties that perplexed them." That was part of his work, carried on in a voluminous correspondence, which helped to bring many into the Church. But no estimate of Newman can rest there.

Why is it that even his most controversial works are still read and studied while those of his contemporaries are all but forgotten? The answer lies in the depth and breadth of Newman's thought. He was unable to treat any subject without going down to fundamental principles which are as relevant today as during his lifetime. "I have been obliged," he said, "to take great pains with everything I have written." He put the whole of himself into what he wrote and he illuminated every subject he touched.

As the years have gone by, so his influence has increased; this is in part due to his remarkable power of foreseeing the problems that would arise in the future—problems that are with us today.

In his own lifetime, as we have seen, he was misunderstood and even traduced; it is the penalty every prophet has to suffer, but his reputation is now world-wide.

A new edition of his works is being published in America; there are societies for the study of his thought in France and Germany and elsewhere; such organizations as the Newman Association are proud to bear his name. His position in the world of Catholic thought could be illustrated by many quotations bearing distinguished names. Let one suffice. Karl Adam in his book *The Spirit of Catholicism* wrote, "Her [the Church's] greatest minds, Origen, Augustine, Aquinas and Newman, made it their life's task to establish a synthesis of faith and knowledge."

Even during his lifetime Newman had the satisfaction of seeing an advance made in matters that had a leading place in his thoughts. Leo XIII's Encyclical of 1879, *Aeterni Patris*, which stimulated the revival of the study of Thomism was welcomed by Newman as a sign, to quote a letter he wrote to the Pope, that the Church was alive to the needs of "a time when there is so much cultivation of mind, so much intellectual excitement, so many new views, true and false, and so much temptation to overstep the old truth."

Time has also shown that the Church's interpretation of the dogma of Papal Infallibility is more in keeping with Newman's moderate views than with the extreme claims of Manning and Ward. It should further be noted that in 1895 the Pope consented to Catholics, under certain safeguards, attending Oxford and Cambridge. How far-seeing were Newman's thoughts can also be illustrated by such Papal Encyclicals of recent years as that on "Biblical Studies" (1943) and on "False Trends in Modern Teaching" (1950). His influence endures for his was one of the formative minds of the Church.

*   *   *   *   *

It would be presumptuous and foolish to attempt to assess the relative influences of these three great men. The biographer, like the historian, can study documents and actions but he cannot record the workings of the inner life, or estimate with assurance the personal influence of one man on another. Any attempt to do so when writing of three priests—for Wiseman, Newman and Manning were priests first and last—is bound to fail. In some of their more intimate papers, a hint is given here and there of the spiritual life that gave meaning to thought and policy and action. The rest is hidden.

We can, however, rejoice that the Church was able to use three men of such diverse personalities and abilities. Each made his distinctive contribution which enriched the life of the Church; controversies and discords are inseparable from the human story, but they lose much of their prominence when seen as part of the greater story of the advance of the Catholic Church in England during the nineteenth century.

* * * * *

Yet there are different kinds of gifts, though it is the same Spirit who gives them, just as there are different kinds of service, though it is the same Lord we serve.

I Cor. 12. 4, 5.

NOTES ON BOOKS

THIS is not, in any sense, a bibliography; it gives the main sources of information, and suggests books that will be found helpful for those who wish to pursue the subject.

General

Bishop Bernard Ward's two volumes, *The Sequel to Catholic Emancipation* (1915), cover the years 1830–50. There is no comparable history of the Catholic Church in England for the rest of the century, but much valuable information will be found in Abbot E. C. Butler's *Life and Times of Bishop Ullathorne*, 2 vols. (1926), and in *The English Catholics: 1850–1950* (1950).

E. E. Y. Hales, *Pio Nono* (1954) gives the general history of the Church and of Italian affairs for the years 1846–78. A more detailed survey will be found in R. Aubert, *Le Pontificat de Pie IX* (Paris, 1952).

Abbot E. C. Butler's *The Vatican Council*, 2 vols. (1930) is an essential book.

Newman

Anne Mozley, *Letters and Correspondence of John Henry Newman during his Life in The English Church*, 2 vols. (1891).

Wilfrid Ward, *The Life of John Henry Cardinal Newman*, 2 vols. (1912).

These two books are the standard works. Anne Mozley's volumes may be supplemented by Maisie Ward's *Young Mr Newman* (1948).

For the Oxford Movement, Dean Church's *The Oxford Movement* (1891), retains its importance. Two more recent books may be noted: *The Anglican Revival* (1925) by Y. Brilioth, and *The Spirit of the Oxford Movement* (1933) by Christopher Dawson.

There is a useful bibliography in the National Book League's pamphlet *John Henry Newman* by J. M. Cameron (1956).

Most readers will begin with the *Apologia*; that might be followed by *The Present Position of Catholics in England*, *The Idea of a University*, and by a volume of Newman's sermons. *Autobiographical Writings* (1956) supplements the *Apologia*.

Wiseman

Wilfrid Ward, *The Life and Times of Cardinal Wiseman*, 2 vols. (1897).

Very little new material has been published since this standard biography.

Of Wiseman's own writings, *Fabiola* (1855) and *Recollections of the Last Four Popes* (1858) can still be read with enjoyment.

Manning

E. S. Purcell, *Life of Cardinal Manning*, 2 vols. (1896), merits many of the strictures passed upon it; it is not only ill-proportioned, but it is, in places, seriously misleading (thereby providing Lytton Strachey with material for his malicious study). The book, however, is indispensable as a documentary source; after Purcell's death, the documents he used were dispersed and most cannot be traced.

Purcell's book can be supplemented and, in part, corrected, by Shane Leslie's *Henry Edward Manning* (1921).

Other corrections and criticisms will be found in *Essays* (1911) by H. I. D. Ryder, who was Newman's successor at the Birmingham Oratory, and also a nephew of Manning; in Maisie Ward's *The Wilfrid Wards and the Transition* (1934), pp. 214–19, and Appendix A, and in the later editions of J. R. Gasquet's *Cardinal Manning* (1896). This last small book gives the view of one who knew Manning well in his later years. Dr Gasquet (a younger brother of Cardinal Gasquet) married Manning's niece.

A. W. Hutton's *Cardinal Manning* (1892) is well worth reading; it gives the view of a sympathetic Anglican. It contains a useful bibliography of Manning's writings.

Of Manning's own books, *The Eternal Priesthood* and the three volumes of his *Miscellanies* should be read.

KEY TO "THE FIRST PROVINCIAL SYNOD OF WESTMINSTER, 1852"

(See illustration facing p. 135)

1   CARDINAL WISEMAN
2   BISHOP BRIGGS (Beverley)
3   BISHOP BROWN (Newport)
4   BISHOP HOGARTH (Hexham)
5   BISHOP TURNER (Salford)
6   BISHOP BURGESS (Clifton)
7   FR. AYLWARD, O.P. (Hinckley)
8   FR. EUGENE, C.P. (London)
9   CANON CROOK (Provost of Liverpool)
10   BISHOP WAREING (Northampton)
11   BISHOP ULLATHORNE (Birmingham)
12   BISHOP ERRINGTON (Plymouth)
13   BISHOP BROWN (Shrewsbury)

14   DOM MOLYNEUX, O.S.B. (Warrington)
15   FR. ETHERIDGE, S.J. (London)
16   FR. PAGANI, I.C. (Rugby)
17   REV. J. WHEBLE (Chelsea), Ceremoniarius
18   MGR. SEARLE
19   REV. FR. GOSS (Liverpool) or C. HARDMAN (Cantor)
20   SIR GEORGE BOWYER, Notary
21   CANON WHITTY (Moorfields), Provost of Westminster
22   DR. CROOKALL (Old Hall), Cantor
23   CANON COOKSON
24   CANON MAGUIRE (London)

25   CANON WHEDALL (Oscott)
26   CANON COX (Southampton)
27   BISHOP GRANT (Southwark)
28   REV. R. BAGNALL (Oscott), Secretary
29   DR. ROSKELL (Nottingham), Theologian
30   REV. J. H. NEWMAN, Cong. Orat. (Birmingham), Theologian
31   MGR. MANNING, Ob.S.C. (Bayswater), Theologian
32   CANON HUSENBETH (Cossey), Provost of Northampton
33   REV. JAS. MOORE (Sedgley Park), Ceremoniarius
34   REV. DR. MORGAN (Oscott)

INDEX

M = Manning   N = Newman   W = Wiseman